PRINCIPAL
SUSPECT

PRINCIPAL SUSPECT

The True Story of
Dr. Jay Smith and the
Main Line Murders

William C. Costopoulos

CAMINO BOOKS, INC.
Philadelphia

Manufactured in the United States of America

1 2 3 4 5   99 98 97 96

Library of Congress Cataloging-in-Publication Data

Costopoulos, William C., 1944–
    Principal suspect : the true story of Dr. Jay Smith and the Main Line
Murders / William Costopoulos.
     p. cm.
    ISBN 0-940159-36-8 (hardcover : alk. paper)
    1. Murder—Pennsylvania—Case studies. 2. Trials (Murder)—
Pennsylvania—Case studies. 3. Reinert, Susan, d. 1979.
4. Bradfield, Bill. 5. Smith, Jay C. I. Title.
HV6533.P4C67 1996
364.1'523'0974818—dc20   96-5989

For information write:

Publisher
Camino Books, Inc.
P. O. Box 59026
Philadelphia, PA 19102

Dedicated to the
Supreme Court of Pennsylvania

CONTENTS

ACKNOWLEDGMENTS

I want to thank everybody in my law office who helped me through, and supported me through, the representation of Dr. Jay Smith. That trial and its aftermath spanned seven years of our lives. Special thanks to David Foster, Bill Kollas, Leslie Fields, Charles Rector, Allen Welch, Skip Gochenour, and Nick Ressetar.

All the material in this book was taken from the trial transcripts, court records, police reports, correspondence, interviews with hundreds of witnesses and personnel, and, of course, endless hours with Jay Smith. These documents exceeded 20,000 pages and everybody in my office reviewed all of them to confirm the legal history and entanglements of this case.

I want to thank Dr. Smith for his patience.

I also want to thank my legal secretaries, with special thanks to Tammy Hair, Ami Gelbaugh, and Tammy Weaber, who typed and retyped the manuscript, and ran the law office on the side.

Finally, I want to thank my wife Jill and our three daughters, Kara, Khristina, and Callista, who never stopped believing in me, even when I stopped believing in myself.

PROLOGUE

I represented Dr. Jay Smith, a former Principal of Upper Merion High School near Philadelphia, who was convicted and sentenced to death for the brutal murders of a fellow school teacher and her two young children. I tried the murder case which I have written about. It is a true story about a seven-year investigation by the FBI and the Pennsylvania State Police— the most massive homicide investigation in American history—that resulted in convictions and an unsolved crime. The children have never been found.

Many people believe that Jay Smith not only killed an innocent woman, disgracing her in her death, but that he also caused those two children to mysteriously vanish from this earth. Those same people also believe that Dr. Smith is responsible for the disappearance of his own daughter and son-in-law.

Jay Smith was a nocturnal creature, an eccentric by all accounts, and the strangest person I have ever come to know. I got to know the "Prince of Darkness," as he was dubbed by the law enforcement community, on a personal level. His eeriness cannot be denied, but I believe he was an innocent man sentenced to die for three murders that he had nothing to do with.

Yet my belief in his guilt or innocence is not relevant. Indeed, some would say my belief is self-serving and suspect. This book is not an effort on my part to prove his guilt or innocence. Readers will come to their own conclusions.

Few life scenarios afford the suspense, the danger, the excitement, and the opportunity for the exercise of pure power (both personal and institutional) of a first-degree murder trial. Too often the adversaries place themselves above the law and lose sight of the fact that their welfare is not what is at stake. What is at stake, in any criminal trial, is the integrity of the system and the fate of the accused.

The story to follow *is* about crossing the line, fixing cases, zealous prosecutions, rigging testimony, planting evidence, and the making and breaking of reputations in the courtroom. This true story is about a fight for the truth, an illusive concept in the courtrooms of America.

· 1 ·

DEATH WITHOUT DIGNITY

At 5:20 a.m. on June 25, 1979, in Harrisburg, Pennsylvania, a police ra-
dio dispatcher received a call from a man who identified himself as
Larry Brown. "There is a sick woman in a car in the parking lot of the
Host Inn," the mysterious caller whispered and quickly hung up.

The unknown caller sounded as if he had a Spanish accent. He was
never heard from again.

The call was automatically recorded and transmitted to the Lower
Swatara Township Police Department. Within 10 minutes, two uniformed
patrolmen pulled into the Host Inn parking lot in a marked car and
cruised around until they saw a red Plymouth Horizon with its hatchback
partially opened. They stopped and peered inside. What they saw in the
predawn of that early summer morning they would never forget, and they
would both be called upon many times to testify to their findings over the
next seven years.

Jammed into the hatchback of the car in a fetal position lay the naked
body of a young white woman. Her knees were pressed up against her
chest, and her head was bent forward. The body was mutilated with chain
marks on her wrists and ankles and bruises on her back. Her eyes were
black and blue, her front teeth had ripped her lower lip, and one officer
thought he saw dried mucus or sperm smeared around her mouth and
nose. Out of habit, he bent over and touched her wrist for a pulse. Since
the Host Inn was in Swatara Township, he called a patrol officer with the
Swatara Township Police Department.

Officer Joseph Ruddy got the call to go to the Host Inn. Ruddy was
visibly upset when he arrived and saw the body of the woman. He had a
nagging feeling of guilt because he had cruised the Host Inn parking lot at
approximately 2 a.m. that very morning and had seen the red Plymouth
Horizon with the hatchback opened. He didn't get out of his patrol car to
examine the suspicious-looking vehicle, but he did make a radio check and
determined the car belonged to Susan G. Reinert of Ardmore, Pennsylvania. Then Ruddy went to the Host Inn's registration desk and was told that
no one by that name was registered there. An emergency call to handle a
fatal traffic accident forced him to leave at 2:10 a.m. without further investigation of the Plymouth Horizon with the open hatchback.

Within a matter of hours after Ruddy's return to the Host Inn's parking
lot, the crime scene had been secured, and investigators from the District

Attorney's Office of Dauphin County, the Pennsylvania State Police Criminal Division, and the Dauphin County Coroner's Office had arrived.

The car was photographed from every angle and dusted for fingerprints inside and out. Every single item in the car was inventoried, and as each item was removed from the car, it was placed into an evidence bag, identified, and readied to be sent to the crime labs in Harrisburg and Washington, D.C. for analysis.

Among the items removed from the car were a program from the First Presbyterian Church, a Cub Scout pamphlet, a deck of playing cards, some notes, a road map, a pin, a hairbrush, three stuffed animals (a lion, a duck, and a monkey), candy wrappers, and some soft drink containers. There was no clothing, no purse, no keys, no items that could help identify the body in the trunk.

But the Pennsylvania State Police were already pretty sure who the victim was. The car registration, previously checked out by Officer Ruddy, indicated that the car did indeed belong to one Susan G. Reinert. The police soon learned from the victim's neighbors and friends in Ardmore that Susan Reinert was an English teacher at Upper Merion High School, which is on the Main Line—an elite suburb of Philadelphia known for its estates and mansions, prep schools, academies, and universities. The picture of Susan Reinert in the school's yearbook looked like the victim in the trunk.

The homicide investigation started out routinely enough, but there was a growing feeling among the officers at the scene that something bizarre had happened. They weren't exactly sure why they felt uneasy, but they did. Maybe it was the fact that the woman had been placed in the car naked in a fetal position, disgraced in her death, a death without dignity. Maybe it was the chain marks on her body. It could have been the strap-on dildo, found in the car; or the simple blue comb, with "79th USARCOM" engraved on it, that lay so conspicuously in the trunk like a calling card. One thing was certain, this was no ordinary murder.

Thomas Dacheux, of the Troop H Identification Unit, photographed the body and had it transferred onto a stretcher and then taken by ambulance to the Community General Osteopathic Hospital.

Within hours, an autopsy was performed on the body by Dr. Robert Bear to determine the cause and manner of death.

★ ★ ★

Date: June 25, 1979 (The same day the body was found)
Time: 9:30 a.m.
Place: Dauphin County Courthouse, Harrisburg, Pennsylvania

The Dauphin County Courthouse is a white bastion of granite on the corner of Market and Front Streets in Harrisburg within blocks of Pennsylvania's capitol dome. A statue of a tall Roman soldier, clutching unsheathed arrows in his left hand and standing on a gargoyle with his right foot, looms over the entrance of the courthouse overlooking the Susquehanna River. The four courtrooms on the third floor and the two courtrooms on the fifth floor are all ornately paneled, with long wooden pews in the gallery for the observers. On the walls of each courtroom are huge oil paintings of jurists long past. Behind each judge's chair is a brass plaque engraved with a motto about justice.

When the criminal term is in session in Dauphin County (15 times a year), the hallways are bustling with witnesses, victims, supportive family members, prosecutors, defense lawyers, courtroom stenographers, tipstaffs, sheriffs, and those defendants who are out on bail and also have their supportive family members with them. In the corners, prosecutors talk to defense lawyers trying to work out deals to keep the cases moving. Many tears have been shed in those hallways.

Tiled corridors lead into huge, marble courtrooms where the noise level suddenly drops. Gone is the buzz of the crowd. The only sound in a courtroom is the voice of a prosecuting attorney calling a case, or of a defense attorney making a plea for mercy for his client, or of the client explaining to the judge what did or didn't happen.

"What time is it?"

"It's after 9:30. He should have been here by now."

"Do you think he'll show?"

"He'll show."

The young deputy district attorney from Delaware County was getting nervous in Judge Morgan's courtroom because Dr. Jay Smith was running late for his sentencing. Smith, the Principal of Upper Merion High School, was no stranger to the criminal court system of Dauphin County. Three of his cases had been transferred from the Philadelphia area on changes of venue because of the extensive publicity on the Main Line. In March 1979, he was convicted of theft and receiving stolen property for a scam perpetrated on a Sears store in Abington, Pennsylvania. On May 31, 1979, he was convicted by a Dauphin County jury of theft and receiving stolen property for a scam perpetrated on a Sears store in St. David's, Pennsylvania. In addition, a weapons and instruments-of-crime charge and one of possession of marijuana with intent to deliver were pending.

And now, on this 25th day of June, 1979, a distinguished high school principal, an educator from Main Line Philadelphia, a lieutenant colonel in the United States Army Reserve, was about to be sentenced like any common criminal.

"It's not that late," Smith's defense attorney answered the young prosecutor from Delaware County who was now pacing. "He'll be here. I talked to him this weekend."

"It's after 9:30."

"Relax."

"I'm relaxed. Judge Morgan might not be."

The back of the courtroom was crowded with other defendants waiting to plead guilty or to be sentenced for offenses ranging from petty theft to drug dealing to rape. Defendants waiting to be sentenced that day by Judge Morgan were upstairs in holding cells, in lockup without bail, and were not free to appear for their sentences on their own.

Also in the back of the courtroom on this day was a gray-haired couple who never missed a day when Jay Smith was scheduled to appear in court. They were still searching for justice and a clue to the whereabouts of their missing son, Edward, and his wife, Stephanie Smith Hunsberger, who was Jay Smith's natural daughter. Smith finally arrived that morning and apologized to the judge. He showed no emotion as he was sentenced by Judge Morgan to a term of two to five years in the State Correctional Institution at Dallas, Pennsylvania, one of the toughest prisons in the East.

"Here are my car keys," Dr. Smith said to his lawyer. "My car is in the lot."

That was all Jay Smith had to say—to anybody—before two sheriffs escorted him to a holding cell on the third floor. Everybody in the courtroom watched as the distinguished-looking gentleman in a gray pinstriped suit was taken from the courtroom. Smith was impassive during the entire proceeding, showing no evidence of pain, tears, trembling, anger, or fear. He would be taken straight to Dallas, in the northern part of Pennsylvania.

The 1,300 students at Upper Merion High School were stunned at what was happening to their principal. The high school and its principal were fast becoming one of the best tabloid stories in town. The school itself was on the Main Line, with more labs, more library volumes, bigger and better playing fields, more sophisticated audiovisual aids, better gym facilities, more functionally designed classrooms, and a grander cafeteria than the vast majority of the private colleges in the Philadelphia area. It was, without a doubt, a top-notch, upscale, public suburban high school that was getting hammered by the press.

But the horror at Upper Merion High School had only begun.

Ten minutes away from the Dauphin County Courthouse, at the Host Inn parking lot, swarms of uniformed police continued to mill around. The local news stations had already gotten word, and the camera crews and reporters were on their way.

★ ★ ★

By 1:30 p.m. the white female body was on the autopsy table at the Community General Osteopathic Hospital in Harrisburg, identified by a card attached to the foot with the name of the deceased being listed as unknown. Dr. Robert Bear had already examined the body externally and was preparing to make the first cut. In attendance at the autopsy were many, probably too many, law enforcement officials. They gathered at the autopsy table like students in a biology lab about to watch the dissection of their first frog. Surrounding the table under a high-wattage examination light were Corporal John C. Balshy, Trooper Thomas Dacheux, Sergeant Joseph VanNort, Trooper Jack R. Lotwick, Trooper Ron Colyer (all Pennsylvania State Police); Detective Ron Fernsler and Patrolman Joseph C. Ruddy of the Swatara Township Police, and Gerald Yeager, Jr., morgue attendant.

Cameras were constantly flashing in the autopsy room. The picture-taking was primarily before the body was cut open, but some snaps were taken as the autopsy progressed. X-rays of the head, neck, and trunk were taken to be kept by the pathologist. Dr. Bear took smears from the vaginal area and from the rectum, as well as two smears from the oral cavity. All the specimens were appropriately labeled as to type and the location where they were found. Then they were given to Trooper Thomas Dacheux.

Corporal John C. Balshy and Sergeant Joseph VanNort were veteran police officers. Neither of them had any idea who might have been responsible for the victim's death, but they'd both been around long enough, and investigated enough murders, to know what was important in a homicide investigation. Corporal Balshy was trying to get fingerprint lifts off the body. In addition, he used rubber hinge-lifters to get between the crevices of the body for the purpose of lifting material that might become relevant under a microscope at a later date.

Corporal John Balshy was a 25-year veteran and wrote the book on death investigations. He had investigated and solved hundreds of homicides and was a qualified forensic expert in Pennsylvania, Texas, New Jersey, and New York, as well as in the federal courts in Colorado and Pennsylvania. Sergeant VanNort had specifically asked for *him*. Balshy looked like a surgeon with his sleeves rolled up and apron bloodied. This patient, however, needed no anesthesia.

Something flickered like a diamond between the toes and Balshy quickly shifted the high-powered ultraviolet light to the feet. His skilled hands went right to it. The particle was granular.

Sergeant Joe VanNort, the tough-fisted, 30-year veteran with the Pennsylvania State Police, would soon take charge of the investigation. VanNort wanted more pictures taken of the abrasions and bruises on both forearms. He looked hard at the dried blood in the mouth and nose. He shook his head at the abrasions behind both knees, behind the neck, and on the right ankle. He motioned for more pictures to be taken of the bruises on the buttocks and between the shoulder blades.

The external examination established that the body was approximately 35 years of age, that of an average, well-developed, well-nourished, white female whose body weight was judged to be approximately 100 pounds with a body length of 158 centimeters. Rigor mortis was absent. Postmortem lividity was noted over the posterior aspect of the neck and trunk as well as over the face, neck, and anterior aspect of the trunk. Both eyelids showed bluish brown discoloration. The face and the anterior aspect of the trunk were free of notable abrasions. Neither of the upper extremities showed evidence of needle puncture wounds. In fact, the body generally failed to show any needle tracks. To Dr. Robert Bear, the absence of puncture wounds indicated that she had not been injected with poison.

Dr. Bear, Trooper Balshy, and Trooper VanNort all agreed that there could have been a puncture wound somewhere that they missed.

There was a slight delay that afternoon. The strike-saw—a high-speed rotary blade used to cut the cranial cap to access the brain—broke, and Balshy had to fix it while the victim stared with eyes wide open. Soon, her brain was scooped into a bucket.

The smell of death filled the room and hung in the air. A young police officer gagged and ran out of the room to throw up.

The victim's hair was abundant and brown. Numerous red and blue bits of material, appearing to be fragments from cloth or a rug, were found in her hair. Under ultraviolet, the red and blue material was readily identified. Samples of it were removed from the body and turned over to the evidence officer. There was marked dark blue discoloration to the face. The right eye was hemorrhagic, and the vessels of the left eye were engorged. The oral cavity contained a small amount of clotted blood, but the teeth did not appear to be loose. There were no lesions of particular note.

Dr. Bear's internal examination of the body produced very little of significance. Anoxia due to respiratory failure was the cause of death entered on the report in the Department of Pathology. Dr. Bear's findings were consistent with asphyxiation.

Sergeant VanNort was furious with the results of the autopsy. They told him nothing. Even he could figure out that she had stopped breathing. VanNort had made up his mind that he wanted a second opinion on the cause of death and fully intended to get one. VanNort wanted to know the *reason* for the clinical shut-down of the body.

Once Dr. Bear completed the preliminary autopsy, the county coroner ordered the body released to the family pending identification. But VanNort called Coroner Bush on the phone and told him to hold onto the body until he could get a second opinion from a forensic pathologist. "Death by asphyxiation" was a useless medical conclusion as far as VanNort was concerned.

Little did Sergeant VanNort know that there was going to be a mix-up over the body within 24 hours.

★ ★ ★

Officer Lou DiSantis, tall with black slicked hair, also a veteran cop, was married with children of his own and dreaded his assignment as he entered the Fidelity Bank at almost closing time. Under one arm was the yearbook that he had secured from Upper Merion High School. He was soon directed to the personnel manager's office in the back, and he did what he had to do. Though Lou was an experienced police officer, he was also a sensitive man, and he hated being a messenger of death.

"Are you Ken Reinert?"

"Yes."

"This is about . . . well . . . this is about Sue Reinert."

"Yes."

"Is this your ex-wife?" DiSantis asked Mr. Reinert as he pointed to her picture in the yearbook.

"Yes . . . but . . . why?"

DiSantis had not ruled Ken Reinert out as a possible suspect, but in his heart he really did not believe that Reinert's shock was being faked. He was visibly stunned at the news, and it was a long, long ride from Philadelphia to Harrisburg for both of them.

Ken Reinert was taken to the morgue in Harrisburg to identify the body. This encounter also gave the police an opportunity to talk to an individual who could give them some leads, if not incriminate himself, in this homicide investigation that would soon be out of control.

"Yes, that's my ex-wife," Ken whispered, shaking his head in utter disbelief, still stunned, as the white sheet was pulled up over her body on the steel table for the last time.

"Are you sure?" he was asked by one of the troopers.

"I . . . I'm sure . . . It's her."

Of course, Ken Reinert was sure. He had been married to Susan Reinert for 16 years before their divorce. Reinert said he had a wonderful marriage until a guy by the name of Bradfield came along and Susan fell in love with him. Susan had asked him for a divorce. That was several years before her murder.

"Bill Bradfield was the bastard that ruined my marriage," Reinert exploded.

One of the troopers quickly wrote down in his notebook—"Bill Bradfield."

"By the way," Ken asked, afraid of his own question, afraid of the answer, afraid of the thought, "My kids . . . Karen, Michael . . . who has my kids?"

Ken Reinert trembled and cried when no one said a word.

★ ★ ★

Somewhere, somehow, communications broke down between the Pennsylvania State Police, the coroner's office, the Community General Osteopathic Hospital, and the undertaker. No sooner had the corpse been fingerprinted than the undertaker was permitted to leave with Susan Reinert's remains. At the request of her brother, Pat Gallagher, the undertaker followed the family's wishes and cremated the remains of the body at once.

"You mean we lost the body!" VanNort screamed.

"What body?" was all the stunned personnel at the Community General Osteopathic Hospital could say.

2

THE SEARCH

"It's hard to imagine how much more difficult those kids made the case. They were always there in the back of your mind . . . you wanted to find them—it was your job to find them; but if you found them buried somewhere . . . in a grave in somebody's backyard or out in the woods, you couldn't tell how you'd react to that, either . . . .It was just so *damn* hard . . . one of the worst things I ever had to go through.

"It really affected everybody. Joe VanNort, the state trooper in charge of this thing—you can't imagine what it's done to him . . . .This is his *life* now."

Special Agent Michael Wald, FBI

Just their pictures were enough to tear your heart out—Michael's toothy grin, his short, dishwater blond hair parted neatly to the side. He was a cute little kid, a church-going Cub Scout, who loved baseball and his mom and dad. Karen—thin, shy, a pretty little girl with a soft complexion and silky brown hair cut short—still loved dolls and make-believe.

The Pennsylvania State Police realized immediately that they were confronting not only the murder of Susan Reinert, but also the disappearance and possible murder of two young children.

Michael was 10; Karen, 11.

Sergeant Joseph VanNort remained in charge, and dozens of state police were assigned to him. VanNort became obsessed, then consumed, with the search for Michael and Karen. He was nearing retirement. He did not want to end his career without finding the children. He did not want to end his career without finding the killer or killers.

VanNort's orders were explicit. Search everywhere. Search homes. Businesses. Cars. Trucks. Question everybody. Follow up on every lead.

"What about anybody's rights?" a young investigator innocently asked.

"Fuck their rights," VanNort snapped. "I said find the kids!"

The task force of the Pennsylvania State Police was relentless and tireless. They searched in teams day and night. They searched homes, trucks, trunks of cars, the New Jersey shoreline, excavation sites, schoolyards, cemeteries, dumpsters, caverns, manholes. They pursued every lead and every sighting. The children were being sighted all over the country, from communes to gypsy camps.

Even news reporters got caught up in the frenzy and search. Some of them even dug shallow, child-size graves on their own time in the dense woods of Chester County. Sometimes off-duty reporters would run into off-duty state troopers or FBI agents doing exactly the same thing, and on more than one occasion, a backhoe was used.

Psychics also tried to help, but to no avail.

Finally, the Federal Bureau of Investigation joined in the search.

Governor Thornburgh's recently appointed commandant of the Pennsylvania State Police was Daniel Dunn, a former FBI special agent-in-charge from the Pittsburgh bureau, where Thornburgh himself had served for many years as western Pennsylvania's United States' attorney. Commander Dunn wanted his old colleagues from the FBI in on this one at once. The Feds didn't need any jurisdictional approval to offer their assistance and lab facilities to Troop H at Harrisburg; they had done it before with the Commonwealth's blessings. The mere fact that Reinert's two kids were missing was enough to raise the federal kidnapping issue.

Sergeant Joe VanNort did not like the federal involvement one bit. He felt they were meddling. He firmly believed that the Feds had no idea how to investigate murder cases.

When any of the special agents wanted to go to the Reinert house, VanNort demanded that a trooper be present. When the agents wanted to bring Ken Reinert or Pat Gallagher into the house for any reason, VanNort became furious because he personally hadn't cleared those two individuals, or anyone else for that matter.

VanNort, 58, was a Marlboro chain-smoking cynic from the old school. This was *his* investigation and his honor was on the line. This was *his* investigation, and the honor of the Pennsylvania State Police was on the line. All cops think that way, but especially old cops.

The search went on.

Ken Reinert's cry for help had launched one of the most massive homicide investigations in America's law enforcement history. The unified army of federal and state police power was unleashed across the country. European contingents were contacted to be on the alert at all airports.

A command post was set up at the state police barracks in Philadelphia, special phones were installed, and stenographers were assigned full time to SUMUR, the federal code name that referred to the massive joint investigation.

Interpol was activated. Eighteen FBI agents were assigned full time as were dozens of Pennsylvania State Police officers trained in homicide investigations. The finest forensic laboratories in the world, plus unlimited resources, were available 24 hours a day.

Nothing. Not a trace. Not even a clue to the whereabouts of the children was uncovered.

Michael and Karen had disappeared.

The last time Susan Reinert and her two children were seen alive was around 9:15 at night on Friday, June 22, 1979—three days before Susan's body was found in the trunk of her car at the Host Inn. Michael and Karen were outside their home playing, picking up hailstones that had pelted the quiet, family street in Ardmore earlier that evening.

Mary Gove, an older lady who lived next door to Susan, remembered seeing the children that night. She also remembered that they went into the house when a severe thunderstorm moved in from the northwest and battered the windows and rooftops. At approximately 9:30 p.m., according to Mrs. Gove, who had been standing at her window watching the storm unleash its fury, she saw Susan and her children run out of their house, across the front porch and into the storm before the three of them climbed into Susan's car. She remembered seeing that Susan was clearly in a hurry. She remembered the lights of the red Plymouth Horizon vanished into the darkness. Bethann Brooks, the teenage granddaughter staying with Mrs. Gove, remembered seeing them too.

Mrs. Gove and Bethann were the last people known to have seen Susan and Michael and Karen alive.

Except for Susan's killers—the children's killers or kidnappers.

★ ★ ★

Because Joe VanNort was the ranking sergeant in the criminal investigations unit, he would normally come into a case after the preliminary leg work had been finished. If he was lucky, there would already be a suspect in the case whom he could interrogate. He was very good at interrogation, in fact, the best. But this one involved missing children and no suspects, and he had been in on the leg work from the start.

VanNort was suspicious of everybody, including Ken Reinert; to Van-Nort, a husband or ex-husband was always a suspect.

"Tell me again," VanNort said, for the hundredth time, at one of his many informal staff meetings as he smoked one Marlboro after another. His small office in Harrisburg was dimly lit, and the heavy smoke in the room shadowed Trooper Holtz and DiSantis who were sitting across from him. VanNort had the sinking feeling that time was running out.

One of VanNort's most trusted men was his younger partner, John J. Holtz, known to everyone as Jack, a 32-year-old trooper who joined the Pennsylvania State Police in 1968 and who had been working for VanNort as a criminal investigator out of Troop H in Harrisburg since 1975. Van-Nort had a lot of faith in his protégé and partner because Jack Holtz enjoyed working up criminal cases.

Holtz was a young, shy traffic cop when VanNort started him on homicide investigations. VanNort liked his younger partner's ambition, his respect for the badge, and his perfectionist tendencies. Because VanNort married late in life and never had any children of his own, the older troopers kidded him that Jack Holtz, who was almost 30 years his junior, was his son.

Jack was 20 years old when he joined the state police at Troop H headquarters. Now, 12 years later, he considered himself a homicide investigator, and in his conservative three-piece suit, he looked the part. Jack Holtz was always well-groomed, with thick salt-and-pepper hair. He was built like a high school basketball center, and had recently gone through a divorce of his own.

"Tell you what again, Joe?" Jack Holtz asked.

"When did Ken Reinert say he saw his children for the last time?" he replied, looking right at Trooper Holtz.

"Friday, June 22, 1979," Holtz answered without having to look at his state police notebook.

"What time?"

"Late that evening, Joe."

"Exactly what time?"

"8:20 p.m."

"What were the circumstances?"

"I'll tell you in one second," Holtz answered, reaching into his jacket pocket for his notebook and turning right to the appropriate dog-eared page. "Ken Reinert saw them on Friday, June 22, for the last time. Michael was active in Cub Scouts and they were having a father and son softball game. They met at the church where the game was . . . his ex-wife, Susan, had dropped Michael off at the church . . . she did not stay for any part of the game. After a couple of innings there was a lot of thunder so they canceled the game and they went inside for the normal Cub Scout pack meeting they were having that night. Ken saw Susan come in and wondered what in the hell she was doing there because he was supposed to take Michael home. Michael then walked out of the church with his mother."

"How was Michael dressed?" VanNort asked, again.

Trooper Holtz, adjusting his aviator glasses, answered his boss dutifully, for the hundredth time. "Michael was dressed in a Phillies baseball shirt, which had pinstripes and a P on it, and blue jeans and sneakers."

"How was Susan dressed when she picked the kids up?"

"She had on blue jeans and a white knit blouse with short sleeves, with various colored stripes running across it red, green, yellow. Maybe sandals."

"Did he see the little girl at that time?"

"Ken said he could see Sue turning the corner in her car with Michael, and he saw that Karen was in the car with her."

"That night?"

"That night."

"Time again?"

"8:20 p.m."

"Did Ken hear from any of them again?"

"Yes, Michael called his dad on the phone at about 8:45 p.m. The kid apologized for having to leave that way, and the kid said he was going away with his mother. Michael then checked with his mother while Ken was on the phone and Ken heard Sue say, 'Just tell him we are going to Parents without Partners.'"

"Was that it?"

"Yes, sir."

"Never saw or heard from them again after that?"

"No, sir."

"Do you believe that, Jack?"

"Yes, sir. I believe that."

"Look, what if Ken Reinert had the shits because his ex-wife picked up the kids whenever she felt like it. What if he wasted her and the kids are somewhere in Europe and it's his intention."

"No," Holtz interrupted, "Joe, I was the one in the morgue that night when Ken Reinert identified Susan's body. He . . . he was in bad shape then. I'm telling you, he was in bad shape. Remember on the way from the morgue to the station house it was me who took Ken Reinert to Arche's Bar and Grill on Route 22. We talked together that night over coffee, face-to-face, and when he asked me who had his kids . . . I'm telling you, Joe . . . the guy was in so much pain. He couldn't have been faking it, Joe."

"I don't think so either, Joe," Trooper DiSantis added. "I drove him back that night from Harrisburg to Philadelphia, and I agree with Jack, the guy wasn't faking it. He just slumped down in his seat, all the way back and I . . . I didn't even know what to say to him."

"All right," VanNort interrupted. "I've heard this from you two guys before. Ken Reinert didn't do it."

"Right," Holtz said.

"Right," DiSantis said.

"Tell me about this guy Bradfield again," VanNort said.

Holtz looked at DiSantis out of the corner of his eye and smiled.

· 3 ·

RASPUTIN

He was a fellow English teacher of Susan Reinert's at Upper Merion High School. Big, bearded, intellectual, with long, coppery blond hair and bedroom blue eyes, he enjoyed poetry and art and music. He knew Latin and Greek and read the classics. The students at Upper Merion High found him articulate and charismatic, and they loved him.

Everybody, it seemed, loved him.

His name was Bill Bradfield, William Sydney Bradfield.

He looked something like Rasputin, the 19th-century Russian monk who acquired influence and power over noble women, educated women, who believed that his mystic powers could ease their suffering and pain. The real Rasputin took full advantage of his "holiness" and adopted a dissolute lifestyle, one of notorious debauchery, that ultimately resulted in his murder by a group of nobles, who first tried to poison him, and failing that, dumped him in the river Neva after shooting him.

It was rumored that Rasputin was very well endowed, and that upon his death, his organ had been cut off by his admirers and preserved in formaldehyde, and that they fled with it after the Russian Revolution from St. Petersburg to Paris.

Maybe the police should have studied Rasputin.

His look-alike did.

Bill Bradfield's name kept cropping up as the state police investigators questioned Susan Reinert's friends, neighbors, and relatives.

According to Ken Reinert, it was Bill Bradfield who destroyed their 16-year marriage. Reinert said that once Susan fell in love with Bradfield there was nothing that he or their children could do to change her mind. To her closest friends and family, Susan Reinert seemed spellbound.

★ ★ ★

Sue Myers also loved Bill Bradfield and expected to marry him. Bradfield, 47, was to be *her* future husband, too. Myers had met him when she came to teach at Upper Merion High School in the fall of 1963, and within a year, they were lovers. Sue Myers and Bill Bradfield had lived together since 1973 near the Reinert residence before, during, and after the breakup of the Reinert marriage. Though there was a lot of love going on at Upper Merion High School, there was no love between Susan Reinert and Sue Myers.

13

On three occasions, Sue Myers had confronted Susan Reinert at school and called her a bitch and a whore. On one occasion in the presence of Bill Bradfield, and on school property, Myers had kicked Reinert. She explained that this had occurred because Reinert had become involved with someone who Myers thought belonged to her. On the weekend Susan Reinert disappeared, Sue Myers was still living with and still expected to marry Bill Bradfield.

To Sergeant VanNort, this moved Sue Myers up a notch on his suspect list.

★ ★ ★

Wendy Zeigler, a former student of Bill Bradfield's, was also in love with Bradfield and expected to marry him. Bradfield and Zeigler had formed a romantic relationship sometime during the summer of 1978, and, toward the end of that summer, Bradfield expressed to Zeigler an intention to marry her. Wendy was only 20 years old, a pretty, shy freshman at a California college. She hoped to be married in a Catholic church and had discussed with her priest the possibility of an annulment of the marriage of Bill and his second wife. Wendy had written to Bradfield, "I love you madly, passionately, eternally, and infinitely . . . I need you to be with me . . . I don't see how I can survive days, let alone years . . . I am meant to be a mother . . . I am ordered to you as a wife, and so what I feel is proper and I thank God I feel this way."

Apparently, Bill Bradfield had been married twice, "sort of, kind of common law-like," Bradfield called them "spiritual marriages," before he moved in with Sue Myers. And he had children with both of his former "spiritual wives." He had two sons, Martin and William, born one year apart, with Fran, the college sweetheart who had left him when the children were five and six years old. Then he had a third son, David, with his second "spiritual wife," Muriel.

★ ★ ★

There was one more woman in love with Bill Bradfield on the weekend in question and her name was Joanne Aitken. She also expected to marry him. Young, quiet, attractive, and bright, Joanne was a graduate student in architecture at Harvard University in Cambridge, Massachusetts. She met Bradfield in the fall of 1974 (the same year Susan Reinert met him), when Joanne had gone to Upper Merion High School to recruit students for St. John's College in Annapolis, where she was working as the Director of Admissions and had the responsibility of recruiting high school seniors. She fell so madly in love with Bradfield that she lost her self-confidence, her strength, and her independence. She wrote to him: "I love you beyond belief," and six months before Susan Reinert's murder she wrote: "How can I

return to Boston without you? I am frightened to act without you around.
I want to have you there to comfort me. I don't care what else happens as
long as I can be with you."

The women who loved Bradfield adored him. Immeasurably. With passion. With romance.

Like Rasputin's women of long ago.

★ ★ ★

Every time a state police investigator reported back to Sergeant VanNort
that another woman was madly in love with William Bradfield and could
not bear to live without him, he would go crazy. VanNort was a career
criminal investigator. He had spent his life running down murderers, psychotics, rapists, drug dealers, pimps, and thieves. He had dealt with a lot of
manipulative ladies' men—Romeo types and even Charles Manson
types—and he questioned a lot of women who fell madly in love with
convicted killers after they were put behind bars for life or were sent to
death row. But this guy, Bill Bradfield, was really getting to VanNort. He
didn't know what it was about Bradfield that was driving these women
crazy, but he intended to find out.

"Maybe he's got a big dick," VanNort said, jokingly.

"I haven't seen it," DiSantis answered, defensively.

Lou DiSantis believed that all Bradfield did was pick on certain types of
women, such as those who were lonely, shy, and riddled with self-doubts,
and that "he would play with their heads to get into their pants." That was
DiSantis's bottom-line explanation.

Bill Bradfield stood six feet three inches tall and weighed 200 pounds.
He was once a college wrestler and managed to keep his big chest and
arms but had gained considerable weight in his midsection. His beard, long
hair, and stature gave him the look of a 16th-century philosopher. His students at Upper Merion High liked that magnetic look. Bradfield was described by those who knew him in and out of the classroom as affectionate,
compassionate, sensitive, and charismatic; some even called him "hypnotic."
They said it was because of his penetrating, steely blue eyes.

And Lou DiSantis was right about Bradfield's women. They were all
lonely, shy, and insecure. All of them were only modestly attractive and had
spent most of their lives in the classroom (either as students or teachers),
studying literature, art, poetry, and music, which is a kind of womb that
shelters one from the real world. The women who loved Bradfield led
cloistered lives and, for whatever reason, were pitifully vulnerable.

VanNort liked Lou DiSantis a lot. He knew that Lou had grown up in
the streets of Philadelphia as a lanky, dark-haired, Italian kid. Philadelphia
made Lou DiSantis street-smart, and to VanNort that was the best training a
police officer could get. DiSantis was also married with two daughters of
his own, who were only two and four, and that added to Lou's emotional
commitment to find out what happened to the Reinert children.

VanNort, however, had reason to believe that Bill Bradfield was much more controlling and manipulative than DiSantis gave him credit for. The information coming back to VanNort indicated that Bradfield's relationships with these women were not steeped in sex. It would have been a lot easier for VanNort to understand those multiple relationships if sex was the bottom line. It was just that Bradfield, according to VanNort's information and instinct, had more in mind than passion for the women he loved, or, more accurately, said he loved.

Bill Bradfield *used* every one of his women.

And both of his male friends, Chris Pappas and Vincent Valaitis.

And, it seemed, all the Bradfield "friends" had a big role to play on the weekend Susan Reinert was murdered and laid to rest in the back of her car.

★ ★ ★

It had been a hot, frustrating summer, that summer of 1979, for Sergeant VanNort. The family and friends of the Reinerts were losing hope with each passing day. By the time school started again in Pennsylvania, and the leaves of fall began their majestic turn, the pain in Ken Reinert's heart surged when he saw children on his street getting on school buses with their book bags.

Every lead, every clue, and every shift in the case led to a dead end. What was worse, because of the multiple jurisdictions involved, federal, state and local, and the enormous number of personnel crossing over onto each other's turf, there were communication failures that resulted in mishandled or lost evidence.

After the episode of Susan Reinert's cremation before a proper forensic examination could take place, it was VanNort's idea to check the 911 tape at the Dauphin County Courthouse. VanNort was interested in testing that tape to compare electronically the voice of the anonymous phone caller with the voices of Susan Reinert's male friends. VanNort also wanted to listen for himself to "Larry Brown" with the Spanish accent who said there was a "sick woman in a car in the parking lot of the Host Inn." All that Van-Nort needed for a promising lead was the original tape.

But just as the hospital had greeted the investigators with "What body?" people at the Dauphin County Courthouse could only stammer, "What tape?"

The tape had been mistakenly erased, and like the corpse, had vanished.

VanNort went into a tirade.

Yet he was still a hard-core veteran who had dealt with major setbacks before in his career, and when those around him seemed to lose faith, old VanNort would calmly tell his men, "Gentlemen, we'll solve this one too, even with the fuck-ups. It's just a matter of time."

"And," VanNort added, with a lopsided, confident grin, "I'm going to get our lover-boy Bradfield, because he loves to talk."

Trooper Holtz and DiSantis were in agreement with that. They had done their homework. They had documented one of the oldest motives for murder—money—and their paper trail led right to Bill Bradfield's doorstep.

★ ★ ★

Susan Reinert's mother had died the year before, in October of 1978, leaving her approximately $30,000 in cash and about $200,000 in property near Ridgeway, Pennsylvania, in upstate Elk County. About a month after her mother died, Reinert drew up a will naming her brother, W. Patrick Gallagher, executor and her children, Michael and Karen, sole beneficiaries. But her will changed radically just seven weeks before her death. On May 4, 1979, Susan Reinert changed her will and named William Bradfield as executor of her estate and sole beneficiary of all her assets. It identified him as her future husband.

The will also contained a clause which directed that William Bradfield should become the guardian of her children in the event of her death.

"Unbelievable," VanNort exclaimed, in amazement, to Trooper Holtz and DiSantis, who had handed him a copy of the will.

"She cuts out her brother as executor by naming Bradfield, she eliminates her children as beneficiaries and gives everything to Bradfield. Then, to add insult to injury, she wants Bradfield to be their guardian in the event of her death," VanNort added, looking over the will on his desk.

"You got it," Trooper Holtz said.

"So he killed her."

"I believe that."

"Or had her killed."

"Yes."

"What else?" VanNort asked.

"Take a look at this," Holtz answered, taking more papers out of his briefcase. "What I have here, Joe, is a life insurance policy taken out by Susan Reinert in March of 1979 for $250,000 with a $200,000 accidental death rider. In her application for her insurance policy, she listed as her beneficiary William Bradfield, and designated him as her 'intended husband.'"

"Jesus," VanNort said as he lit up another Marlboro cigarette with the butt of the one he had just finished.

"There's more," Holtz continued, excited. "On June 8, 1979, 17 days before she was murdered, Susan Reinert obtained another life insurance policy in the amount of $100,000 from New York Life Insurance Company. The beneficiary of that policy was again William Bradfield. On June 20, 1979, five days before she was murdered, Susan Reinert bought a third life insurance policy in the amount of $150,000 from New York Life Insurance Company, again naming William Bradfield as her beneficiary and, in her application, again designating him as her 'future husband.' All life insurance policies were one-year term life policies, which means that they had no residual cash value and would only have cash value if, in fact, Susan Reinert died within that year."

"Just to get into their pants, huh," VanNort said jokingly to DiSantis. DiSantis just shook his head.

"Quite the lover-boy," VanNort added.

"Yes, sir," said Holtz.

"Yes, sir," said DiSantis.

"Is Sue Myers cooperating?" VanNort asked.

"Yes," Holtz answered.

"What about his two boyfriends, Vincent Valaitis and Chris Pappas?"

"Yes," Holtz answered.

"Do they love him too?" VanNort asked sarcastically.

"They're loyal."

"What about Wendy Zeigler? Is she cooperating?"

"Not yet, Joe."

"What about Joanne Aitken?"

"No. She . . . she's the toughest one of the bunch," Holtz said, with a lot of regret in his voice.

"Put the heat on all of them!" VanNort snapped.

* * *

The paper trail made of money and wills and insurance policies led to Bill Bradfield's doorstep all right, but when they followed it further, which VanNort and Holtz and DiSantis did over the next 15 months, it took them right into Bradfield's house, occupied by him and Sue Myers, and then into Wendy Zeigler's closet, and then back to Bradfield's house, and ultimately into Bradfield's pocket.

The state police and the FBI agents practically lived in the Reinert house on Woodcrest Avenue in Ardmore. They waded through every scrap of paper and pieced them together like a puzzle. The puzzle, when finished, did not show the children or give a clue as to their whereabouts, nor was it a picture of violence with a killer and blood, but the picture was clearly one of grand theft by none other than William Sydney Bradfield.

And to VanNort, this picture was a prelude to murder.

In February of 1979, Susan Reinert withdrew $25,000 in cash from a savings account which she had at the Continental Bank in Montgomery County. This was practically all the money she had in her account, inherited from her mother, who had just died that previous October. It took Susan six trips to the bank, specifying on most occasions that she wanted $100 bills, but it took her a lot of shuffling and talking to make those withdrawals, because of the advice and resistance of the bank officials.

Susan Reinert did not want cashier's checks or certified treasurer's checks, which bank officials offered. She told them "he" would only take cash. The bank withdrawal records found in her home noted, after each withdrawal, that the money either went to "B" or to "Bill."

Once that border to the puzzle had been completed, getting the $25,000 in cash into Bill Bradfield's hands was the next phase. The document which could help the authorities do that was a signatory card to a safe deposit box at a local bank which bore the signature of the young student who was madly in love with Bradfield, Wendy Zeigler.

Wendy Zeigler, however, would hold out for a long time for the man she trusted and loved.

· 4 ·

PRINCIPAL SUSPECT

"The military was my life. Except for being an educator and a principal, it was my whole life. I was a colonel in the army reserves and was being considered for general. I have always felt that being a general was the best kind of achievement that you could make. I went to all the military schools – the officer's infantry school, general staff college, the war college – I am a graduate of all those schools. At the time that my world fell apart, I was very close to my lifetime goal of general. I was right next door to it."

Jay Smith

Dr. Jay Smith was the principal of Upper Merion High School for 12 years before his world fell apart. Some say he self-destructed and deserved everything he got. Others aren't so sure. Some say he should have been put to death for the murders of Susan Reinert and her children. Others say he was an innocent man, the victim of Bradfield's trap and an overzealous prosecution.

He was a private man, 50 years of age, tall, erect, proud, always poised. His face was pallid, almost rubbery, with a dark, receding hairline and seemingly lifeless eyes. If one's "eyes are the window of the soul," then Jay Smith's window was hard to see through. He could make anybody feel uncomfortable in his presence, even if he didn't want to, so he had a habit of looking away when he spoke.

Jay Smith seldom fraternized with faculty or staff or anyone else, because he was a loner. But he was a respected spit-and-polish colonel in the United States Army Reserve. His military superior, General John Eisenhower, son of the late president, praised Colonel Smith's intelligence and administrative ability as commander-in-chief of personnel. The two of them would ride together from Valley Forge to their reserve duty near Lansdale, two Sundays a month, from 1973 to 1975, and Eisenhower never thought that Colonel Smith was strange. In fact, according to General Eisenhower, all that Smith ever did was talk about his work.

The enigmatic principal had been born and raised in Chester, Pennsylvania and had been the undisputed boss of Upper Merion High for 12 years. To the staff and student body, he was a thoroughly competent administrator in a demanding school district. The school flourished under his administration and attracted dedicated educators like Susan Reinert.

Upper Merion forms the northern tier of the traditional Main Line. The foremost town in the area is King of Prussia, which hosts the prestigious King of Prussia shopping malls, home to Macy's, Bloomingdale's, Tiffany's, Strawbridge and Clothier's, and hundreds of other exclusive retail stores. The suburbs are quiet neighborhoods with an abundance of Gothic churches and synagogues throughout. Close by is the National Historic Park at Valley Forge with tree-lined rolling hills, restored bunkers used by George Washington's men during the Revolutionary War, and museums that will forever preserve American history.

Then on August 18, 1978, Jay Smith sent shock waves through the conservative Upper Merion community and made his own history.

★ ★ ★

It was almost midnight. In the parking lot of the Gateway Shopping Center, a young couple sitting on a curb eating pizza saw a man with a hood over his face and a gun in each hand sneaking up on a parked van. The young couple crept away and called the police.

Within minutes, a sergeant and a lieutenant, in a marked car with red lights flashing, pulled over the brown Ford Granada mid-sized car described on the radio broadcast. The arresting officer, Lieutenant Carl Brown, approached the car from the passenger side and saw a .22-caliber pistol laying on the seat. The driver, still wearing his hooded mask, inched his right hand over and picked up the gun.

"Drop it!" the lieutenant yelled, frightened.

The hooded driver obeyed. He was ordered out of his car and the hood was torn off his head. The driver was a tall, middle-aged man with a receding hairline. He was identified as Dr. Jay C. Smith. Dr. Jay C. Smith was expressionless.

Even the picture on his driver's license, confirming his identity, was a blank.

On the passenger seat lay an open black bag containing a .38-caliber, a .22-caliber, and a .25-caliber handgun, all loaded. A further search of the car by the police produced four .22-caliber cartridges, seven .25-caliber cartridges, 10 high-speed Mohawk .22-caliber cartridges, a box containing another 50 high-speed Mohawk cartridges, and a military-style blue raincoat with eight cartridges in one of the pockets. Police officers also found five black empty plastic garbage bags tied with rubber bands, a pair of white gloves, one Biger .22-caliber rifle, a Colt Cobra revolver, and a black-and-red bolt cutter. And there was an oil filter with two bullet holes in the top that turned out to be a homemade silencer.

Under the seat was a notebook that said, "Brinks 3:30, 7/26 Wanamaker's, King of Prussia."

There was a syringe in that car and another syringe in Smith's pocket. A lab report showed the second syringe was loaded with Placidyl, a tranquilizing drug that produces sleep if taken orally, but if injected causes unconsciousness within a minute.

Smith told the cops that he was looking for his daughter, Stephanie Hunsberger, and her husband, Eddie, whom, he feared, were being held in a van at the Gateway Shopping Center parking lot by heroin dealers. Smith also claimed that the drug-loaded syringe belonged to his son-in-law, who was an addict.

Lieutenant Carl Brown either didn't believe him or didn't care and arrested Jay Smith on the spot.

While Smith was at police headquarters, he was allowed to make a phone call, and an officer standing behind him overheard the conversation.

"Get everything out of the basement, especially the file cabinet," Jay Smith whispered. "Yes, tonight. I said tonight."

* * *

August 19, 1978.

At 1 a.m. two detectives were staked out in an unmarked car at the Smith residence on Valley Forge Road. It looked like an ordinary, middle-class, brick house in a quiet, suburban, middle-class neighborhood.

At 2 a.m. a 1974 tan-and-white Plymouth pulled up to the rear of the Smith house. It was a clear night with a full moon, so visibility was good. The detectives watched as a man made five or six trips carrying boxes from the basement of the Smith home to the trunk of his car. Then they moved in on him.

Their suspect identified himself as Harold Jones, "a friend of Dr. Smith's." Jones cooperated immediately and fully. He said he was a former librarian, and he made it clear that the police had his permission to search his car and take what they wanted. "I only did what I was told to do by Dr. Smith. Everything in the trunk belongs to Dr. Smith. None of it is mine," Jones uttered, terrified.

The boxes taken from Smith's basement and found in Jones's trunk held manuals issued by the War College in Carlisle, Pennsylvania and three paintings that belonged to Upper Merion High School. Plus two pounds of marijuana.

Getting a search warrant that night for the Smith residence was easy.

In the house the police found an additional 580 grams of marijuana and vials of contraband pills and capsules. There were stolen office machines, more paintings from the school, and four gallons of nitric acid—apparently taken from Upper Merion High's chemistry lab.

The cops in the basement found five more oil-filter silencers along with a pair of latex gloves. The basement walls were punctuated with bullet holes.

There was also a collection of pornographic and bestiality magazines, among them *Animals as Sex Partners, Animal Fever, Carla's Puppy Love, The Four-Legged Lovers, The Bestial Erotics, Herbie's Dreams,* and *The Canine Tongue.* In another part of the basement was a bunch of explicit swinger magazines, both straight and gay.

In addition to stolen military ID cards, they found a pile of blue combs bearing the name of Smith's Army Reserve unit, 79th USARCOM.

Of far greater interest to the swarms of police in the Smith residence were Brink's security guard uniforms, a dark blue Brink's security hat, two silver badges, and an employee identification card bearing a photograph of Dr. Smith with the name "Carl S. Williams" beneath it.

The reason?

In December 1977, a man wearing a Brink's security guard outfit entered a Sears store in the Neshaminy Mall, Bucks County. After showing a phony ID card, he left with $100,000 in cash and personal checks. Only after he had departed with the money and the real guard had shown up did the store officials realize that they had been scammed.

Police also suspected Smith in the theft of $34,000 in cash and $19,000 in checks from another Sears store in the town of St. David's, because the same thing had happened there. A man wearing a Brink's security guard outfit had entered the Sears store, displayed a phony ID card, and after being given the cash and checks, had politely thanked the bookkeeper and vanished.

"Upper Merion High School is not going to be ready for this," one officer said, shaking his head.

The Upper Merion Police Department threw the book at Dr. Jay Smith. And the highly respected Principal of Upper Merion High School was charged with possession of instruments of crime, unlawful possession of firearms, and possession with intent to deliver marijuana and other unlawfully controlled substances. He was also charged with the theft of $53,000 from the Sears store in St. David's, Pennsylvania and with posing as a uniformed Brink's security guard with false credentials to effectuate the scam. A second charge of theft was brought alleging the same modus operandi at the Sears store in Neshaminy Mall. The police leaked information to the media about the search of the home and added plenty of fuel to that leak with wild rumors of strange sexual interests.

Overnight, Dr. Jay Smith became a media sensation and the best tabloid story in town.

★ ★ ★

The officer was right. Upper Merion High School was not ready.

Hundreds of frantic parents wrote letters to the administration and attended a specially called meeting within that same week. They demanded an explanation and immediate action. The meeting room was packed with hostile parents, and the school board members had their hands full. There were no *Robert's Rules of Order* that night.

"How could a man who has served as the high school principal for 12 years have led such an incredible life?!" one mother screamed.

"We . . . we can't answer that, ma'am," a defenseless school board official answered.

"How could you do this to us?!"

"We didn't . . . we . . . we can't answer that."

"Didn't you do a background check on him, for God's sake?!"

"Where were you when all of this was going on?!"

"How could you have allowed him to be in charge of our children?!"

"We . . . we . . . we can't answer that, ma'am."

The school board officials tried to handle the irate crowd of mothers and fathers but could not answer any of their questions. It was all they could do to keep a riot from breaking out, because no one could explain any of it. Dr. Jay Smith was bizarre. And people were talking about him—in their homes, in the streets, in laundromats, in bars, in grocery stores, but especially at the school.

Immediately following that meeting, within one week after his arrest, Dr. Jay Smith was suspended by the school board and his 12 years of dedicated service as the esteemed principal of Upper Merion High went out the window. It's not that the school board had any choice, presumption of innocence or no presumption of innocence. Dr. Jay Smith was presumed guilty as hell.

At least his military reserve unit didn't move in, but his lifelong dream of a promotion to general was suddenly over.

And after Jay Smith's arrest and the sensationalized tabloid stories that followed, everybody avoided him like the bubonic plague. With one brief exception from Upper Merion High, and he came to Smith's aid.

That exception was Bill Bradfield who wrote to Smith at the Chester County Prison, before Smith was released on bail, offering to send him books and help him in any way that he could. Smith wrote back asking him for a copy of *Warriner's Book of Composition and Grammar*, a copy of *Ivanhoe*, and a copy of *Moby Dick*.

Smith was leery of Bradfield's kind offer because he considered Bradfield an adversary and had never really liked him. It's just that at the time, Smith was in no position to be choosy.   Vincent Valaitis remembered Bill Bradfield coming to him one day sometime after Smith's arrest. Bradfield told him Jay Smith was innocent of the St. David's robbery and that the police were twisting evidence and unjustly harassing him.

Valaitis remembered that Bradfield also said, "I know he couldn't have robbed the Sears store at St. David's because the day the theft occurred I was with him. That was the day I bumped into him at the shore. The realization came to me last night in a dream. I dread getting involved in

Smith's case, but I have no choice. After all, it's my moral responsibility to tell the truth."

Vincent Valaitis loved Bill Bradfield and believed in him, but he wasn't sure about the dream part.

★ ★ ★

Jay Smith's arrest also ended his private life forever and completely. Between the law enforcement officials (at the federal, state, and local levels), the television and radio stations, and the scores of newspaper reporters always looking for a different angle, a different spin, everything in Jay's past came to light, usually on the front page of the *Philadelphia Daily News* or the *Philadelphia Inquirer*.

Maybe in the past his co-workers hadn't been sure if Jay Smith was married, or if he had children, but Smith's married life fascinated the tabloids.

Jay had been married to Stephanie for 28 years. She was a little older than Jay and had grown up in the college town of West Chester. She had worked hard all her life and had helped put Jay through college. Even at the height of Jay's career as a colonel and principal, she was employed at a local dry cleaners and worked at the front counter.

Stephanie Smith, unlike her husband, was not a private person. She loved to gossip to everybody about everything, and her favorite topic was her married life that wasn't all that great. Stephanie was constantly threatening to leave Jay. Her unstable marriage got bad enough at one point that she hired a divorce lawyer and felt it necessary to turn over to him a dildo, which he thought was an unusual piece of evidence in a divorce case.

Stephanie Smith was a little unusual herself. She was over 50 years old and still wore white go-go boots with tight mini-skirts or hot pants, and her hair was always dyed and spiked. Maybe she'd had the body for it once.

Jay and Stephanie had two daughters—Stephanie, named after her mother, and Sheri. They were troubled girls from a troubled home and, to add to their problems, for the past two years their mother had been dying from terminal cancer. The way the doctors at Bryn Mawr Hospital explained it, their mother was suffering from "raging leukemia" and there was very little hope.

For a time, the younger Stephanie was a student at Upper Merion. It was common knowledge that she was a drug user and she soon dropped out of school. It was also rumored that young Stephanie was involved in prostitution to support a heroin addiction.

And if that wasn't enough, she married Eddie Hunsberger, a handsome young man seeking drug rehabilitation. His parents, Pete and Dorothy, lived in North Wales, Pennsylvania and Eddie was their only child.

February 28, 1978 was the last time that Pete and Dorothy saw Eddie and Stephanie alive.

Eddie Hunsberger's parents insisted that Jay Smith had murdered the couple.

After a nationwide search, the police said that Smith's son-in-law and daughter had vanished and were presumed dead.

· 5 ·

ALIBI

All four of them—Bill Bradfield, Sue Myers, Chris Pappas, and Vincent Valaitis—said they couldn't have had anything to do with it because they were at the shore together. They said they had gone to Cape May, New Jersey late that Friday night and didn't get back until Monday afternoon. They said they were "shocked" to learn that Susan Reinert had been murdered and couldn't believe that it happened.

"I couldn't believe it," Bradfield said. "It was a tragedy."

From the day that Sergeant VanNort took over the Reinert case, he wasn't convinced of anyone's innocence, especially Bradfield's, because to VanNort a lover is always a prime suspect—and he didn't care where Bradfield said he was or who Bradfield said he was with, or who Bradfield said was with him.

"Check it out" was all VanNort had to say to Holtz and DiSantis.

"And remember," he added, "interview everybody—*everybody*—and separate those four . . . and believe only what you have to believe because there's going to be a lot of lying going on."

In no time, the Pennsylvania State Police were in Cape May interviewing everybody and showing them pictures of the kids. The local Cape May detectives were brought in to assist, and the canvassing went into the boarding houses, motels, seafood restaurants, and the quaint retail shops throughout Cape May's historic district. Many officers and detectives looked more than once at the rolling ocean tide and wondered.

The state police quickly learned that on the previous Tuesday, June 19, 1979, Bradfield had traveled to Cape May to procure lodging for himself, Susan Myers, Chris Pappas, and Vincent Valaitis for the weekend beginning that following Friday. Bradfield had been accompanied on this trip by Joanne Aitken, who at that time was living in the Congress Hotel in Philadelphia. Ms. Aitken had been at the Congress Hotel for approximately 30 days prior to going to the shore with Bradfield. She was registered as Mrs. William Bradfield.

Joanne Aitken was by far the most resistant and challenging of the Bradfield women. She was in her early thirties, with dark, straight hair, parted in the middle, pulled straight back behind her ears; no makeup, no jewelry, no high heels. Ms. Aitken was a graduate student at Harvard University that year and was by all accounts very, very bright. She was always one step ahead of Holtz and DiSantis, and the Feds, and the lawyers.

Holtz and DiSantis worked her and worked her, and she never told them anything. When asked what she had been doing for 30 days at a cheap hotel in Philadelphia, she told them, "I was studying Philadelphia's architecture . . . getting to know the city."

When they asked her where she was on Friday evening, June 22, she told them, "I would say somewhere in Philadelphia . . . I don't remember."

When they asked her where she was on Saturday, June 23 . . . and Sunday, June 24 . . . and Monday, June 25, her answer was the same: "I don't remember."

When they threatened her with prosecution for withholding information, or cajoled her, or tried to win her sympathy, she wouldn't even tell them that she didn't remember. It's not that she was flippant or cocky or daring. She just wouldn't tell them anything.

When Bradfield went to Cape May with Joanne on June 19th, he secured accommodations for himself and his other three friends at the Heirloom Boarding House. Bradfield informed the proprietor, Marian Taylor, that he and his friends would be there on the evening of June 22nd. Bradfield told Taylor that they would be arriving late and that she should leave the room unlocked for them.

Sue Myers always loved going to the shore with Bill Bradfield, especially Cape May, where the vast ocean held memories of years gone by, when she had been a little girl playing on the beaches in the hot sand and sun. She still loved walking those beaches with Bill, who had promised her so many things on those moonlit nights, like a beautiful marriage, and beautiful children, which seemed so elusive to her. The waves, she once thought, were like his promises that kept washing away.

"When he talked of love to me," Sue once told a friend, "I felt I was the only person in the universe to him. When he'd hold me, I was convinced of it beyond all doubt."

Sue Myers heard all the stories at school about Susan Reinert and hated her for it. Sue still intended to marry Bill and have children with him and that's all there was to it.

Sue would have preferred going alone with him to the shore that weekend, but rather than not go at all, she agreed to have his friends, Valaitis and Pappas, come along. She did not know that Joanne Aitken helped make the arrangements. Normally, whenever Bradfield planned a trip, Sue Myers was in charge of making the arrangements and his initiative for this weekend was unusual.

★ ★ ★

Friday, June 22, 1979.

During the early morning hours, without saying a word, William Bradfield left the residence he shared with Sue Myers. He gave her no explanation of his proposed activities, though he had been living with her at the time for six years.

At some point, Chris Pappas and Wendy Zeigler told the police that Bradfield was with them all day, first with Chris Pappas and then with Wendy Zeigler. Bradfield spent the early part of that afternoon in a cheap hotel with Wendy. Then he turned $25,000 in cash over to her, asking her to hide it in her closet.

"Why?" Wendy asked, innocently.

"Just in case Smith kills Susan Reinert in the next couple of days," Bradfield answered after some thought, and continued, "Reinert has this silly will in which I am named beneficiary. I don't know why, but, well, my assets might be frozen, so I want you to hold onto my cash until I get back from New Mexico, which is going to be in the fall."

"I see," Wendy said, confused.

And that was it. She did it for Bradfield. She hid the cash in her closet, because she loved him and trusted him.

At approximately 8 p.m., Bradfield drove Wendy Zeigler to her girlfriend's house. Thereafter, he was unaccounted for until 11 p.m. VanNort was very much interested in this gap because Susan Reinert and her children were last seen alive leaving their residence at 9:20 p.m. that evening.

At approximately 11 p.m., Bradfield had returned to his residence to meet Sue Myers and Vince Valaitis. Valaitis described Bradfield as being somewhat upset and irritated, and said that he uncharacteristically hurried them along to leave the apartment. After packing what remained for the trip in Bradfield's Volkswagen, the three of them drove to Chris Pappas's apartment, where they picked up Chris.

Though Vincent Valaitis was 29 years old at the time, he looked 17. He was tall with dark hair and wide shoulders. He wore glasses and was studious-looking. The students at Upper Merion called him "Clark Kent," the alter-ego of Superman. Valaitis was a fellow English teacher at Upper Merion High and a good friend and confidant of Bill Bradfield. Superman he was not. He was a devout Catholic who had almost gone into the seminary and was the living definition of naiveté. In fact, a more naive person would be a real find in today's day and age. Like the other Bradfield friends and lovers, he was vulnerable and plagued with self-doubts.

Chris Pappas was no different. A former student of Bradfield's, Pappas was also a friend and confidant. He taught at Upper Merion. At 25, he was insecure and had problems. Soft-spoken, black-haired Chris Pappas looked Italian but was Greek. He was of medium height, with a sturdy build.

Pappas drove the Volkswagen all the way to Cape May with Susan Myers in the passenger seat. Bradfield, exhausted and dozing off, sat in the cramped back seat with Vincent Valaitis. According to Valaitis, during the trip Bradfield began to talk about Susan Reinert. Bradfield told Valaitis that Jay Smith was going to kill Susan Reinert that weekend. Bradfield stated that he had driven to Reinert's house that evening and had followed Smith while Smith circled the block around Reinert's house 14 times. He claimed that he then lost Smith in a hailstorm. Bradfield indicated that he had done everything he could to protect Susan Reinert. How he could have lost Smith circling the same block was a question that Bradfield could never answer.

Not one of them—Bradfield, Myers, Valaitis, or Pappas—could explain why they never said anything to the authorities.

★ ★ ★

Saturday, June 23, 1979.

At approximately 3 a.m., the four vacationers arrived in Cape May.

"That's right," Valaitis told authorities at one of his many interviews. "We . . . we went to breakfast in a restaurant and then drove to a rooming house at approximately 4:15 a.m. When we got there, we discovered that the room we had rented was occupied by another individual. Bradfield tried to wake up the proprietor at that time but was unsuccessful. I slept with Bradfield in the hall of the rooming house, while Myers and Pappas went for a walk until the rooming house opened. Later that morning, Bradfield got us two rooms at the room house. Bradfield and Myers took the one room, and I took the other one with Pappas.

"That Saturday evening, the four of us had dinner together. After dinner, Bradfield insisted that I accompany him to the Catholic church where the two of us lit candles and prayed for Susan Reinert."

"You lit candles for Susan Reinert?" Holtz asked, incredulous.

"Yes," Vincent answered.

"And prayed for her?

"Yes."

"Unbelievable."

★ ★ ★

Sunday, June 24, 1979.

Early that Sunday morning, according to Valaitis, he and Bradfield attended Mass and again, they both lit candles for Susan Reinert.

Holtz considered asking them if they lit extra candles for the children.

Later in the day, Bradfield directed Pappas to call Wendy Zeigler in Montgomery County in order to find out if anything "newsworthy" had occurred. Pappas took this to mean that Bradfield wanted to know whether or not Susan Reinert's death had been reported in any newspapers. When he made the call, Pappas was informed that nothing had appeared in the newspapers, and he assumed that Reinert had not been killed. He dutifully reported this to Bradfield.

Throughout the weekend in question, Bradfield was careful to insist that receipts were obtained for every purchase made by any of the four individuals in his group. When they left the Heirloom Boarding House, he also asked the proprietor to give him a receipt for Friday, as well as the days he actually spent at the shore, and asked her to place the names of all four individuals on that receipt.

★ ★ ★

Monday, June 25, 1979.

It was time to go home, but not for long for William Sydney Bradfield, or for Chris Pappas.

Joanne Aitken was waiting somewhere in the Philadelphia area—she didn't remember where—to drive Bill Bradfield to the airport. She did remember that Bradfield picked her up in his car and that she dropped him off at the busy Philadelphia International Airport late that night. She also remembered that on the way to the airport, Bradfield asked her to drive his Volkswagen to New Mexico and meet him there, which she agreed to do. Bradfield had preplanned a trip to New Mexico where he was going to spend the summer with Chris Pappas and Joanne Aitken.

Prior to leaving Cape May that morning, however, Pappas and Bradfield cleaned out the interior of Bradfield's car and placed multiple documents in an envelope. On the way home, they made a stop at an apartment complex with a dumpster, and Pappas threw the envelope in the dumpster at Bradfield's direction.

According to Pappas, during one of his many interviews, none of the trio of Bradfield's friends questioned him about this.

That evening, Pappas met Bradfield at the Philadelphia Airport, and they flew together to Santa Fe, New Mexico. Joanne Aitken arrived in New Mexico approximately one week later in Bradfield's car.

★ ★ ★

VanNort drove straight to Cape May, New Jersey to do his own looking around within days of Reinert's murder. He met with the local detectives and then personally paid a visit to Marian Taylor, the owner of the Heirloom Boarding House where Bradfield and his friends had just spent the weekend.

No, the proprietor said, she could not account for their whereabouts that weekend, only that they were there and she showed VanNort a copy of the receipt to prove it. And no, she had not seen the children pictured in VanNort's photographs or any children for that matter.

On the way back from Cape May, VanNort double-checked the distances and times from the Host Inn to Philadelphia and from Philadelphia to Cape May. From Cape May to Philadelphia was less than two hours; from Philadelphia to the Host Inn, he clocked one hour and 50 minutes going the speed limit.

No problem, VanNort noted.

VanNort and Holtz were ringing Sue Myers's doorbell within 24 hours after Reinert's autopsy. Myers had some explaining to do. Vincent Valaitis just happened to be there, and the heat was on. Not even Valaitis knew how much heat a veteran like VanNort could put on him. Sergeant VanNort, when it came to interrogation, could set a roaring fire.

On July 4th, Joe VanNort and Holtz flew to Albuquerque, New Mexico, rented a car, and drove to Santa Fe. Soon they were on the beautiful campus of St. John's College and felt away from it all, but not for long. They met with the college's vice-president, Dr. J. Avlt, and told him that they wanted to talk to William Bradfield and Chris Pappas. Sergeant VanNort made it clear that he wanted to interview them separately, and that he wanted to speak to Chris Pappas first.

VanNort and Holtz learned that Bradfield was taking a course in the science of natural mathematics at St. John's. It was a discussion of Plato and the creation of the cosmos. Professor Steven Crockett was impressed with Bradfield's intelligence and thought he was the best student in the class. Bradfield eventually got an "A" as he did in all of the seminars he had ever taken. Joanne Aitken frequently joined Bradfield's classes and Chris Pappas was always close by with his own books.

Professor Crockett saw Bradfield talking to the Director of the College, but had had no idea that the conference was about two out-of-state homicide detectives waiting to question him.

It was Holtz who read Bradfield and Pappas their rights. Both of them were visibly nervous. Bradfield, controlling his voice, nodded that he understood but refused to talk to them. On the advice of Bradfield, Chris Pappas did the same.

"We've come a long way to talk to you about a very serious matter, Mr. Bradfield," Holtz said gently.

VanNort just watched, scrutinizing Bradfield's reaction.

"Chris Pappas, Vincent Valaitis, Sue Myers, and I were in Cape May on Friday, Saturday, Sunday, and Monday, the entire weekend of the murder. That's all I have to say. Submit your questions to my attorney in Philadelphia. I'd like to help in this investigation, but I can't say when I will be able to provide my attorney with my answers. My first concern at this time is with my studies," Bradfield said.

Holtz was livid.

VanNort said nothing. He showed no emotion but he was furious. This was a homicide investigation and that kind of thing was to be expected. VanNort knew in time that he was going to get him.

★ ★ ★

Fall, 1979.

When summer school ended in New Mexico, Bill Bradfield and Joanne Aitken and Chris Pappas would be back. Joanne would return to graduate from Harvard, Bradfield would return to Upper Merion, if he didn't get canned. Chris Pappas would do the same.

What Bradfield didn't know when he got back was that VanNort and Holtz were working Valaitis. For weeks, the police had been showing Valaitis material and evidence that indicated Bradfield had been lying and was involved in the murder. Vince felt the anger and humiliation swelling in his chest, but the overriding emotion was fear.

Something that VanNort was very good at instilling.

Sue Myers was the first of the Bradfield women to break. She told Bradfield one night, crying, "I can't stand the thought of going to jail. I'll kill myself if I have to go to jail. They told me I was next. They told me that you were going to kill me next."

VanNort did, in fact, tell Sue Myers all those things.

Sue Myers may or may not have believed that Bradfield was going to kill her, but she definitely believed that VanNort, Holtz, and DiSantis were capable of putting her in jail. That's all she needed to think about for a while. Though she loved Bill Bradfield and had lived with him since 1973—though she adored him immeasurably, with passion, with romance—Sue Myers had no intention of going to jail for him.

It's not that Bill Bradfield's magnetism was wearing off.

It's that VanNort's magnetism was getting to her.

6

MEDIA FRENZY

First there was Jay Smith's arrest and conviction for weapons and theft and drugs. He was sentenced in Dauphin County on June 25, 1979. Then there was Susan Reinert's bizarre sexual murder and the vanishing of two innocent children. Susan's body was found outside the Host Inn in Dauphin County on June 25, 1979. Then the media found out about the incredible and unexplained disappearance of Jay's own daughter and son-in-law.

And if that wasn't enough, there were allegations of orgies and satanic cults and sex between teachers and students in the classrooms. Then there were "leaks" by the police that Dr. Smith was into mass pornography and swinger's sex clubs and satanism. There were even rumors reported that Smith sometimes wore a red Satan costume during his escapades.

And the media went wild!

Reporters from the *Philadelphia Bulletin* suspected devil worship and went right to the presses with it on Sunday, August 26, 1979.

SATAN CULT DEATH?

Teacher may have been sexually assaulted, tortured, before she was slain, probers say. The murderers of Upper Merion High School teacher Susan Reinert may have been members or associates of a Satan worship cult, investigators have told reporters. Mrs. Reinert may have been stripped, tortured, and sexually assaulted as she lay on a makeshift sacrifice altar during a black Mass devil worship ceremony on the weekend of her murder last June. Federal and state investigators have found evidence of the existence of the cult in the Upper Merion area.

Cult members were described by one investigator as "intellectual professionals." They did not balk at using animals in sex exhibition and encounters, the investigators said. Investigators said they were not sure if Susan Reinert was actually a member of the cult or whether she attended the black Mass rituals and other ceremonies out of curiosity, but they said they were certain Mrs. Reinert knew about the cult and the identity of many of its members.

Satanism or devil worship is as old as Christianity itself. Its members traditionally dress in dark hooded robes and gather at a narrow altar to witness Satan, usually a cult ringleader in Satan garb, perform a sexual sacrifice on an unclothed maiden. Literature about the cult attests that in modern times the ceremony has included the use of sexual stimulation devices. Satan performs sado-masochistic acts on his victim who is tied up and heavily drugged while other cult members hold lighted candles and chant ancient prayers of Satanic worship.

Some of Smith's papers, letters, and diaries that were made public last week in a copyrighted story in a Montgomery County newspaper, indicated that Smith engaged in sexual activities while wearing such costumes as military fatigues and a Satan outfit.

When word was leaked to the press, again by the police, that in addition to routine items found in Susan Reinert's car there had been a strap-on rubber dildo, another banner headline and story was generated.

SEX RING LINKED TO MURDER; SWINGER'S GROUP PROBED

State police have uncovered explosive new evidence in the Susan Reinert murder case linking the Upper Merion teacher to a bizarre sex ring. Officials have categorically refused to disclose any details publicly about the group. But sources said yesterday that Mrs.Reinert's knowledge of the love cult may have been a motive in the slaying.

The individuals contacted by reporters have said that as many as 20 to 30 men and women regularly participated in "swinging sessions" that included homosexual and sado-masochistic acts. However, it could not be determined whether Mrs. Reinert actually participated in any of the orgies.

One police source said that Mrs. Reinert may have been killed because she was about to expose the existence of the group and its members, most of whom are "professionals."

With school about to resume at Upper Merion High that fall, the frenzy was at a fever pitch. At least four teachers were under investigation for criminal offenses. As many as a dozen more were suspected of involvement with, or knowledge of, a love cult. Newspapers featured front-page pictures of an irate mob of parents about to lynch a harried school board president and the school superintendent. Other headlines read, THE ABC's OF A SCHOOL GONE BAD ... THE SCHOOL FOR SCANDAL ... LIFE IN THE SUBURBS IS SUDDENLY SCANDALOUS ... SEX, DRUGS, TROUBLE—UPPER MERION HIGH.

★ ★ ★

Joe VanNort was going crazy. Every time he read about Satan, or orgies, or cults, or hooded burnings, or exotic sex practices, he lost valuable time and men. His own men and the FBI would go on wild goose chases looking for the devil and cults. VanNort refused to buy into these media creations which his own men helped create with their damn leaks. He had the news clips on his desk, and he noted that the sources of the media were "probers," or "investigators," or "a police source." His own men were setting certain fires the media was fanning and VanNort was furious because of it, with his men, with the media, and with the stories.

"I ain't chasin' no devil except that long-haired hippy son-of-a-bitch!" VanNort told Holtz, irate, in his office one day with newspapers strewn all over his desk.

"I agree with you," Holtz said.

"We're going to get him, Jack. Trust me. He talks too much, and we've got his friends and lovers right where we want them ... just about."

"I agree with that too," Holtz said, equally determined.

"Good. No more devil chasing."

"Right, Joe, but ... "

"But what?" VanNort asked.

"This guy, Jay Smith," Holtz said cautiously. "He's capable, and we found a blue 79 USARCOM comb in the trunk under Reinert's body. Smith was in the 79th U.S. Army Reserve Command, and he had combs like that in his home. In addition, Smith shows up for sentencing in Harrisburg on the same day Reinert's body was found in Harrisburg."

VanNort watched Holtz closely as Holtz reminded him that Bradfield had testified for Smith at Smith's "Brink's trial" in Harrisburg one month before Reinert was murdered. In May 1979, Bradfield had provided Smith's alibi at the principal's trial involving the Sears store at St. David's in 1977. Bradfield told the jury that on the day of the incident he had actually run into Smith in Ocean City, New Jersey, spent time with him there looking for a mutual friend, and even shared a meal with him.

Bradfield's alibi didn't work. The jury deliberated less than two hours before returning a verdict of guilty. VanNort had read in a local paper that the jury foreman was interviewed by the press as to the alibi testimony of William S. Bradfield, and the juror was quoted as saying, "We sure didn't believe *that* teacher!"

The juror's comment was in all the newspapers the next day.

Bradfield's testimony at Smith's trial, which helped get Smith convicted because Bradfield had no credibility, was no motive to VanNort for Smith to kill; in fact, he thought that Bradfield's alibi for Smith was crap, a way for Bradfield to get closer to the guy he was going to set up.

VanNort was relying on 30 years of experience and his instincts, which seldom failed him. Smith was a fallen and disgraced man—portrayed by the media as capable of anything. He was a sitting duck for a guy like Bradfield. VanNort knew that Holtz wanted Smith, but he wasn't convinced of anything at that point.

First of all, VanNort was not impressed with the comb in the trunk under Susan Reinert's body. It was much too obvious. A guy like Smith, who was capable, wasn't leaving a calling card.

Secondly, Smith showing up in Harrisburg to be sentenced hours after Reinert's body was found in Harrisburg was far too obvious. Smith was too smart for that if half of what the media said about him was true.

In addition, there was no motive for Smith to do it, and guys like Smith needed a motive. The two Brink's holdups were for money, and there was no violence. To VanNort, that was just a scam of deception, and that's all there was to it.

"It's too obvious," VanNort told Holtz. "It looks more like a setup to me by our friend Bill Bradfield, but everybody is a suspect, Jack, including Smith. Remember that, but I'm telling you it's too obvious. Smith was a nut, and Bradfield is a manipulative, scheming son-of-a-bitch."

"How do you explain the disappearance of his daughter, Stephanie, and Eddie Hunsberger?" Holtz asked.

"I can't," VanNort answered, frustrated.

★ ★ ★

It was late spring, 1980.

Ten months had gone by.

And after all that time, after all that energy and manpower, after one of the most massive investigations in Pennsylvania's criminal history, no one had been arrested, indicted, or charged with anything. All hope for the children was lost. The Reinert case seemed to be languishing.

In addition, the police troops were being pulled out. The FBI removed 16 of the original 18 agents who had been assigned to the case, and the Pennsylvania State Police cut their full-time manpower in the investigation back to three, which left Sergeant VanNort, Trooper Jack Holtz, and Trooper DiSantis in the field alone.

Not completely alone, however, because an army of media stayed in the field with them.

The murder of Susan Reinert and the disappearance of her two children became one of the most written-about and discussed unsolved murders in recent history. The newspapers kept it on the front pages with running editorials, and the TV and radio networks kept it as their lead story. The word on the street was that ex-cop-turned-author Joseph Wambaugh was considering the murder of Reinert as a possible book or movie.

It's just that at that time there was no conclusion.

Then it happened.

VanNort saw it coming but didn't tell anyone. William Bradfield made a mistake, just like VanNort said he would, and although it took Bradfield a year to make the wrong move, it was a move that the authorities would later describe as "the mistake that proved William Bradfield's undoing." It was a move by Bradfield that would ultimately land him in one of the toughest prisons in Pennsylvania for the rest of his natural life. It was June 1980, approximately the anniversary date of Reinert's execution, when William S. Bradfield quietly moved to probate the will and collect on the insurance policies that named him as executor and sole beneficiary of Susan Reinert's $1.1 million estate. In order for Bradfield to collect, he would have to go to court and testify under oath in a civil proceeding. Bradfield would also have to testify about the $25,000 that was missing and unaccounted for, and therefore owed to the estate of Susan Reinert. Joe Van-Nort and Jack Holtz couldn't wait to be there.

VanNort and Holtz were going to probate court as interested spectators, very interested, in the hopes of getting their own inheritance.

VanNort and Holtz were sitting on their investigation, which established that Bradfield had $25,000 of Sue Reinert's money. If Bradfield had said it was a loan, or that she had given it to him to invest, or that she had given it to him to hold and the estate could have it back, or even that she had given it to him for a gift, then Bradfield would have once again checkmated Van-Nort and Holtz as he had done in Santa Fe, New Mexico one year ago.

However, when Bradfield took the witness stand in probate court, he did not know how much, or what, the state police had already uncovered. He didn't know that VanNort and Holtz had discovered from Susan's cash withdrawals, and her notations and cooperating witnesses, that she had passed the money to him.

On June 10, 1980, at a quiet orphans' court hearing, the trap for Bradfield was set, and he stepped right in. The effective examination of William Bradfield that day was done by attorney John Reilly, the court-appointed executor of Susan Reinert's estate.

Q. Please state your full name for the record.
A. William S. Bradfield.
Q. What was your relationship with Susan Reinert in May and June of 1979, sir?
A. We were very good friends.
Q. Were you anticipating marriage?
A. I was not. No, sir.
Q. Did you ever discuss marriage with her?
A. Often.
Q. Did you ever spend evenings with her?
A. Yes, sir; often.
Q. Overnight?
A. Never.
Q. Never?
A. No.
Q. Do you know what Susan Reinert inherited from her mother?
A. No, sir, I don't.
Q. Do you know what Susan Reinert inherited from her mother's estate in terms of cash?
A. No, sir.
Q. You didn't know she had any cash in the bank?
A. No.
Q. You didn't know that at all?
A. No, sir.
Q. Did Susan Reinert ever give you any money to invest?

A. No, sir.

Q. Mr. Bradfield, did Mrs. Reinert give you sums of money periodically from January 1979 until the period immediately preceding her death?

A. No, sir.

Q. She never gave you any money whatsoever?

A. No, sir.

Q. By the way, were you aware that Susan Reinert had taken out extensive insurance policies naming you as beneficiary, sir?

A. No, I was not.

Q. Isn't it a fact, sir, that you had promised to marry Mrs. Susan Reinert upon obtaining the divorce?

A. No, sir.

Q. That is not a fact?

A. No, sir.

Q. Now directing your attention to February 19, 1979, or shortly thereafter, did Mrs. Reinert give you $1,500 in cash, sir?

A. No, sir.

Q. No, sir?

A. No, sir, Mrs. Reinert never gave me any money.

Q. Never gave you any money?

A. No, sir.

Q. Did she give you $1,500 after February 21, 1979?

A. Mrs. Reinert never gave me any money.

Q. For purposes of investment?

A. No, sir.

Q. What about March 2, 1979? Did she give you $5,000 at that time?

A. No, sir.

Q. March 7, 1979, did she give you $5,000 at that time?

A. No, sir.

Q. Mrs. Reinert never gave you any money?

A. No, sir.

VanNort and Holtz were sitting in the back of the courtroom. If William Bradfield didn't know that, he should have. He should have remembered they had been his visitors in Santa Fe.

When Bradfield's testimony was concluded at the orphans' court hearing, Holtz looked at VanNort and whispered, "We got him."

VanNort nodded.

The big mistake Bradfield made was denying any knowledge of the money. He even denied knowledge of Reinert's will and insurance policies.

Bradfield had told so many lies under oath—about the money, the will, the insurance policies, Susan Reinert, himself—that a prosecution based on theft was going to be a piece of cake for VanNort and Holtz. The next court proceeding for William Bradfield wasn't going to be in orphans' court probating a will. It was going to be in the criminal courts of Delaware County, and the charge was going to be the theft of $25,000. All Holtz needed to do was tie up some loose ends.

The *Philadelphia Daily News* had this to say in an editorial:

> Putting it gently, Susan Reinert had an impressive amount of life insurance. Spectacular Bid is insured for more. So, presumably, is Streisand. But for a schoolteacher the figure's a bit high.
>
> What Bradfield is suggesting has a charm all its own. Susan Reinert, under the mistaken impression that she was going to marry Bill Bradfield, tiptoes out, purchases three quarters of a million dollars worth of insurance, didn't tell him a thing about it, didn't tell him about her estate, didn't tell him she changed her will, didn't tell him she has made him sole beneficiary of the estate and the insurance. Now if Mr. Bradfield could only put that to music we could all dance down the yellow brick road.

At the close of those proceedings, no one in the courtroom knew that Chris Pappas, Bradfield's friend and former student, had been following both press and television accounts of the probate hearings and was now haunted by the information that he had previously withheld—information about $25,000 in cash that he had wiped fingerprints from and had helped William Bradfield hide—not to mention what Bradfield had told him about chains and locks, guns, acid, and cutting up bodies.

Pappas couldn't take it anymore.

• 7 •

PRESSURE

The questioning by the police, the notoriety of Susan Reinert's death, the horror of the missing children, and over a year of lies and hiding had finally gotten to Chris Pappas. And Pappas remembered the horrible visit he got from VanNort and Holtz in Santa Fe. Every time there was a loud knock at the door, or the phone would ring, Pappas got sick in his stomach. He still loved Bradfield, but he couldn't take it anymore, and he made the call.

VanNort and Holtz wasted no time sitting down with Chris in the comfortable environment of VanNort's office. Maybe it wasn't so comfortable for Chris when VanNort put the heat on him. Chris Pappas sang like a canary to a full house with VanNort and Holtz at front and center. They silently cheered and clapped after every song. The words and music were flawless.

"What did Bradfield tell you about Susan Reinert's will before she was murdered?" VanNort asked.

"He . . . he showed me the document. I didn't read the entire will, but it was a will. It mentioned that he was the beneficiary," Pappas answered, reluctantly.

"What can you tell us about the $25,000, Chris?" VanNort asked ever so gently.

"Bill Bradfield never told me he got the money from Susan Reinert," Pappas answered, "but in the trunk of his car—he showed me—it was filled with gym bags and briefcases and just lots of things. There was a bottle of acid in there and a large sum of money in different locations. Some of it had been in a gym bag. Some was in different briefcases. Some was in the glove compartment of the car."

"How was it packaged?"

"Some of it was loose. Most of it had rubberbands around it. They were all $50 and $100 bills."

"What was done with it?"

"We took it to my apartment, and then Mr. Bradfield took out his handkerchief and wiped off all the bills. He said that he was trying to remove any fingerprints that might appear on them."

"Why did he do that?"

"He said it was for my benefit, and that if my prints were on the money, I could be involved in some sort of an investigation."

41

"Did you count the money while you were there?"

"I did."

"How much money was there?"

"I recall $28,500."

"What did you do with the money?"

"We put it in a safe deposit box at either the Southeast or Southwest National Bank in West Chester, Bill Bradfield's name was on the signature card, and my name was on the signature card along with Wendy Zeigler's," Pappas answered, nervous but relieved to be finally telling the truth.

"Wendy Zeigler's?" VanNort repeated, shaking his head knowingly.

"Yes."

VanNort and Holtz huddled. Holtz whispered to VanNort that they might need Wendy Zeigler, but she was in California going to school, and every time they tried to talk to her, she either clammed-up or gave them the run around. VanNort whispered back that he personally would take care of Wendy Zeigler, but they had Chris Pappas on a roll and VanNort didn't want that ball slowing down.

"Chris," VanNort said reassuringly, "I want you to sit back and relax."

"I can't seem to do that," Pappas said, still sick in his stomach at what he was going through.

"You better try," VanNort said calmly, "because now we're going to talk about your little trip to the shore."

★ ★ ★

The investigation of Dr. Jay Smith was not letting up either.

The former principal of Upper Merion High School had been convicted in Bucks County for posing as a Brink's security guard and robbing a Sears store at the Neshaminy Mall; then because of the massive publicity in Delaware County, the St. David's Brink's robbery was transferred to Dauphin County, where Smith was convicted again by a jury for posing as a security guard and executing that theft. In addition, Smith was convicted of weapons and related charges and was sentenced in Harrisburg on the day Reinert's body was found. The bottom line for Jay Smith since June 25, 1979 (after multiple appearances in front of several tough sentencing judges) was a six-to-12-year sentence in a hard-core state correctional institution.

Dr. Smith was out of circulation but not out of sight.

In August 1980, the cops obtained a search warrant from the state of Delaware to search Smith's blue Capri, which was parked at his brother's home in Wilmington.

Jay Smith's brother, William, who lived in a conservative, quiet neighborhood, was shocked and embarrassed when he got home that day. He was greeted by Joe VanNort, John Balshy, Jack Holtz, some other Pennsylvania State Police officers, a Delaware state cop, and a deputy attorney general. The interest level of the Pennsylvania State Police was not waning.

The search of William Smith's home, which included going through all of the belongings he was holding for his imprisoned brother, produced another bogus Brink's identification card with Jay Smith's picture on it, which at that point meant nothing. The search of the blue Capri revealed a little lapel tab—a green metal pin with a white "P"—which came from the Philadelphia Museum of Art. Identical pins were handed out by guards at the museum to show that admission had been paid. Different colors were issued on different days.

Everybody was disappointed with the results of the search, because no one knew at that time the importance of the little green pin with a white "P."

Corporal John Balshy, the husky, white-haired, pipe-smoking, bespectacled forensics man that VanNort wanted on the case, was also disappointed and frustrated. He was nearing retirement and felt that time was running out for him to help bring the case to a conclusion. For 25 years he had served the Commonwealth and was rarely foiled in a complex homicide investigation.

Balshy was looking forward to fishing Pennsylvania's freshwater streams for rainbow trout and getting caught up on his reading, maybe teaching a little, and enjoying his six children and future grandchildren after 30 years of a good marriage. But he hated leaving his life-long police buddies with this unsolved triple murder.

★ ★ ★

He had spent 14 years with the Los Angeles Police Department. He was the author of nine internationally acclaimed best-sellers: *The New Centurions, The Blue Knight, The Onion Field, The Choirboys, The Black Marble, The Glitter Dome, The Delta Star, Lines and Shadows,* and *The Secrets of Harry Bright.* He was a cop's cop and an author's author. He was also a charming, good-looking, charismatic, and unassuming guy—everybody loved him when they met him.

His name was Joseph Wambaugh, and he had flown in from California. He came to the Main Line in January 1981, when the Reinert case was already two years old and still unsolved. Word traveled fast that Wambaugh was in town, especially among the cops, because he was a legend and a hero in their story-telling world. Wambaugh was also the idol of many news reporters, would-be authors, and millions of readers because of his quick wit and writing style. He could describe a complex personality in one word and make anyone a hero or a demon with the stroke of his pen.

Wambaugh carried with him money and power and tickets to stardom.

It was no secret that this famous author and moviemaker was interviewing many people, including none other than William Bradfield and Joseph VanNort. Wambaugh liked the Reinert story a lot and could see Bradfield as an intriguing figure in his next best-seller—but there would *have to be* a conclusion. The two "Joes" went to VanNort's mountain cabin three hours north of Harrisburg to discuss the investigation. They spent an enjoyable weekend getting to know each other. They really hit it off together for all the right reasons and planned to do business—but there would *have to be* a conclusion.

★ ★ ★

On March 26, 1981, Sergeant VanNort received a letter from an inmate requesting a meeting to discuss the Reinert murder investigation. The inmate's name was Raymond Martray, a 37-year-old ex-cop from Connellsville, Pennsylvania. Martray had been a patrolman and a detective for Connellsville City for approximately eight years. He was married with three children. Martray wrote the letter from SCI-Dallas, a hard-core prison in Pennsylvania.

VanNort then contacted Trooper Nickle of the Uniontown station to get more background information on the inmate who was soliciting the meeting.

Trooper Nickle advised VanNort that Raymond Martray was a former police officer who organized a group of off-duty city policemen to commit burglaries in the same community they were sworn to protect. Martray was described to VanNort as a guy you had to watch because he was "a mastermind, very intelligent, clever, and next to genius." But this intelligent, clever genius was not only convicted of those burglaries after a trial by jury in his home county, he was also convicted of perjury and then was thrown in jail for a minimum of four years.

With Jay Smith.

On April 9, 1981, Raymond Martray was interviewed by Sergeant Van-Nort, Trooper Holtz, and Trooper Nickle at the Holiday Inn on West Main Street in Uniontown, Pennsylvania. Martray tried to get friendly—Van-Nort wasn't interested—and then he proceeded to tell the officers he had a strong feeling that Jay Smith had been involved in the Reinert murder.

"You're in with Smith at SCI-Dallas?" VanNort asked.

"Yes," Martray answered.

"Well, it's nice of you to tell us your feelings, but do you know anything? Did Smith tell you anything that we might be interested in?" Van-Nort asked.

"Sort of, sir. Smith commented he was glad the taped phone conversation was destroyed. Smith said Reinert's body was cremated and the investigation was mishandled."

"What else did Smith tell you?" VanNort asked, suspicious of this convicted perjurer.

Martray acknowledged at that time that Smith had never admitted to participating in any murder, but nevertheless Martray believed he might have, based on Smith's expressions and comments during their conversations. Martray told his audience that he believed Smith was a criminal genius. Martray said that Smith would talk as though Bradfield was a friend at times and on other occasions just the opposite. According to Martray, Smith had said that the Reinert children were somewhere between here and New Mexico.

During the interview, Martray claimed Smith had stated that Reinert had to have had a reason for leaving the house. Bradfield could have called her. Martray stated several times that he had so much information in his head that he was unable to relax and recall everything at once. He said he was also unable to take notes because Smith searched his cell when he wasn't present.

VanNort and Holtz both knew that jailhouse snitches can be found in any high-profile case and are a dime a dozen. They knew that a guy like Martray wanted to go home to his family and would sell his soul to do it, let alone Smith's.

"Every single thing you have told us, Mr. Martray, is practically a quote from a magazine article titled 'Murder on the Main Line' in this month's issue of *Philadelphia Magazine*," VanNort said, confronting Martray angrily, unimpressed with Martray's information.

"Really!" Martray said, acting surprised.

"You do have that magazine, don't you?" VanNort asked, sarcastically.

"Yes," Martray answered, sheepishly.

But Martray would not give up.

Three weeks later on April 28, 1981, Sergeant VanNort received a telephone call from Martray who related that Smith had told him about the Brink's robberies. Martray said that he wanted to meet with the authorities again and go over some more information that might interest them.

Sergeant VanNort, Trooper Holtz, Trooper Nickle, Sergeant Fayock, County Detective Hurzock, and FBI Agent David Kwait interviewed Martray again at the Mount Vernon Hotel in Uniontown, Pennsylvania. At that meeting, Martray said he had recalled further information about his conversations with Smith. According to Martray, Bradfield contacted Smith and said he was scared that Reinert might not support his alibi. Bradfield felt Reinert was going to blow the whistle and requested Smith to take care of Reinert. Martray thought this contact came on the same day the Reinert children disappeared.

"This guy must have read *Philadelphia Magazine* for the second time," VanNort said to Holtz. Holtz was not so quick to dismiss Martray. Martray was feeding Holtz's personal mission to get Jay Smith.

According to Martray, Smith claimed he got Reinert out of the house by telling her that Bradfield had been in a bad accident and for her to meet Smith at the hospital or in an emergency room. Martray said that Smith had explained that there were three ways to get rid of kids: (1) use a rowboat to dump them in the river; (2) eat them; or (3) find a newly dug grave with a casket already buried and place the bodies on top of the casket and replace the dirt.

"What do you think about this guy," Holtz asked VanNort, hoping for his blessing.

"Let's just say I'm leaning your way about our boy Jay Smith. But it's got nothing to do with Raymond Martray. That much I can tell you," VanNort answered, and meant it.

★ ★ ★

It was the moment that VanNort and Holtz and DiSantis had been waiting for. It wasn't *the* moment, but back in May 1981, it was going to have to do, and they were going to enjoy every minute of it. VanNort and Holtz and DiSantis were about to arrest William Bradfield for theft by deception and theft by fraudulent conversion.

Their unmarked car crept up the lane to the old stone farmhouse where the Bradfields lived. Mrs. Nona Bradfield answered the doorbell and was clearly frightened. She was in her mid-seventies, frail, with gray hair and blue-gray eyes. She was Bill Bradfield's mother and the first to be told.

"Mrs. Bradfield, we have a warrant for your son's arrest," Holtz said.

"Just a minute, please," she said politely, but nervously.

She made them wait outside while her son got dressed in a three-piece suit for the occasion. When Bill Bradfield came down the steps to greet the officers, he had a topcoat draped over his arm but did not look as confident as he had in Santa Fe.

It was not a good day for Nona Bradfield. As she watched, Holtz took the topcoat and frisked her son, while VanNort read him his rights.

"Are you arresting me for murder?" Bradfield asked, obviously frightened.

"No," VanNort answered, "just theft by deception, theft by failure to make required disposition of funds received, and conspiracy."

Bill Bradfield was visibly relieved but his mother wasn't as she watched the Pennsylvania State Police handcuff her son and escort him to the car.

Bradfield was taken to the police barracks, fingerprinted, and photographed. Bill Bradfield was a perfect gentleman throughout the processing. So were VanNort and Holtz.

"Are you going to arrest any of my friends?" Bradfield asked softly.

"Yeah," VanNort answered, without hesitation. "It looks like we have to charge Wendy Zeigler for conspiracy."

"I . . . I wish you'd let me call her first," Bradfield said, misty-eyed. "She's such a fragile child."

Bradfield was right about Wendy Zeigler, and VanNort was counting on it.

Wendy Zeigler was young, fragile, innocent. She was not an accessory to the crime of theft because she never knew the $25,000 was Susan Reinert's. All she did was put the money in her closet on the weekend in question because Bradfield told her to.

Both the state police and the FBI knew that Wendy Zeigler was innocent. What she was guilty of was not cooperating to the satisfaction of Van-Nort, and that grated on him. VanNort had everybody else in line, sort of—except Joanne Aitken—and resented the fact that this young whippersnapper was lying and holding out to protect her guru boyfriend.

To VanNort, it was time for a little pressure.

"I'm arresting her along with Bill Bradfield and charging her with theft by deception and conspiracy," VanNort announced, after thinking about it for a while.

"You can't do that," Special Agent Matt Mullen of the FBI protested, trying to talk some sense into VanNort, because everybody knew she was innocent. "She's just a kid, Joe. She just did what Bradfield told her to do. You can't do it."

"She's been holding out on me, and don't give me that kid stuff," Van-Nort snapped, resenting the FBI's lofty involvement.

"That's not a crime, Joe," Mullen said defensively. "You can't do it."

"You watch me."

VanNort had had about as much as he could take from Bradfield's lovers and friends. He didn't want to hear about Wendy Zeigler's civil rights either. He never lost sight of the fact that two innocent children were still missing and probably murdered in cold blood. All he wanted was Wendy Zeigler's cooperation, and if he had to get a little rough on her, exert a little pressure, then that's how it was going to be.

VanNort didn't care that Wendy had to fly in from California to surrender herself at the magistrate's office. VanNort and Holtz took her to a women's jail for mugshots and fingerprints before she was released to her parents on $10,000 bail.

It wasn't long before VanNort got a telephone call from the District Attorney of Delaware County. Wendy Zeigler had agreed to become a witness against Bill Bradfield, if VanNort would agree to drop the charges against her.

"Of course, I will," Joe VanNort said, smiling. "Why she's just a kid."

★ ★ ★

Date: July 28, 1981
Time: 9:30 a.m.
Place: Delaware County Courthouse, Media, Pennsylvania
Case: *Commonwealth v. William Sydney Bradfield*; Theft by Deception;
           Theft by Failure to Make Required Disposition of Funds Received

The small courthouse was packed with observers and the media. It was only a theft trial, but people knew what was going on and wanted more. Judge Robert A. Wright warned everybody in the courtroom that any mention of a murder investigation would result in a quick mistrial. Bradfield was represented by John Paul Curran and his law partner, Charles Fitzpatrick. The Commonwealth was represented by Edward J. Weiss. The media was represented by themselves, and they were very well represented.

The three-day trial in Delaware County was plenty exciting but uneventful. The media was finally getting a firsthand look at some of Bradfield's lovers and friends whom they had been writing about for over two years.

The manager from Susan Reinert's bank first told the jury about Reinert's $25,000 cash withdrawals. He stressed to the jury that in spite of his resistance and offering her treasurer's checks and a certified cashier's check, Reinert insisted on cash, in 50s and 100s, "because *he* only wanted cash."

Then Chris Pappas took the witness stand and looked Bill Bradfield right in the eye. He told the jury about wiping their fingerprints off the $25,000 with a handkerchief—money that had been retrieved from gym bags and briefcases and envelopes in the trunk of Bradfield's car. He told the jury how he put it in a safe deposit box to keep it hidden. He *did not* mention anything about chains and locks or guns or acid or cutting up bodies.

Sue Myers was next. The jury and observers could tell that she still loved the man she had lived with for six years. She described their relationship, she told the jury he promised her marriage, she explained that she handled all of their financial affairs, and she made it clear that Bill Bradfield never had $25,000 that *she* knew anything about.

Then the picture of innocence everybody was waiting for, especially the media, took the witness stand. She looked like the child that she was, and no one could understand her relationship with a teacher who was old enough to be her father. She was called to the witness stand by Bradfield's prosecutor, District Attorney Ed Weiss.

Wendy testified tearfully that she had graduated from Upper Merion High School in 1978. "Bradfield was my teacher. He taught me English, Latin, Greek, and the Bible. At first it was just a student-teacher relationship. Then we became romantically involved. He promised me marriage, and I wanted to marry him. He told me his relationship with Susan Reinert was platonic. He told me Sue Reinert had a romantic interest in him, but he had no romantic interest in her."

Then Wendy Zeigler—like Chris Pappas and Sue Myers—put it on him. Her reluctant testimony was brought out by the precise questioning of District Attorney Weiss.

Q. Directing your attention to Friday, June 22, 1979, did you receive a call from Mr. Bradfield on that day?
A. Yes.
Q. Approximately what time?
A. 11 a.m.
Q. Without getting into your whereabouts that day or what you did, would you tell the jury whether Bradfield showed you cash that day?

A. Yes.

Q. Did he?

A. Yes.

Q. Did he tell you where this money came from?

A. He said he had saved it.

Q. Did he give you the money to hold for him?

A. Yes.

Q. What did you do with it?

A. I hid it in my closet.

Q. How much money did he give you to hold for him?

A. About $25,000, I believe.

Q. How long did it remain in your closet?

A. For the rest of the summer.

Q. Why did you do it?

A. He asked me to.

Though exciting, the trial was uneventful because Bill Bradfield, on the sound advice of his lawyer, did not testify. John Curran figured Bradfield had done enough damage to himself in orphans' court several months ago.

It was also uneventful because the verdict was engraved in stone while the jury was being picked. The jury was out less than one hour, and when Bradfield was found guilty of both theft counts, the courtroom broke into applause.

· 8 ·

RISING STAR

Just as the police had their ongoing problems over jurisdiction and who was in charge, even within the same department, there were power struggles and jealousies over who was in charge and who was to do what—four Pennsylvania district attorneys with independent jurisdiction couldn't figure out whose case it was, either. No one knew where Susan Reinert had been murdered. No one knew where the bodies of Karen and Michael had been disposed of, or even if they were dead. Susan Reinert lived in Delaware County, Pennsylvania; William Bradfield lived in Chester County, Pennsylvania; Jay Smith's home and the Upper Merion School District were both located in Montgomery County, Pennsylvania; and Susan Reinert's body was discovered in Harrisburg, Dauphin County, Pennsylvania.

Joe VanNort, and then Holtz and DiSantis, did not have the power to prosecute, nor did they know to whom to turn.

And the public kept demanding that something be done. The public didn't care who the prosecutor was going to be or what county it was tried in. It was an outrageous killing. Two innocent children were unaccounted for. Where was the justice, for God's sake?

A fiery prosecutor would soon surface from the political arena in Harrisburg. He would take control of the case, eliminating the jurisdictional squabbles, and would be determined from the outset to bring William Bradfield and Jay Smith to justice.

In November 1980, the Commonwealth of Pennsylvania had an election to determine who would become the first elected Attorney General of Pennsylvania. The new position carried with it the legislative power to accept cases from local district attorneys where they lacked the resources to prosecute a criminal matter or where there were multiple-county jurisdictions involved—such as in the Reinert case. The newly elected attorney general was also given the legislative authority to empanel a statewide investigative grand jury with subpoena and contempt powers.

LeRoy S. Zimmerman, the highly respected district attorney from Harrisburg, became the first elected Attorney General of the Commonwealth of Pennsylvania.

I was proud of Roy when he won that powerful position, and I attended his historic swearing in. Roy Zimmerman was my first boss when I began my legal career in 1972 as an assistant district attorney in Harrisburg. I tried a lot of cases under his tutelage.

"The courtroom is a pit," Roy used to say. "You must have respect at all times for the judge, for your adversary, and for the system; but you cannot try cases on your knees. Do you understand what I am saying?"

I understood *exactly* what he was saying.

I respected and liked Roy a lot, because he was a real courtroom barrister. He looked the part, too. At that time, he was 40 years old, a big, handsome man with dark, short hair slicked to the side. He was clean-shaven and always wore a conservative, two-piece suit with matching tie and wing-tipped shoes. He could win a case in his opening argument. If his opening didn't get that jury to fall in love with him, by the time he was done cross-examining or closing, there was nothing to talk about. "Guilty," "Guilty," "Guilty," was all he ever heard from a jury foreman.

LeRoy Zimmerman took the oath to uphold the laws of the Commonwealth of Pennsylvania on January 1, 1981. The newly elected Attorney General of Pennsylvania, the Honorable Leroy Zimmerman, pursuant to the powers vested in him by law, was asked to take over the "Reinert case" which thereby ended the confusion between the district attorneys of at least four counties. Then in August 1981, Roy Zimmerman personally went to Rick Guida, a former prosecutor who once worked for Roy, and asked if he would be willing to assume the role of a full-time special prosecutor with the Office of the Attorney General.

Roy wanted Rick Guida to take over the Reinert case. Roy had personally trained Rick 10 years before, when Rick was a young assistant district attorney in Roy's office in Harrisburg. Richard "Rick" Guida, under Roy Zimmerman's tutelage, tried over 70 jury trials and successfully prosecuted major murder cases and coordinated in-depth investigations into the most complicated crimes. He earned Roy Zimmerman's admiration and respect. Roy was sorry to see Rick go into private practice back then, but there just wasn't enough money an assistant district attorney could make to keep him.

I also knew Rick Guida. He was an excellent prosecutor. We started our careers together, sharing an office as fellow prosecutors, and Roy considered us his sharpest litigators. Rick was an excellent choice, at least I thought so at the time, to take over the Reinert case.

"Rick," Roy said, smoking one of his big cigars, with his feet up on his desk in his huge oval office overlooking the Susquehanna River, "if you accept this position I'm offering you, you will personally be in charge of the Reinert case. You will be in charge of coordinating the investigation and eventual prosecutions which are imminent."

"The Reinert case?!" Rick was excited as he stood in front of Roy's desk. He had become bored with the rigors of private practice over the past several years.

"You heard me, Rick," Roy said, smiling, setting the hook.

"That's a big one, Roy," Rick said, unable to conceal his excitement.

"They don't get any bigger, Rick. You have to take it."

"I will," he answered, without hesitation, and extended his hand to shake Roy's to lock in the offer.

* * *

One of the biggest setbacks of the Reinert investigation struck quietly on October 1, 1981. It happened without warning on the firing range at the Pennsylvania State Police Academy and was a real tragedy for the Commonwealth of Pennsylvania. On a crisp, fall afternoon the guns up and down the firing line were cracking loud and clear. Old Joe VanNort was on the pistol range qualifying when he felt a sharp pain in his chest. He dropped to his one knee, pistol still in hand, and then collapsed. All firing on the firing range ceased. Sergeant Joseph VanNort, age 58, a 32-year veteran, was dead.

VanNort was buried with all the pomp and ceremony he rightly deserved. The state police were in full dress—dark gray trousers, gray shirts, black gloves, brimmed hats, and black leather holsters with guns. An American flag draped the casket. VanNort's uniformed comrades carefully folded it before it was handed to his widow. Then guns were fired in salutes. Many loved ones wept openly as the casket was lowered into the ground. It was a sad, sad day.

If a monument were ever to be created by the Pennsylvania State Police, one of the oldest and most honorable law enforcement agencies in the country, it would be to Sergeant Joseph A. VanNort. His epitaph would read, "Served with Honor, Integrity, Without Fear."

* * *

October 1, 1981 was also Rick Guida's first day on the job as Chief of the Special Prosecution Section for the Office of the Attorney General. His offices were on the 16th floor of Strawberry Square in Harrisburg. On that very same day, while he was hanging pictures on the wall and organizing his desk, the lead investigator in the Reinert murder case, Sergeant Joseph VanNort, suffered a massive heart attack and subsequently died. Rick Guida had lost the expertise of a very good man that morning. I will always wonder how history might have played out if Joe had been there for Rick.

At 33 years of age, Rick Guida took over the command position of the Reinert case from the standpoint of prosecutor. He put pictures of Karen and Michael on his desk to remind himself why he was there. Like those before him, Rick became an obsessed man, consumed, aggressive, determined to do whatever had to be done.

Rick was a chain-smoking courtroom performer. He was a good-looking guy, a little nervous, a little edgy, a little short with people, but all the girls in the office loved him. Rick had never married. He walked with a confident swagger and always dressed to kill (like his mentor, Roy) in expensive, dark suits, fashionable ties, and shoes that matched his belt and briefcase. He was ready for the courtroom at all times. His build was that of a middle-weight, but in the courtroom he could fight like a world-class heavyweight.

Rick Guida and Jack Holtz became inseparable partners and good friends during the Reinert case. Holtz was one month younger than Guida when Jack inherited the file from VanNort on October 1, 1981. Holtz was truly grieved by VanNort's death, wept privately, and was honored to be a pallbearer for him. He did welcome, however, the opportunity to be top gun in the biggest homicide case in his career. One of the first things Holtz did upon VanNort's death was to go through all of Joe's personal files, page by page; he then took them home.

Holtz's new full-time partner was Trooper Lou DiSantis from the Belmont Barracks in Philadelphia. That team made sense because they were both on the case from day one, and they liked each other and worked well together. But Jack Holtz made no bones about it to anybody. He made it clear to Lou, and to the feds, *he* was now in charge.

In the months that followed VanNort's death, Holtz met with Guida literally every day, either in Rick's office or while traveling back and forth between Philadelphia and Harrisburg. Holtz's "debriefing" and "teaching" included going over boxes and boxes of investigative reports from the state police and FBI files. He personally delivered them to Rick's "war room" on the 16th floor of Strawberry Square. Several large filing cabinets and a special evidence closet had to be set up in Guida's office for the material he received, most of which had already been pursued and exhausted or discredited.

Not all of it, however.

William Sydney Bradfield had just been convicted of the theft of Reinert's money and was very much on the front burner for a murder charge when Guida got involved. And Dr. Jay Smith was Holtz's ultimate target.

★ ★ ★

Date: December 23, 1981
Time: 9:00 a.m.
Place: Delaware County Courthouse, Media, Pennsylvania

Bill Bradfield had been out on bail since his conviction five months before, but two days before Christmas, he had run out of time and delays and money for appeals.

"May it please the court," the young District Attorney of Delaware County respectfully said, "now is the time and place for the sentencing of William Sydney Bradfield, who was convicted in this courtroom by a jury of his peers last July 1981. All post-trial motions have been dismissed by this court, and now is the time and place for sentencing, your Honor."

The small courtroom was packed again to witness the sentencing about to take place. The media was well represented.

Honorable Judge Robert A. Wright had tried the case and heard the witnesses. In less than one hour, the jury had convicted Bradfield of theft, and specifically, of stealing $25,000 from Susan Reinert's estate.

Bradfield's lawyer, John Paul Curran, impressed upon the court that Bill Bradfield led a good life, that he had never been in trouble before, that he came from a good family, and that this conviction cost him his teaching position at Upper Merion High School.

Judge Wright had reviewed the pre-sentence report prepared by the probation department. Everything Bradfield's lawyer was saying was true. Everything the district attorney had told the jury was also true. And accordingly, Judge Wright, without expression from the bench, sentenced Bill Bradfield to a term of four months to two years to be served in the Delaware County Prison, "and furthermore," Judge Wright added, "bail is hereby increased from $75,000 to $150,000."

John Curran was outraged at the increase in bail. Usually, in a criminal case a defendant has a right to reasonable bail after he is sentenced pending appeals.

But there would be no release on bail for Bill Bradfield.

There would be no appeals.

Bradfield just stood there, stunned, angry, hurt, and scared—emotions the sheriff's department dealt with every day—as they took him from the courtroom and delivered him to the Delaware County Prison. He would do his four months, and for the first time spend Christmas behind bars.

★ ★ ★

Rick Guida looked out the window of his 16th-floor office and could see the sun setting on the Capitol complex across the street. Harrisburg is a government town with modern federal and state buildings—an unusually grand Capitol modeled after the one in Washington, D.C., the Federal Courthouse, PennDot (the Pennsylvania Department of Transportation), the State Museum, the State Library, the Dauphin County Courthouse— all within a few blocks of each other. Hundreds of nearby businesses and local restaurants exist to service the thousands of government workers who control the city from 9 to 5. Harrisburg is all business and politics during the day.

At night, however, there is very little to do in the city where Rick Guida had been born and raised. The social scene of bars and restaurants had very little to offer a bachelor like Rick. But at that point in his life, he didn't have time anyhow. He was just about ready to indict Bill Bradfield for the murders of Susan, Karen, and Michael Reinert. For 18 months, Rick worked day and night, seven days a week, often alone.

Guida felt he had a great case against Bradfield *before* he had gone to jail. He had the will, the insurance policies totaling $750,000, the theft of

$25,000, and the cooperation of Bradfield's most intimate friends and lovers—Chris Pappas, Vincent Valaitis, Sue Myers, and Wendy Zeigler.

But Guida also wanted what all good prosecutors want in any criminal case—a confession from the defendant, no matter what the source—because confessions seal verdicts.

It was soon after Guida's involvement that Jack Holtz and Lou DiSantis contacted officials at the Delaware County Prison to see if William Bradfield had spent time with any particular prisoner to whom he might have confessed. "Yes," they were told, "Bradfield had spent time in a cell with Proctor Nowell, a 23-year-old, uneducated black man from Chester County, who had been in and out of prison from the age of 16 on weapons, stolen property, and aggravated assault convictions."

A guy like Proctor Nowell was sure to know the system, and did. On February 25, 1983, Nowell made the call and met with Holtz, DiSantis, and Guida. What he told them that day, after he was taken out of maximum-security prison, would be repeated within a month in front of the third Multi-County Investigating Grand Jury which was sitting in Harrisburg.

★ ★ ★

March 23, 1983.

Guida got what he wanted.

The Multi-County Investigating Grand Jury, having received and reviewed documentary and testimonial evidence pertaining to the death of Susan G. Reinert and the disappearance of her children, Karen and Michael, recommended that William S. Bradfield be charged with appropriate criminal violations, to wit: Murder—3 counts; Conspiracy to Commit Murder with a Person or Persons Unknown—3 counts; Solicitation to Commit Murder—3 counts; Kidnapping—3 counts; Conspiracy to Commit Kidnapping with a Person or Persons Unknown—3 counts; Solicitation to Commit Kidnapping—3 counts; and Obstructing Administration of Law or Other Governmental Function—3 counts.

★ ★ ★

April 6, 1983.

It was 5 a.m. and still dark.

Bradfield had been out of the Delaware County Prison for over two years on the theft charges. He was now going back.

The arrest team consisted of Jack Holtz, Lou DiSantis, four other troopers, and Rick Guida. They walked up the street in the quiet neighborhood of Birdsboro, looking all around with great caution, dressed in heavy flak vests and carrying loaded shotguns.

Noriega himself would have been intimidated.

Bill Bradfield was staying at a friend's house. He was sleeping with his English setter who had been hurt. The officers pushed open the door to his bedroom, flicked on the lights, and with their shotguns aimed at Bradfield and his pup, they went through the ritual.

· 9 ·

JUSTICE

Date: October 11, 1983
Time: 9:30 a.m.
Place: Dauphin County Courthouse, Harrisburg, Pennsylvania
Case: *Commonwealth v. William Sydney Bradfield*
Charge: Murder

Judge Isaac J. Garb, President Judge of Bucks County, had been hand-picked by the Pennsylvania Supreme Court to preside over the high-profile Bradfield case in Harrisburg, Pennsylvania. He was a man in his mid-fifties, learned in the law, but in addition, as a former assistant U.S. prosecutor and public defender, he knew the blood that could be shed on a courtroom floor in a high-stakes, no-limit courtroom drama. The prosecution was asking for the death penalty for Bradfield, and the stakes don't get any higher than that.

Deputy Attorney General Rick Guida represented the Commonwealth, and he was ready.

The defense attorney for Bill Bradfield was Joshua Lock, who was Guida's age and the former Chief Public Defender of Dauphin County, and he was ready, too.

Thus began a *voir dire* that lasted five full days. Ninety-five prospective jurors took the witness stand and underwent a rigorous examination by Rick Guida and Joshua Lock. Those selected were known as "the Bradfield jury" and had the awesome responsibility of determining a fellow citizen's guilt or innocence in a triple murder; specifically, for the deaths of Susan Reinert and her two children who had never been found. If they found Bradfield guilty, then they would deliberate again to determine whether he should be put to death.

Jury selection is involved and tedious, but especially in a death penalty case, it is critical. A lot has been written about the best way to pick a jury. The defense looks for jurors who are most likely to acquit, and the prosecution looks for jurors who are most likely to convict. Defense attorneys contend that employment and social positions are relevant; railroad men and their wives are excellent jurors; and persons of Irish, Jewish, and south-

57

ern European extraction are more desirable as jurors than people of British, Scandinavian, or German extraction. But they are rules of thumb and that's all they are, and usually the most one can do is rely on instinct and experience and then hope and pray.

Finally, after five days of questioning, nine men and three women were chosen. They were law-abiding, God-fearing people—civic-minded, uninfluenced by anything they may have seen, read, or heard outside of the courtroom. They were free of fear, sympathy, prejudice, or bias. At least that's what they said, and they were sworn in by Judge Garb to render a verdict based solely on the evidence.

★ ★ ★

Rick Guida's case took nine days, from October 15th to October 24th. The early testimony came from expert witnesses who talked about a red fiber found in Susan Reinert's hair that was consistent with fibers found in a red carpet in Jay Smith's house. An FBI lab specialist testified that a strand of hair found in Smith's basement was consistent with Susan Reinert's hair. A trooper testified that a blue comb with the inscription "79th USAR-COM" was found under Susan Reinert's body in the car.

Guida could not link Bradfield to those items and did not intend to, but he was laying the groundwork for the theory that Bradfield participated in a conspiracy with Jay Smith or with a person or persons unknown—not necessarily having anything to do with Smith.

Joshua Lock seized upon those physical items like an attack dog to put the crimes on Smith. Lock intended to play out the hand he was dealt, which meant Smith did it, or somebody else did it—because Bradfield didn't. Because Bradfield had been at the shore for the whole weekend in question, Josh felt he had a good hand. He was a competent lawyer, and like many other people involved in the case, he devoted a piece of his life to it. He had spent 28 days in the prison visiting room with William Bradfield and practically closed down his private office to prepare. In addition, Joshua Lock believed Bill Bradfield, who was very good at deception.

But Guida's case wasn't based solely on forensics.

There was the will naming Bill Bradfield as the sole beneficiary of Susan Reinert's estate, and stating that he was to be the guardian of her children if anything happened to her. And there were the life insurance policies totaling $750,000 that Bradfield was to get—but only if Susan Reinert was dead. Then came the $25,000.

And poor Wendy Zeigler was back on the stand.

Every time Guida showed a witness a legal document that would make Bradfield a millionaire, but only if Susan Reinert was dead, the defense took a hit. Those hits were damaging, very damaging, but not fatal.

But then came the friends and lovers.

Pappas told the jury that he was friends with Susan Myers and Vincent Valaitis. Pappas told the jury that he knew Wendy Zeigler. He went on to tell them that he met Joanne Aitken. Yes, Pappas said, he knew Susan Reinert. Then his testimony made the jury sit up. Guida's questioning of Pappas was crisp, fast-moving, incisive, effective.

Q. Did Bradfield know Smith?

A. Yes.

Q. What did Bradfield tell you about Smith?

A. He said that Smith had confided in him. He said that Smith wanted to kill the people who were investigating him.

Q. What did Smith tell Bradfield about Susan Reinert?

A. Bradfield said that Smith told him that Smith intended to kill a number of teachers of which Susan Reinert was one.

Q. Did he tell you why?

A. Yes.

Q. What was the reason that she was to be killed?

A. Bradfield said that Smith was angry with Reinert because they had an affair and that Reinert had jilted Smith.

Q. Did you ever talk to Mr. Smith about this?

A. No.

Q. Did Bradfield ever show you anything that he said Smith gave him?

A. Yes.

Q. What type of items are we talking about?

A. He gave me items such as a ski mask and chains and locks. He also gave me a .30-caliber carbine, which he said he got from Smith.

Q. Did Mr. Bradfield ever give you any acid which he said he got from Smith?

A. Yes.

Q. When did that occur?

A. That occurred around April of 1979.

Q. What did you do with the .30-caliber which he gave you?

A. He told me to remove the serial numbers from it because Bradfield felt that Smith might have stolen it from Bradfield and altered it, and Bradfield didn't want it to be traced to him.

Q. Did you do that?

A. Yes.

Q. Why?

A. He asked me to.

Q. Did you ever suggest to Bradfield that he go to the police?

A. Yes, but Bradfield talked me out of it, because he said Smith knew people in high places.

Q. Now, you mentioned items such as chains, small locks, tape, ski masks. Did Mr. Bradfield ever tell you after he gave them to you what these things were for?

A. He did.

Q. What did he say to you about that?

A. He said that Smith had a way of apprehending and overpowering an individual. He used those items in order to accomplish that.

Q. Did Bradfield ever show you how to immobilize a person?

A. Yes.

Q. Tell us about that.

A. Bradfield said this is how Smith would do it. Bradfield demonstrated by wrapping my hands in the chains and then locking the device.

Q. Did that work?

A. Yes.

Q. Did Bradfield ever practice the whole routine on you?

A. Yes.

Q. Tell us about that.

A. He had a blue parka with four pockets as I recall, and it had in one pocket, the tape. Another pocket he put the chains and in another pocket he put the ski mask, and in another pocket he had placed bags—plastic bags.

Q. Bradfield did this?

A. Yes.

Q. Now, Mr. Pappas, did you go to Cape May on the weekend in question with Mr. Valaitis, Susan Myers, and William Bradfield?

A. Yes.

Q. Did he tell you why you were to go along?

A. Yes.

Q. What did he tell you?

A. He said that it was important for me to go along because he might need an alibi for that weekend. He said that he wanted to be in the company of myself and several others, just in case anything happened to Susan Reinert that weekend. He wanted to be able to say that he was with me, that he was totally disassociated with her murder. We were supposed to go to Santa Fe that weekend, but he wanted to be close by, just in case Jay Smith was going to kill Susan Reinert that weekend. He wanted to be close by to help her if she needed him.

Q. Did you go to the shore on that Friday, June 22nd?

A. Yes, down to Cape May.

Q. Were all four of you together at the shore.

A. Yes.

Q. Did he talk about Susan Reinert over that weekend?

A. Yes.

Q. What did he say?

A. He expressed concern that she was going to be killed that weekend.

Q. Did you help Mr. Bradfield clean his car out that Monday morning?

A. Yes.

Q. Tell us about that please.

A. We cleaned his car out.

The jury of nine men and three women watched Pappas in stunned silence. Every time he pointed the finger at Bradfield from the witness stand, the jury would follow his finger with their eyes and glare at Bradfield with utter contempt—especially the women.

The gallery was with the prosecution all the way.

Judge Isaac Garb showed no emotion from the bench, but took copious notes.

Chris Pappas testified in detail that they had washed the car, going through it carefully, gotten all the papers and letters out, including correspondence from Susan Reinert, and, on their way back from the shore, they had made a stop and threw everything in a trash dumpster. Then Pappas testified that he got back to his parents' home on June 25th around noontime. That same evening, he met Bill Bradfield at the Philadelphia airport because of their summer school plans in New Mexico.

Q. And did you fly directly to New Mexico from the airport?
A. We did.
Q. Which airport are you talking about?
A. Philadelphia.
Q. How many days after you arrived in New Mexico did Joanne Aitken show up with Bradfield's car?
A. I say it was about a week, 10 days.
Q. When did you find out that Susan Reinert had, in fact, been murdered?
A. I found out on Tuesday, the 26th.
Q. And who told you?
A. William Bradfield.
Q. Did he blame Jay Smith?
A. Yes.
Q. What did he say at that time about Jay Smith?
A. He said that apparently Jay Smith had gone through with his threats and had killed her.
Q. Did he ever change that story?
A. Yes.
Q. When?
A. About a week later, he said maybe somebody else other than Jay Smith had killed her, that he suspected a person by the name of Alex who lived in Carlisle, Pennsylvania, and that Alex was supposed to be some kind of kinky sex partner with Susan Reinert.

Then Susan Myers took the witness stand. She told the jury that she was still a teacher in Upper Merion School District and had been there for 24 years. Yes, she said, she knew the man in the courtroom by the name of William Bradfield. She told the jury that they had become romantically involved around Christmas, 1963; the two of them traveled in Europe together in the early '70s; and she told the jury that they returned in September 1973, and then lived together until 1980.

Q. Did you become aware of any romantic relationship that Bradfield had with Susan Reinert?

A. Yes.

Q. And when did you learn that?

A. The fall of 1974.

Sue Myers learned about that romantic relationship when she walked into his room after school to go home with him, and there was a book lying on his desk with a note in it from Susan Reinert indicating that there was something more than friendship going on. When she confronted him, Bradfield denied it and told her "that he was doing research in order to write poetry" and that seemed to satisfy Sue Myers at the time.

In the courtroom, however, Sue Myers was in a lot of pain telling the world how she had been cheated on and lied to by her lover.

In October 1978, Bradfield also told Susan Myers that Smith was going to kill a number of school officials, including Susan Reinert. At the time that he made this disclosure to Myers, he told her to have faith in him and not question his whereabouts and to be obedient. He told Sue Myers, again around Christmas, 1978, that Smith was going to kill Susan Reinert.

From January 1, 1979 until Susan Reinert's disappearance, Bradfield continued to inform Sue Myers that Smith was going to kill Reinert.

Q. Ms. Myers, do you know an individual by the name of Jay C. Smith?

A. Yes.

Q. How do you know him?

A. He was the Principal at Upper Merion High School.

Q. For how long?

A. Approximately 10 years.

Q. What did Bradfield tell you about Smith?

A. He said he had committed some thefts and he had murdered.

Q. What else did he tell you?

A. In the fall of 1978, Mr. Bradfield told me that Dr. Smith intended to kill Susan Reinert.

Q. Ms. Myers, directing your attention to Friday, June 22, 1979, were there plans made to go to Cape May?

A. Yes.

Q. Who was to go on the trip with you?

A. Chris Pappas, Vince Valaitis, Mr. Bradfield, and me.

Q. Did you know what the purpose was?

A. No.

Q. Did he mention to you that he needed an alibi?

A. No.

Q. Did you know that he was going to be starting school on that Monday in Santa Fe, New Mexico?

A. Yes.

Vincent Valaitis testified and corroborated Myers's story. Bradfield had told him, too, that Susan Reinert's life was in danger for a period of time. No, he did not go to the police either, because he trusted Bill, and Bill had told him that he could protect Reinert and stop Smith from doing it.

Q. Did Bradfield, after the fact, ever get upset and do something which you felt was unusual?

A. Yes.

Q. Tell the jury about that conversation.

A. Well, he was upset, and he said, "All right, if I'm going to be blamed for this, I'll admit to it," and he took a piece of white paper, and he drew a square on it, and he drew a line, and he said, "All right, I took the kids and I gave them to ... " Then I interrupted him, and I said, "Don't do that," and I grabbed the paper from him, and I said, "Don't make things up," and I threw it away.

Q. Did you know whether he was making that up or not, Mr. Valaitis?

A. I didn't know if he was making it up.

Q. And after Susan Reinert was murdered, Mr. Valaitis, why did you wait until August 22nd to begin going to the police and telling them what Bradfield told you?

A. Well, I was being told that the lawyers did not want us to speak to the police, and almost immediately, the newspaper articles began to implicate us and all kinds of sordid things were coming out, and I was very frightened, and I did not know what to do.

Q. But the question is, what finally made you decide to do it?

A. I couldn't stand it anymore.

Guida held back Proctor Nowell until near the end. He wanted Bradfield's confession ringing in the jury's ears when he rested his case. Guida and Holtz had spent a lot of time preparing Proctor Nowell for this day. They had reviewed his grand jury testimony with him, and Nowell repeated it for the Bradfield jury, almost verbatim.

Rick Guida did the questioning. It was skilled, paced, and deliberate.

Q. Please state your full name for the record.

A. Proctor Nowell.

Q. Were you in the Delaware County Prison with Mr. Bradfield?

A. Yes.

Q. Did you have the opportunity to talk with Mr. Bradfield on a number of occasions?

A. Yes.

Q. Was there an occasion when Bradfield was returned to the Delaware County Prison because a bail reduction he requested was denied?

A. Yes.

Q. What was your conversation on that occasion with Mr. Bradfield?

A. I said, "How did you make out in court today?" And he said, "Well, man, they're fucking me over. They denied my bail reduction." So, I said, "Well, all that money you was makin' as a teacher, couldn't you use that to make bail." And he said, "I owe. I lost 30 acres and two cars. I was forced to close down a store in Montgomery County. If I wasn't in a financial bind, I wouldn't be here now, nor would any of this shit have had to happen to Susan."

Q. Go on.

A. Then Bradfield said, "I was there when they were killed, but I didn't kill anyone." And I said, "Damn, Bradfield, the children too?" And he said, "None of this was meant for the children, only for Susan. It was a shame they had to suffer like this, but there couldn't be a stone left unturned."

Q. What did you do after that?

A. I just stayed away from him 'cause I didn't like the idea of him saying that about the kids.

Q. Mr. Nowell, when you were originally questioned by the police, did you give them this information?

A. No.

Q. Why did you then, later?

A. I told the trooper, "I don't know nothing about it." And then the one trooper said, "Well, why don't you think about it. This is concerning two men and some kids." So . . . I went back to my cell and I thought about it, like the trooper said, and I thought about how I had two kids. That's why I did it.

Nowell told the jury that he agreed to cooperate because he had children of his own, and after he thought about that, he made the call.

Proctor Nowell had done just fine. At least Guida and Holtz said they believed him.

· 10 ·

NEVA

Joshua Lock had gotten hammered for nine straight days. He fought back every day like a true courtroom fighter, but every witness either put him on the ropes or knocked him down.

Josh kept getting up, intending to go the distance. His approach was intellectual and scholarly, but with a lot of emotion and passion, which was always his style; however, for the past nine days, no approach could offset the *facts* of the case.

Susan Reinert had been murdered. The children were gone. Bradfield was the beneficiary of her estate, of her insurance policies, of her money, of her jewelry, but only if she was dead. Bradfield knew of Reinert's death weeks before it happened and never told the authorities. His "alibi" was not a coincidence. And the testimony of Proctor Nowell that Bradfield confessed was now before the jury.

Nor could Josh get away from the fact that *his* alibi witnesses were the Commonwealth's witnesses, and though they alibied him, sort of, every one of Bradfield's most trusted friends and lovers incriminated him beyond recovery. Because of Josh's personal involvement and his belief in Bradfield's innocence, he was taking the proceedings much too emotionally and had lost a lot of weight during the trial because of it.

Josh had one hope left for the final round. His only chance to win an acquittal for Bradfield rested with the credibility of one witness. This witness was either going to knock out the prosecution cold or end it for the defense. It was the moment everybody was waiting for—the Court, Rick Guida, the media, the gallery, the jury, and Josh himself—and he called him.

Rasputin was going to testify!

When Bill Bradfield stood up to take that long walk to the witness stand, there was a hushed silence in the packed courtroom. Spectators had arrived before daylight that day anticipating this moment of truth. Bradfield was dressed in a three-piece blue suit, and looked tired if not beaten. The look of prison pallor had already set in. Josh's direct examination was well-prepared and emotional.

Q. Please state your full name for the record.
A. William Bradfield.
Q. Mr. Bradfield, would you please keep your voice up so the jury can hear you.

A. Yes, sir.
Q. How old are you?
A. Fifty.

Bradfield went on to tell the jury that he graduated from Haverford College in 1959 and had a master's in liberal education from St. John's. He described himself and Myers as "not a real romantic pair for many, many years." He said that his relationship with Myers ceased to be intimate in 1973 or 1974, which is when he moved in with her.

Bradfield repeatedly was told to keep his voice up during his two full days of testimony. It kept fading out. In one afternoon session, he became ill and complained of nausea and dizziness, and that session was cut short.

Bradfield admitted to being romantically involved with Wendy Zeigler, though he denied having sex with her. He denied any romantic involvement with Susan Reinert and testified that he had never even taken her to a movie, show, dance, party, play, or concert. He was very evasive about Joanne Aitken.

Bradfield's assessment of Chris Pappas's testimony and that of Vincent Valaitis, Sue Myers, and Wendy Zeigler was that they were basically telling the truth. He testified that he did go to those extraordinary lengths to protect Susan Reinert from Jay Smith and that he went to the shore that weekend to get some distance. Josh Lock then ended his lengthy and protective direct examination by going to the ultimate issue.

Q. Did you kill Mrs. Reinert?
A. No, I did not.
Q. Did you plan to kill Susan Reinert?
A. No.
Q. Did you kill either of her children?
A. No.
Q. Did you plan to do either of those things?
A. No, I did not.
Q. Are you responsible for their deaths?
A. Absolutely not. I never hurt Mrs. Reinert or her children in any way.

★ ★ ★

During the court recess after Bradfield's direct testimony, Rick Guida must have smoked a pack of cigarettes in the hallway. He too had lost some weight during the trial. His hands shook somewhat when he lit a cigarette, and though he was nervous, he was ready. His jitteriness was obvious to everyone.

Finally, it was Rick Guida's turn. He had waited a long time for the opportunity to cross-examine Bradfield, something Rick was very good at. Josh ended with questions that went to the ultimate issue, and Rick began his cross by going to that issue—with a fiery explosion.

Q. Who *did* kill Mrs. Reinert, Mr. Bradfield?

A. I don't know.

Q. In 1979, you told a number of people that Jay C. Smith was going to kill her, and you were so afraid that you went to the shore just to have an alibi. Now, don't you think Jay C. Smith killed Susan Reinert?

A. I don't know who killed Susan Reinert.

Q. Do you *believe* that he did, Mr. Bradfield?

A. Do you want me to speculate?

Q. Sure, just tell me what you think.

A. He may have.

Q. He may have. Now what about this other person that you identified in the summer of 1979, while you were in New Mexico? Do you think he may have killed Mrs. Reinert?

A. I think he may have.

Q. Who was that? What was his name? If you think somebody else killed her, I'd like to know how you know that.

A. Mrs. Reinert mentioned the name in the winter of 1979, the name Alex, among four names that she mentioned over the years as men whom she'd gone out with and met through her association with Parents Without Partners. She mentioned four names only. No last names. Jay, Alex, Ted, and Graham. She said they were into group sex, that they were advocates of bondage and discipline. And they were advocates of deviate sexual practices, such as urination during the sex act and oral sex, and stuff like that. That's where I learned about them. In the spring of 1979, I baby-sat for her, and she came in at 4:30 in the morning and said she had seen him. He was the next-to-the-last person that I heard her mention.

Every time Lock objected to a question to protect Bradfield, and Lock tried repeatedly, Judge Garb overruled him without hesitation. Guida had tried enough cases in his time that he could sense Bradfield was going to be *the Commonwealth's* best witness.

Q. The question was, do you think somebody else did it other than Jay C. Smith? Yes or no, please.

A. I think someone else may have. Yes.

Q. Even in spite of all of those threats that Jay C. Smith made, is that right?

A. Yes.

Q. And why do you think that Jay C. Smith didn't do it?

A. Because I found out more from the newspapers. First, that it was in Harrisburg—that's where she said Alex was from. Secondly, it seemed to involve some kind of sexual misuse. There was a dildo found in her automobile.

Q. Where was that found? Where was that dildo found?

A. Found?

Q. Yes. Where was that found?

A. I don't remember. It was part of the things that were recorded early on. Thirdly, the thing that made me really wonder about Dr. Smith is that nothing he had ever told me indicated that he would kill in this way. It didn't seem to be his style. There were chain marks on her. And, in addition to this, under her body was found a comb from the same outfit as Dr. Smith, and that certainly didn't make any sense to me, that he would do it.

Q. Does it make any sense that Alex, an unnamed person, would come all the way to Harrisburg to get Jay C. Smith's comb and plant it in Susan Reinert's car? Does that make any sense?

A. I never thought he planted it there.

Q. Then how do you think it got there?

A. Well, Susan told me that she was meeting somebody named Jay. This was one of the reasons early on that I thought there was a relationship between her and Dr. Smith. His first name was Jay. Later, after I'd been arrested, I found out that there was another man named Jay that she knew of.

Q. You didn't answer the question. The questions was, How do you think that the comb got there? How did Jay C. Smith's comb get into the car, unless it was planted there by Alex from Harrisburg?

A. I wondered about it. Perhaps he lost his comb. Why the comb was where it was, I'm not sure.

Lock was sitting tight. He could only hope that the jury would hear Bradfield out, give him a chance, understand the pressure he was under, honor the presumption of innocence. It's not that Bradfield wasn't trying to explain everything. It's just that his past movements, the things he had been saying, his friends and lovers, everything about him, was very, very strange, strange as in incredibly bizarre!

Bradfield testified that he moved in with Sue Myers in 1974, but their intimacy had stopped at that point. Yes, he lived with her for six or seven years without intimacy, but Sue Myers offered him the comfort of a home base; it was the place he felt the most at home; it was not because they were intimate.

Yes, Bradfield testified under cross-examination that while living with Sue Myers he was "seeing" Joanne Aitken and Wendy Zeigler because he cared very much for both of them, and yes, he cared very much for Sue Myers, too.

Q. You were concerned about Jay C. Smith's threats, is that right?

A. Yes.

Q. But you never told Susan Reinert about Smith?

A. Not directly, no.

Q. Did you tell her about the chains?

A. No.

Q. Locks?

A. No.

Q. Ski masks?

A. No.

Q. Trash bags, did you ever tell her about that?

A. I never saw any trash bags.

Q. Never? Now, you heard Mr. Pappas tell us that you actually went out and bought some of these trash bags?

A. You have to remember that someone like Chris has been interviewed year after year by the FBI and by the state police and by the federal grand jury and the state grand jury. And Chris Pappas must have, judging from the material that we have, must have had 75 interviews. It's understandable that after four and a half years Chris would, last month, suddenly remember trash bags. I'm not suggesting necessarily that it was something that he made up, but it's simply something that did not happen.

Q. So you're telling us that the FBI and state police planted that information and told him to say it, encouraged him to lie. Is that what you're telling us?

A. Yes, I think it's merely as simple as that. Chris has misremembered the trash bags. I never had trash bags in any of my pockets. I never spoke to Chris about trash bags, and I never tested any trash bags, and Dr. Smith never showed me any trash bags.

The jury was listening intently to Bradfield, but he wasn't evoking any sympathy, and they didn't seem to like him throughout his testimony. One juror would whisper to another, or they would exchange glances between themselves, and though nobody can ever "read" a jury, they weren't expressionless either. The jury that would decide Bradfield's fate didn't look like they were believing him about anything.

Because cameras were not allowed in the courtroom, the television stations had artists in the gallery doing pastel sketches of Bradfield, as well as Judge Garb, Rick Guida, Josh Lock, and the jury.

Q. Let's go back to the pockets, Mr. Bradfield. We're talking about your blue jacket now?

A. Yes.

Q. Did you have tape in that jacket pocket?

A. Sometimes I did.

Q. Did you have chains in that jacket pocket?

A. Yes, I did.

Q. Did you have gloves in that jacket pocket?

A. Occasionally, I may have.

Q. Why did you have a jacket with all of these things in the pockets? What were you doing with tape, chains, gloves, and locks?

A. We were trying to test them against some kind of reality to see whether this man was telling me an absolutely bizarre fabrication. We were trying to see whether they really worked. I'll explain to you about the gloves.

Q. Let's take the tape. Did you tape up Pappas to see if it worked?

A. Yes.

Q. Did you use the chains?

A. Yes.

Q. Is it the same jacket you had on the night of June 22, 1979, the night that Sue Reinert was murdered?

A. Yes, and almost every other evening. I wore it constantly.

Q. Mr. Bradfield, after Dr. Smith had indicated to you that he was going to do dangerous things, a lot of dangerous things, you thought he was a threat, did you not?

A. I wasn't certain that he was. None of us was ever certain. He was not simply deranged. It's easy to look back now after a murder and see danger. But it was not easy to see for any of us at that point, to conclude that such bizarre tales were really real.

Q. They weren't just tales, Mr. Bradfield. You saw him with a sawed-off carbine, didn't you?

A. Yes.

Q. He had a silencer for the gun, didn't he?

A. Yes.

Q. And you don't think that indicates that he might be dangerous. Is that what you're telling us?

A. It indicates that he *might* be dangerous.

Q. Given that belief, Mr. Bradfield, why did you appear as an alibi witness for him, when he was tried for the St. David's Brink's job, and attempt to have him absolved of his criminal activity?

A. Because I knew where he was at a time when he was accused of being somewhere else, and he could not physically have been able to make it from Ocean City, New Jersey, at around three o'clock to a Sears store in St. David's by, I think it was a quarter to five or five.

Q. Mr. Bradfield, didn't you and Chris Pappas have a contingent plan to murder Jay C. Smith?

A. We did.

Q. So you testify for him as an alibi witness and contemplate actual *murder* in order to stop him from committing the crime. Is that right?

A. That's correct.

Guida was all over the courtroom floor, enjoying another moment in the sun. He was playing to a full house and a jury who seemed to be with him, and a judge who was not interfering with his cross-examination, because Bradfield chose to take the witness stand to put his credibility on the line. Prosecutors are generally afforded great latitude in cross-examining a defendant who gives up his right to remain silent.

Q. Did you telephone Susan Reinert at home on the last night of her life, Mr. Bradfield?

A. No.

Q. Were you concerned that she might be injured that weekend?

A. I had been concerned for some time.

Q. Did you telephone her at all during the day of June 22, 1979?

A. No.

Q. Did you telephone her after you say you saw Jay C. Smith on the night of Susan Reinert's death and tried to follow him?

A. No.

Q. Why not?

A. I had done all I really thought I could do.

Q. But you told us how you used to call her and sit by her house and do all of those things to the point where you were exhausted. Why didn't you just pick up the phone and call her and see if she was all right sometime on this day since you were preparing for the eventuality that she might be murdered that weekend?

A. I had really come to the end of what I could do. Looking back, I wish I had.

Q. You just didn't have one more telephone call in you. Is that what you're saying?

A. I just didn't do it.

Q. Vince Valaitis says that in the car on the way down to the shore, you told him that you had followed Smith around Reinert's block 14 times and lost him in a hailstorm, and that this was the weekend that it was going to happen. Did you tell Valaitis that, Mr. Bradfield? Did you tell Valaitis that you followed Smith around Reinert's block 14 times and lost him in a hailstorm?

A. I said that I should have followed him. I said that I should have circled Sue Reinert's house 14 times.

Q. Did you call Susan to say goodbye?

A. I said goodbye to Susan when I last saw her.

Q. When was that?

A. It was the week preceding her death. It was at school.

Q. The week preceding her death in school? I am talking about at her house. Did you see her there the weekend before her death? Did you see her there?

A. I can't recall specifically whether I did or not.

★ ★ ★

It was on the morning of October 28, 1983 that Joshua Lock began his impassioned closing argument. For nearly four hours he addressed the jury.

Lock tried to impress upon them that there was evidence that Smith had done it, because Bradfield hadn't. Lock pointed out that a car very similar to Susan Reinert's had been parked one night at Jay Smith's house in the spring of 1979, and it was not too far-fetched to think that she may have been seeing Dr. Smith on the sly. Lock didn't dispute the hair on Dr. Smith's floor or the red fiber, and the blue comb spoke for itself.

At one point during Josh Lock's closing argument, he put his hands on the rail of the jury box and told the Bradfield jury, "William Bradfield, ladies and gentlemen, aligned himself in characteristic fashion with two people whose lives did not appear to be on converging paths: Jay Smith and Susan Reinert. At one point, those lives converged, and it was exactly as if someone had taken those two live wires and crossed them. Who was caught in the middle?"

Rick Guida wasn't going to let that one go by.

His summation to the jury was also intense, and powerful.

Guida addressed Lock's argument with a great deal of convincing logic for the Bradfield jury, but instead of putting his hands on the rail, Rick's oratory style was to pace back and forth. "In this case, the defense has made a lot of the name Jay C. Smith, and they have suggested to you that this is a possible person who killed Sue Reinert," Rick argued and continued.

"That is possible. That certainly is possible. It is possible that Jay C. Smith helped the defendant. It is possible that Jay C. Smith was there along with the defendant when they were killing. That's certainly possible.

"What the Commonwealth tried to do in this case is show you why the chair beside the defendant *isn't* filled, why there are not two co-conspirators in this particular courtroom. What would you have if Jay C. Smith were here, if the Commonwealth was required to prove beyond a reasonable doubt that Jay C. Smith had conspired with William Bradfield to kill Susan Reinert? What would you have?

"Basically, you would have four things. You would have a comb, 20,000 which were distributed in 1978, all over the place—at shopping centers, reserve units, all over southeastern Pennsylvania. What does that comb in and of itself mean? It might be a small circumstance, but the comb was available to anyone in the Philadelphia area, including Bradfield.

"What about the fiber in her hair? The FBI told you that fibers are not fingerprints. A match on fibers depends on how much carpet was made of the same color and where the carpet is. Remember, the fabric can be very easily transferred. So, the fibers, for whatever they are worth, the fibers in Susan Reinert's hair matched Jay C. Smith's rug, and that's not a fingerprint. It could have matched thousands of rugs. We don't know. It is a circumstance. But who had access to those fibers? Who was in Jay C. Smith's house for several months? Bill Bradfield was, ladies and gentlemen.

"Then we have a hair, a hair of Susan Reinert's found in the basement of Jay C. Smith's home, a hair that fell out of her head. Now Mr. Malone, the hair and fiber expert from the FBI, came and talked to you and told you specifically that you lose 100 hairs a day. One hundred. One year after Susan Reinert died, one of her hairs is found in the basement of Jay C. Smith's house. Is it logical or fair in terms of the Commonwealth's ability to prove him guilty beyond a reasonable doubt? Wouldn't the explanation be that if a man was sleeping with Susan Reinert three nights a week and that he was at the home constantly and that he was in Smith's basement by his own admission on several occasions, that one, just one, of her hairs might have fallen off his clothing?

"This is what would happen if the Commonwealth had taken upon itself to prove that Jay C. Smith was in fact a conspirator of William Bradfield. I am not ruling out that possibility, but what I am telling you is that that evidence, those three pieces of evidence, would be insufficient to prove beyond a reasonable doubt that Jay C. Smith was involved. Why? Because the rest of the evidence, the rest of the entire evidence, every other fact concerning Jay C. Smith, every statement, everything that has been identified as his, every fear, every single statement, came from one person, and that is the defendant. He is the man who says it all. So, what you would have to do is trust Bill Bradfield's word beyond a reasonable doubt in order to be convinced beyond reasonable doubt that Jay C. Smith was his co-conspirator. When you sit back and look at this case, perhaps I suggest to you that you can answer for yourself why there isn't another chair in this courtroom."

Rick Guida's closing made a lot of sense. He was absolutely right. Smith had not been indicted when Bradfield was indicted because the Commonwealth did not have enough evidence on Smith.

Whether the Commonwealth had enough evidence to convict Bill Bradfield was another matter that would soon be addressed by the jury.

★ ★ ★

The jury retired to deliberate at 8:22 p.m. They were back in the jury box in one hour and 15 minutes with their verdict. It was one of the fastest verdicts in a death penalty case ever recorded.

Everybody in the packed courtroom knew what that meant when the jury filed in smiling at the prosecution's table. William Bradfield was found guilty of conspiracy to commit three first-degree murders. There was obviously no doubt in that jury's mind.

Rick Guida, now triumphant, was prepared to go to the jury with the death penalty. Joshua Lock objected and made a convincing argument, claiming that there were no aggravating circumstances presented that would *legally* justify the death penalty.

Judge Garb, in a move that took a lot of judicial strength in a case like the one at hand, agreed with Lock and dismissed the jurors.

"I am satisfied that the State has failed to prove aggravating circumstances," he ruled without fanfare. "And by so doing, I am directing the verdict of life imprisonment as a matter of law."

The court held that the prosecution had not proved that William Bradfield did any of the actual killings and that there was insufficient evidence to show that he had contracted with a crime partner to have it done. Therefore, as a matter of law, aggravating circumstances had not been established, and Judge Garb took the death penalty question from the jury.

★ ★ ★

The only question left for Judge Garb to answer was whether the life sentences would be concurrent or consecutive. He answered that at the time of formal sentencing:

> It doesn't matter which theory you may adopt regarding the killing of the children. Whether they happened to be there and therefore were witnesses to the actual act, or whether it was part of the grand design in the first place. But it's somewhat diabolical that the children's bodies have *never* been found.
>
> I heard you, Mr. Bradfield, express the prayer that they be found alive somewhere. I think we would have to be naive to assume that this is likely to happen. There are good reasons why the bodies of the children are not to be found. It is somewhat an article of faith by investigators that the best clues actually come from the victims. So of course it makes perfectly good sense to deny the investigator the advantage of those sources of evidence.
>
> Of course, with respect to the body of Susan Reinert, there were other considerations because the motivation for murder was the acquisition of her estate. And so as I view it, a word which hasn't been used in describing these events does apply: "diabolical," a triple homicide, regardless of where you draw that subtle line regarding the motivation for killing the youngsters.
>
> Now, what do we have on the other side? Well, we have a great deal of evidence as to what you are. I don't care to deal in caricatures. It doesn't advance the cause to talk in terms of whether you are a charismatic Rasputin or a noncharismatic Rasputin. Perhaps that is a redundancy anyway.
>
> I also don't know how Dante defined evil. Yes, I suppose there's a difference between an evil person committing an evil act and a nonevil person committing an evil act. I'm not sure which is more egregious. I don't care to characterize you as evil or not evil.
>
> I guess it must be said that you are some kind of an anomaly to us. You have heard and I have heard what has been said today about you. It is said that your interests were such that they were willing to take three lives for something in excess of $700,000 and not for any other reason.
>
> We find that you are a person of unusual quality, highly creative, intelligent, and with more than just a modicum of charm. But I think it is safe to say that you are also extremely destructive. The inflection in and of itself is of a cold and calculating mind, bereft of human sympathy and compassion, that you are bent upon achieving your end at all cost. Now that is what I see.
>
> It seems to me that you have manifested those qualities which demonstrate that you are an extremely dangerous person by virtue of your actions, and for that reason it seems to me that the sentence that is imposed must be one that affords the community the maximum of protection.

Therefore, I will impose the following sentence:

On indictment number 908, that has to do with the conviction of homicide in the first degree of Susan Reinert, it is ordered that you pay the cost of prosecution and that you undergo imprisonment in the state correctional institution for the rest of your life.

On indictment 908a, having to do with the conviction of homicide in the first degree of Karen Reinert, it is likewise ordered that you undergo imprisonment in the state correctional institution for the rest of your life—that to run *consecutively* to the sentence imposed on indictment 908.

On 908b, that being the conviction of criminal homicide in the first degree of Michael Reinert, it is ordered that you undergo imprisonment in the state correctional institution for the rest of your life—that to be served *consecutively* to the sentence imposed to number 908a.

★ ★ ★

The weight of the law was delivered full force that day by Judge Isaac Garb. The sentences were consecutive, which meant Bill Bradfield would never get out of prison.

Bradfield just shook his head no, no, no as the sheriffs moved in to take him away.

Joanne Aitken sat in the back of the courtroom and cried softly.

Bradfield's other friends and lovers were nowhere to be found. They had deserted him.

They say that in our justice system the pendulum has swung from therapeutic rehabilitation toward punishment and vengeance. The real Rasputin must have felt the pendulum in his day had swung pretty far too, especially when a group of nobles dumped him in the river Neva after shooting him.

The real Bradfield was also dumped into a river like the Neva that would slowly carry him to his death: Graterford State Correctional Institution—a deep, dark, gray-walled dungeon not far from Philadelphia—where he would spend the rest of his life in exile.

· 11 ·

SHORING UP

The conviction of William Bradfield of conspiracy to murder Susan Reinert and her two children received nationwide attention, but not like it did in Philadelphia and Harrisburg, where the Bradfield verdict was banner headlines and the lead story on all television networks. It was an honest verdict for Rick Guida who had tried the case and tried it well, and he was basking in the glory of prosecutorial stardom.

"Rick *lived* for the ink, as far back as I can remember," one of his closest childhood friends said of him. "Why he would have given up a $500,000-a-year job for the publicity."

That, in a nutshell, was Rick Guida. He had produced, choreographed, directed, and starred in his own show, and there was nothing wrong with Rick loving the publicity the case had generated. If the publicity drove him to investigate the case the way he did, if it drove him to prepare day and night, if it caused him to look his best and try his hardest in the courtroom, well then, in many ways that's the criminal justice system at its best. At least it's one prosecutor at his best as long as the truth doesn't get compromised.

Jack Holtz was in his glory too, and he also deserved it, and like Guida loved the publicity that winning the Bradfield case brought him.

But in any high-profile case, prosecutors and police officers and criminal defense lawyers must beware. The call of the media is seductive and tempting and insidious.

Lawyers, as officers of the court, must never lose sight of the fact that what is at stake in a criminal trial is the fate of the accused and the integrity of the system.

★ ★ ★

The Bradfield verdict, though a good one for the attorney general's office and the Pennsylvania State Police, answered very few questions for the public.

Who had actually killed Susan Reinert and her two children? Who was the executioner? Was there more than one killer? Could there have been four or five accomplices working in concert? Where were the children?

The Bradfield verdict did nothing to answer *those* questions. The Bradfield verdict satisfied the public that Bradfield conspired with a person or persons unknown to have the Reinert family killed and disposed of, but

76

the Bradfield trial intensified the mystery of who it was that Bradfield conspired with.

Was it Dr. Jay Smith, the Prince of Darkness, the eccentric who was still in prison for wearing Brink's security guard uniforms and scamming two Sears stores? Wasn't Smith that former principal of Upper Merion High School who had mass pornography in his home and guns and drugs and ski masks and syringes in his pockets? Wasn't Smith also the one, according to newspaper and magazine accounts, whose daughter and son-in-law had also disappeared—like the Reinert children? Was it possible that all those missing persons were together?

Jay Smith must have been the one who had conspired with Bradfield. Though his past was not evidence of murder, his past sure fit the bill of guilt.

Plus, at the Bradfield trial, Chris Pappas and Vince Valaitis and Sue Myers and Wendy Zeigler had some wild and crazy things to say about that weirdo, Smith. Each of them had testified that Bradfield had said that Smith had committed multiple murders, and that Smith had vowed to kill Susan Reinert.

The prosecution also had hard forensic evidence in its file that incriminated Smith. There was the blue 79th USARCOM comb found in the trunk; there was also a hair found in Smith's basement that was consistent with Susan Reinert's hair; and there was a red fiber taken out of her hair at the autopsy that was consistent with a red rug in Smith's basement.

But Rick Guida had had that incriminating evidence long before the Bradfield trial and must have had some gnawing uncertainties about the case against Smith when he tried Bradfield in October 1983.

Guida needed more evidence to get a conviction, to win the big one, and the word was out that Jay Smith was the big one.

★ ★ ★

There was also the little lapel tab, the green metal pin with a white "P," which was found in the search of Jay Smith's car in August 1980. This lapel tab was found by Trooper Dove during the search of Smith's car, but at the time nobody knew of its significance. It was subsequently learned that pins like that were handed out at the Philadelphia Museum of Art when admission had been paid, and different colors were issued on different days.

A follow-up investigation into that pin established that Karen Reinert had gone to the Philadelphia Museum of Art with her school class and was issued a pin exactly like the one found in Smith's car. Each of Karen's classmates was issued a lapel tab on the day they went to the museum. The tabs were green with a white "P."

The only downside to that bombshell piece of evidence, and it did have the potential of being a bombshell, was that over 600,000 pins like that were issued yearly by the Philadelphia Museum of Art. To make it a bombshell piece of evidence would require some work, some shoring up, or a break, but it was still a solid piece of evidence the Commonwealth could use to indict Jay Smith.

But Rick Guida and Jack Holtz were not just interested in an indictment. They knew the system well enough to know that they could get a grand jury to indict Smith based on Bradfield's statements to his friends and lovers, the forensic evidence, the pin, and the jailhouse confession, which Raymond Martray was now providing them. They also knew the system well enough to know that they would have to strengthen their case against Smith to get a conviction in a court of law. Jay Smith was not a lightweight, and unlike Bradfield, he was a very private person who talked to no one.

★ ★ ★

But Ray Martray had come through for the Commonwealth with a "Smith confession" *after* VanNort died. While VanNort was in charge of the investigation and did the questioning of Martray, all he could provide was information out of the March 1981 issue of *Philadelphia Magazine*. But on October 13, 1981, 12 days after VanNort's death, Trooper Holtz and DiSantis re-interviewed Martray at the Fayette County Courthouse. At that meeting he recalled additional information pertaining to comments made by Smith and told Holtz and DiSantis, "Smith said he called the police to notify them about Reinert's body and used a Spanish accent."

The caller using a Spanish accent was also mentioned in the *Philadelphia Magazine*.

"Smith told me more," Martray quickly added, because he did not want to lose their interest again. "Smith told me the kids weren't to be there. Smith said he had to take care of the kids, too. Smith also said he had been in the Host Inn several times and that it was a high-class place. Smith said police overlooked that a person could have taken a bus from the Host Inn to Philadelphia."

"Did Smith give you any idea concerning the children's whereabouts?" Holtz asked, hoping for something that wasn't in the magazine.

"Smith often said that you should look for a grave with fresh flowers on it. Smith said you could open the grave and bury a body," Martray answered, coyly.

On December 29, 1981, there was another meeting with Martray at the Holiday Inn in Uniontown. This time, Trooper Holtz and DiSantis were accompanied by Rick Guida. They also had with them Richard Beswick, a Fayette County detective; and Detective Matt Hunchuck. Martray had a big audience and realized that he was now being taken seriously.

"Have you remembered anything else, Mr. Martray?" Holtz asked, as he took charge of the questioning.

"Yes, I have. As a matter of fact, I have," Martray answered quickly.

"Go on," Holtz said, prodding.

"The conversations we had about the murder were held in the grand-stands of the recreation area at the prison. Smith told me, 'I took care of her.'"

"Did he tell you that once or more than once?"

"The second and third time we discussed this case, Smith said, 'I killed the fuckin' bitch Reinert.'"

"Smith said that?"

"Yes."

"When did he tell you that?"

"Around July 1980."

"Why didn't you tell us that before?"

"I was afraid of what Smith might do to me if he found out that I told you this."

"What else did Smith tell you?"

"I asked Smith, 'Why were the kids killed?'"

"What did Smith say?"

"He said, 'If you were to do something and there were witnesses, what would you do?'"

"Did he tell you how he did it?"

"No."

"Did he tell you where the children were," Guida asked, interrupting.

"No."

"Are you willing to take a polygraph?"

"I . . . I'm not sure. I want to wait a few days to get my mind together," Martray answered, after an obvious pause.

On January 13, 1982, Martray's mind was together, and the law enforcement boys brought him in for a polygraph examination by a skilled examiner, Special Agent Lawrence Bria of the FBI. Every time Martray was confronted by the examiner concerning his statements about what Smith had told him about the Reinert case, he immediately backed off from his answers and on each occasion said that he could not recall specifically what he had been told by Smith.

Martray impressed upon the examiner that he didn't have any notes, but the examiner wasn't impressed.

There were follow-up attempts by Jack Holtz to pin down Martray concerning specific statements made to him by Smith concerning the Reinert killing. Holtz reminded Martray of what he had told him and Guida just the other week.

"Don't you remember what you told us in Uniontown two weeks ago, Ray?" Holtz asked, pleading.

Martray then became more and more general rather than specific in his recollection. He finally stated that he wanted to review *Holtz's* notes concerning his previous statements, so he could finally decide what Smith had said to him.

"He wants to review *your* notes, Jack," the examiner quipped sarcastically. The examiner didn't like Martray one bit, and Holtz felt he was losing a star witness.

At that point, the article entitled "Murder on the Main Line," which appeared in the March 1981 issue of *Philadelphia Magazine*, was shown to Martray by the examiner. Agent Bria made it clear that in his opinion most of the information furnished by Martray was coming from the magazine article rather than from specific conversations with Smith.

"You did read this magazine article, didn't you?" Agent Bria asked.

"Yeah . . . I read it."

"And you're familiar with its contents?"

"Yes."

At that point Martray started to sweat and became even more general concerning conversations he had had with Smith about the Reinert case. He continued to indicate that the reason he could not be specific was that he hadn't taken notes, and the reason he didn't take notes was that he was fearful that Smith would search his cell.

"Well, did Smith tell you he killed Susan Reinert or didn't he?" the examiner asked point blank, and Holtz held his breath.

"He led me to believe he killed her. He may not have used those exact words. I did not take any notes. There were many conversations," Martray finally conceded.

Ray Martray flunked the polygraph examination. Holtz wrote down it as inconclusive.

* * *

Raymond Martray's "confession from Smith," though uncorroborated and coming from a convicted perjurer, would get better in time. Jailhouse confessions *do* get better in time, especially as you get closer to trial. Guida would have felt a lot better about that confession if he could just get Smith to repeat it or say something incriminating to Martray, anything at all, *on tape*. Guida and Holtz decided they would put Martray to their own test.

On February 10, 1982, Trooper Holtz met with Assistant Attorney General Guida, who okayed the consent wire tap on Martray. The game plan was for Martray to bait Smith into an admission on tape, while Martray was wearing a body wire, or whenever the two of them might talk on a telephone that was tapped. A confession or an incriminating statement, or even a slip-up, would have been the kiss of death for Smith—and Martray's redemption.

Ray Martray was released from jail and allowed to go home to his wife and three children. That also put him in a position where he could accommodate and cooperate with the Pennsylvania State Police in the following manner:

(1) Martray would report to Trooper Nickel every day by phone or in person; (2) Martray would obtain a P.O. box for all mail received from

Smith; (3) a double tap would be installed on Martray's phone to tape conversations with Smith, one tap to be controlled by Martray and the other by the Pennsylvania State Police; and (4) in the event of a face-to-face meeting with Smith, Martray would wear a taped body device monitored by the police. It was agreed that Martray would be released from prison when the above preparations had been met.

Martray engaged Smith in one conversation after another, baited him, tried to trick him, joked with him, pled with him, but to no avail. Smith steadfastly maintained *on tape* that he had nothing to do with Sue Reinert's death or the death of the children. Reels and reels of tape were being consumed by Holtz and Guida. Days turned into fruitless weeks and weeks into fruitless months.

On one hot day in July 1982, the police instructed Martray to wear a body wire and go visit Smith at SCI-Dallas. Holtz and an electronics technician were hiding in a paneled truck within filming distance of the prison yard. The game plan was to videotape and record Martray and Smith standing outside the prison visiting area. The telephoto lens zoomed in on the subjects as they stood behind the barbed fence, and the camera inside the truck quietly began rolling.

Martray acted like a nut, waving his arms, getting in front of Smith, hopping around, cutting Smith off in mid-sentence, and talking over him. Smith appeared calm and didn't get to say much about anything even when he wanted to. He certainly didn't say anything incriminating.

Jack Holtz was furious at Ray Martray.

Three months later, they tried it again. The only difference this time was that it was a lot cooler outside. But Holtz and the technician inside the paneled truck got plenty hot again at Martray's overdone performance.

At one point during this cinematic audition, Martray blurted out that he was going to "take care" of Bill Bradfield.

Jay Smith simply said, "What for? I had nothing to do with the murder, Ray, you know that."

Jack Holtz was steaming. He knew these tapes and videos would have to be turned over to Smith's defense lawyers after he was indicted. They had already made up their minds that they were going to indict Smith, but their case seemed to be going to hell on tape and on film.

Whenever Martray reported back to the studio, he would simply shake his head and explain to Holtz that Smith was a criminal genius and that he liked making "self-serving statements."

Martray was pulled from the set and was put back on the phones. His filmmaking days were over.

★ ★ ★

In one of the many telephone calls between Jay Smith and Raymond Martray, the two were talking about the William Bradfield murder trial, *during* that trial.

"He's putting it on you, Jay," Martray said with anxiety.

"But Ray," Smith answered calmly, "the only thing Bradfield could say about me was, 'I called Susan out, drove her up to the house where Smith was, and that he gave her a shot of morphine and killed the kids.'"

"Puts you right in the middle, doesn't it?" Ray Martray said, coaxing, praying for Smith to say something incriminating.

"With three bodies? Now what the fuck do you do with three bodies? How did I get rid of them? How did I get her up to Harrisburg by myself and then get myself back with only her car? See what I mean?" Smith answered, bewildered by Martray's ignorance.

Martray couldn't get Smith to say anything incriminating. In fact, during that conversation Smith sounded like he really could be innocent.

"In the newspapers," Smith continued on the phone, "the one thing in the whole case that baffles me is this: Here's a name to keep in mind, Joanne Aitken."

"Yeah, I've heard her mentioned many times."

"Yeah. Now Bradfield was shacking up with this woman for the month of May, the month right before Reinert died, okay?"

"Uh huh."

"Now she drove Bradfield's car to New Mexico."

"Right."

"And shacked up with him out there. Now I think that event of her driving Bradfield's car to New Mexico is significant. Another thing the papers said is somewhere on the way out there she called Bradfield, and that's when she learned Reinert was dead. What if she had those two kids' bodies in that car and dumped them off somewhere? See what I mean?"

"That would be an excellent summation," Martray said, on tape. He was audibly distraught.

"Joanne Aitken sponsored his bail. See, the critical thing is if Reinert leaves her home at 9:30 Friday night and goes with Bradfield, and he shows up two hours later, maybe he killed her, gave her to Aitken, and Aitken then takes her body to Harrisburg and comes back. Bradfield goes down to the shore, okay."

"Uh huh."

"And then Aitken had the two kids, and she takes them to New Mexico when he flies out there. See, Ray, the thing is here's another thing you have to keep in mind. I have a theory that the attorney general must have something else on Bradfield. I have a feeling he must have something else up his sleeve that would link Bradfield to the actual night of the murder. The only reason he would have picked on me to blame is that I was an obvious target from all the bad publicity. So he dreams up this secret love affair with Reinert and the hit man stuff."

"They got the hair and the comb," Ray Martray said, grasping.

"But they still got a problem with why did Smith do it," Jay said. "The only thing they can say is Bradfield was an alibi for him, and then to pay him back, Smith killed the three people."

By the end of that conversation, Holtz and Guida were convinced that Jay Smith was never going to make any real admissions over the telephone or on film, and they were right. But they could not ditch Ray Martray either, whether they believed him or not, because he was the only jailhouse snitch they had.

* * *

On November 10, 1983, less than two weeks after Bradfield's conviction, Jack Holtz and Lou DiSantis traveled to Wilkes-Barre, Pennsylvania to meet with Charles Montione after learning from Raymond Martray that Montione might also provide a confession or an incriminating statement to bolster Martray's. Charles Montione, who was in prison for armed robbery and burglary, was taken to the Wilkes-Barre Holiday Inn. There Montione agreed to cooperate, in exchange for some favors, and according to Holtz's notes, this is the information Charles Montione provided:

> Smith told Montione that he would be arrested for five murders, Susan Reinert, Michael and Karen Reinert, and Stephanie and Eddie Hunsberger. Smith felt that he would be arrested after he appeared before the grand jury. Montione recalled that once Smith wanted a picture from *Hustler* magazine. Smith stated that the picture must be one with a girl on her knees with the head down and her ass exposed, but her legs must be together with the cunt closed, because this is the way Reinert's body was found in the car. Montione also stated that at one time Reinert had her hands tied behind her back. Montione recalled that he showed Smith several pictures from magazines before Smith found the right one. He also recalled Smith stating that the best way to kill someone is by injection because the police will think it was an overdose. (It should also be noted that Montione stated he did not know the cause of Reinert's death.) At the end of this interview, Montione furnished the officers with handwritten notes that he made detailing numerous conversations that he had had with Smith.

Holtz felt Montione was believable. He was soft-spoken, 24 years old and a former medical student. Holtz and Guida felt they could sell him to a jury. He seemed to be an honest, truthful young man, a lot like Proctor Nowell.

Within weeks after Montione's interview, another jailhouse snitch, Joseph Weiss, a convicted robber, called Holtz and DiSantis. Weiss, a 48-year-old white inmate with sentences totaling 30 years, told them he had a detailed confession from Jay Smith, and he too gave them one, but Weiss's "Smith confession" had some details to it and none of those details checked out. He would have been a lot better off if he had just given a "general confession"—no details, nothing to check out—like Nowell and Martray and Montione had done.

* * *

There were more taped conversations between Raymond Martray and Jay Smith, who repeated for the listeners, again and again, "I wasn't involved. I did not murder Susan Reinert. You know that I had nothing to do with it."

The last recorded telephone conversation was on February 3, 1985.

"What if Holtz and DiSantis come back to me?" Martray asked.

"Tell them that you want to talk to them openly, but you want a video tape and somebody representing Jay Smith present."

"Okay, what if they ask me to take a lie detector?"

"Well, say you'll take a lie detector, but you don't want to take a lie detector unless you consult with someone from the other side."

"Okay, how do I handle it?"

"How do you mean?"

"Well, I mean, you know, we went over that, but . . . "

"It's certainly in order."

"Jay, I'm . . . I'm worried about the big question. You know: Did Smith tell you he did it?"

"What I'll do is this then, I'll have my people tell them that you're not taking any lie detector test."

"I got you," said Raymond Martray.

"See, you're not going to do anything unless it's consulted with Jay Smith's lawyer."

Guida would argue that was an incriminating statement from Dr. Smith. Their library of tapes and videos of Smith's denials and assertions of innocence would be dismissed as "self-serving."

★ ★ ★

Everybody agreed that their case was not going to get any better. Six years had gone by.

Guida went to the grand jury in June 1985 and got the indictment of Jay Smith for murder.

On June 25, 1985, exactly six years after Susan Reinert's body had been found in the trunk of her car outside the Host Inn, Jay Smith was arrested for the murder of Susan, Karen, and Michael Reinert. Smith's arrest was on the very day he was to be released from serving his previous sentences.

That's what Holtz wanted.

But Jay Smith would strike back.

· 12 ·

ENGAGED TO DEFEND

September 18, 1985.

Over the past 13 years, I had been in his chambers many times. It was a big office overlooking the ominous Susquehanna River, and his big mahogany desk matched the paneled walls. The enormous red tufted leather chairs made those who sat in them feel small but important. Judge William W. Lipsitt, a senior judge who had a long tenure in Dauphin County, was a quiet man with a surprisingly sardonic laugh who tried to be fair to everybody at all times. And I always liked him a lot.

Judge Lipsitt watched me the whole time he was talking to me, peering at me over his reading glasses. He had never asked any favors of me in the past.

In our system of justice, when one is accused of a crime—no matter how offensive the crime may be—that person has the absolute right to a lawyer. If the defendant cannot afford a lawyer, one will be appointed for him by the court. The downside to being indigent is that the accused must accept the court-appointed lawyer whether he likes him or not.

"Bill," Judge Lipsitt began softly after polite amenities, "I want you to represent Dr. Jay Smith. I have the responsibility of appointing him an attorney because he's indigent, and I haven't been able to get one on this side of the river."

"Why not?" I asked, wanting to know.

"Well," Lipsitt continued, "It's a triple death penalty case, it's going to be time-consuming, costly, stressful, and Dr. Jay Smith is pretty strange."

"Why doesn't the public defender's office take it?" I asked.

"Because they were involved with Josh Lock in the defense of Bill Bradfield, and that would be a conflict of interest," Judge Lipsitt answered.

"Why me?" I pursued.

"This is a death penalty case, Bill, and I want a fair trial. You know your way around the criminal courts. You also have the resources. I also thought of you because it's your kind of case," the judge responded.

"There's a lot of publicity in this case," I said, smiling.

"Lots," he agreed, shaking his head knowingly.

"But no money?" I added, already knowing the answer.

"We'll pay your costs, transcripts, whatever experts you need, but as far as your fees are concerned, they will be nominal, very nominal. I'll do what I can."

"Do they have him, judge?" I asked, wanting to know, hoping it was a triable case.

"I'm not sure," he answered.

"Okay," I said.

"Okay, what?" Judge Lipsitt asked, wanting to make sure I understood my commitment.

"You knew I would take this case when you called me," I answered, laughing.

"You're right," the judge said, shaking his head and blurting out his sardonic laugh.

When I told Judge Lipsitt that I would defend Jay Smith, I realized I had, in an important way, come full circle in my career. I began my career in Dauphin County in 1972, as an assistant district attorney to LeRoy Zimmerman. Thirteen years later here I was, back in Dauphin County, ready to defend the biggest case of my career against Rick Guida, my former fellow prosecutor, who was now LeRoy Zimmerman's top gun in the Pennsylvania Attorney General's Office.

★ ★ ★

The drive back to my Lemoyne law office, just across the Susquehanna River from Harrisburg, didn't give me much time to think about what I was going to tell my law partners and associates. My telling Judge Lipsitt okay was no small commitment for them either in terms of time, money, and energy.

Our office in the Borough of Lemoyne is a Victorian building with Corinthian columns and ornate wrought iron. At the entrance are two sitting lions to welcome those in need. I had been practicing law out of that building since I left Roy Zimmerman's office in 1973, and I had always considered myself a serious player in the courtroom. Our office, at that time, was a family of six lawyers, three secretaries, and a great paralegal.

It was time for a staff meeting in our formal conference room. And I had plenty of explaining to do. The entire office attended since they were going to pay the price. Everybody sat around the long oak table that dominated the room—except my paralegal who stood and paced.

"You're not serious?" Dave Foster, one of my partners, asked. Foster had been my partner for five years, and he was a talented courtroom lawyer. The 36-year-old, blond, athletically built Foster was family oriented—and he had a mortgage.

"Yeah, I am. I told Judge Lipsitt I would do it."

"Bill, you're nuts. You have no idea what you're getting us all into."

"Do I ever, Dave?"

"No."

"Well then?"

Leslie Fields, the only female lawyer in our office, was sitting beside Dave, smoking a cigarette, with half a cup of coffee in front of her. Leslie was in her early thirties, petite, with long auburn hair and doe eyes. She was a consummate tort lawyer, an extreme liberal, and she was concerned about this commitment.

"This is a death penalty case, Bill," Leslie said, worried.

"I know," I answered, knowing her worry was not misplaced.

"Everything about this case worries me," Leslie continued. "The involvement of this office, the bad publicity, the consumption of time, the money, not to mention the death penalty issues."

"I know you're right, Leslie," I said, speaking to everybody there. "It's not that I just made a commitment, but this is what I do. This is what I've devoted my life to for the past 15 years. I see a lot of opportunity here to do something."

The conference room fell silent. My fellow lawyers, my paralegal, and my support staff knew me on a personal level as well as a professional, and they agreed to let me call this one.

"Where's Nick?" I asked, breaking the silence, and everybody knew that I had made *my* decision.

Nick Ressetar was my law clerk; actually, he was the law clerk for all six lawyers in our office and had been for several years. I wouldn't trade him for any team of law clerks with the United States Supreme Court.

"Nick, have a seat."

"Okay."

"We're going to represent Jay Smith."

"Yeah."

"You know the program, Nick," I said, joking.

"Yeah. I do everything—the research, the writing, the pretrial motions, the briefs, the trial memo, points for charge. You get all the credit, and I get nothing."

"You got it."

"Okay."

That's what I loved about Nick. Everybody in my office said he looked like my son because of his jet-black hair and well-groomed beard, but Nick and I both hated that. I felt he was too short and too old. He was 26 and not good-looking or muscular enough to be my son, and Nick always said that if I was his father, he would kill himself.

We had a good office.

Outside it was a typical mid-September early afternoon. The fall has always been my favorite time of the year. I take as much time off as I can to spend on my mountaintop estate between Harrisburg and Carlisle. My wife, Jill, and our three daughters have always enjoyed the privacy afforded by our mile-long driveway and gated entrance. White-tail deer are plentiful on our ranch, year round, and are constantly crossing the driveway. But in the fall, especially in the fall, the big oak trees turn fiery red and the proud buck show up with their majestic horns.

I was 42 years old when I agreed to represent Jay Smith. My workout regimen kept me energetic. I was in good health. My family was in good health. My practice was successful. I was hoping, as I looked outside from my office window onto Market Street, that I was not making a mistake.

★ ★ ★

With one phone call, I learned that Jay Smith was being held in the maximum security division of the State Correctional Institution at Camp Hill. He would continue to be a maximum security prisoner because he was facing the death penalty, and that meant handcuffs, shackles, and solitary confinement. I had no idea how a 56-year-old man, a one-time esteemed principal and respected colonel in the army, could take that.

SCI-Camp Hill was five minutes from my office. The prison was surrounded by thick wire fences with rolls of barbed concertina wire along the top. High brick towers were strategically placed at different locations and manned 24 hours a day by uniformed guards with rifles. My father-in-law used to be one of those guards. It was a tough prison, with tough guards, and tough inmates. In 1989, the inmates rioted and burned the place to the ground.

I hated going there. It was such a pain in the ass to get into even as a visiting lawyer. To get through the metal detector, I had to take my shoes off, remove my jewelry, give them my wallet, empty my pockets, and take my belt off. They went through my briefcase. All the preliminaries sometimes took an hour. Then I had to wait in the outer waiting room for Jay Smith to be brought down.

I had been told before my first visit that I would be talking to inmate Smith through a solid glass barrier, by telephone, and that he would remain handcuffed and shackled. Finally, after a 30-minute period in a noisy waiting room where inmates with contact visits were all over their loved ones, the guard at the desk nodded to me that Jay Smith was in the glass booth.

Smith watched me through the glass without saying a word as I sat across from him. I took a hard look at him too, and noticed his haunting eyes, the stress in his face, and his disheveled, thinning hair and receding hairline. He looked older than his newspaper photos, but he didn't look bad to me, and he didn't look frightened. In fact, there was a certain calm about him that I really liked, almost admired.

"Mr. Smith, my name is William Costopoulos, and I have been asked by Judge Lipsitt to represent you," I said over the phone to start the conversation. It's awkward talking to somebody through a glass. The person across from you doesn't seem real.

Jay Smith just nodded his head, yes.

"All I can tell you is that I'll do what I can for you."

"I know who you are," Smith said.

"I guess that's good," I said half jokingly. "I . . . we're going to have to talk, not so much in detail today, but at some point. Today, I just wanted to introduce myself, since I'm going to be representing you."

"Pleased to meet you, Mr. Costopoulos," Smith said, pronouncing my name wrong.

And that's how the conversation started. He gave me a lot of background information on himself. I didn't ask him whether he was guilty or not. I didn't really care at that point, but I knew what his position had been all along. I told him my private investigator and good friend, Skip Gochenour, would be out to see him a lot more than I, and that he should talk to him and answer all of his questions. He said that he understood, and that was about it.

I did have one question that I had to ask before I left, because I was curious.

"Jay," I asked as I was getting up. "Can you tell me anything about your daughter, Stephanie?"

"I don't know where she is," Smith answered softly.

★ ★ ★

The preliminary hearing for Jay Smith had been held on July 30, 1985—six weeks before my involvement. Glenn A. Zeitz, a capable Philadelphia lawyer, appeared for Smith. Rick Guida was the prosecutor. It was a discovery hearing and was not to determine Smith's guilt or innocence. Zeitz did an excellent job in questioning the witnesses. That hearing was videotaped for posterity, and Guida gave me a copy of the tape.

I couldn't wait to watch it.

One night, after Jill and the girls had gone to bed, I put another log on the fire, took out a note pad and watched the preliminary hearing from beginning to end. Stanley "Skip" Gochenour, 40, one of my best friends of all times and the best homicide investigator money could buy, was with me. The two of us had been in a lot of courtroom wars together, and I seldom went into battle without him at my side.

Skip was a short, red-headed, cigar-smoking, barrel-chested tough guy, in addition to being knowledgeable and bright. He had a college degree and had gone to the best homicide seminars in the country. He was a former police officer with Northern Regional Police Department and had successfully investigated hundreds of murder cases. He carried three concealed handguns at all times—one in a shoulder holster, one on his belt, and one on his calf. I swear he slept with them.

Skip took a lot of notes as we watched the preliminary hearing. I forgot to take any.

"What do you think, Skip?" I asked, after Martray and Montione had testified in my living room.

"They're lying sons-of-bitches," Skip snapped.

"They're dangerous," I said.

"Sure they're dangerous. Any confession is dangerous, and though I don't know whether Smith is guilty or not, not yet at least, there is no way in hell Dr. Jay confessed to fellow inmates. That's absolute bullshit."

Skip was right on all counts. Martray was 41 at the time and looked distinguished with his business suit and gray hair. Zeitz cross-examined him hard, but Martray maintained under oath that he was given no deals or favorable consideration. Guida and Holtz attested to that fact by their silence, but I intended to ask them.

Charles Montione bothered me more than Martray. He was a younger, better-looking Italian boy, with gold jewelry, who wore a white, open-necked silk shirt under his sport coat. Unlike Martray, he didn't seem as eager to please. Montione worried me.

"Skip," I said.

"I know," he said, interrupting me. "Go see Jay Smith. Get all the facts. Run all the witnesses down, wherever they are. Go to Strawberry Square and meet with Holtz and Guida. Get all the police reports, the pathology reports, the forensic evidence, the statements. Bust my ass. Do it all. You get the credit, and I get nothing."

"You got it," I answered, laughing out loud, because I knew he was right, just like Nick was.

★ ★ ★

The media hype was constant. Rick Guida was getting excited. Because of a shortage of space at the Dauphin County Courthouse, he made arrangements with the Court Administrator of Cumberland County to try the case in the old courthouse in Carlisle, Pennsylvania.

Carlisle was 20 miles from Harrisburg, a quaint, small town, and the home of the athlete Jim Thorpe, Molly Pitcher, Dickinson Law School, the Army War College, Bessie's House of historic ill-repute, and my parents.

Guida's arrangements were first-class, too. He put a sound system in the 140-year-old courtroom that ended up costing the attorney general's office $2,696 and a new $1,000 carpet also billed to the attorney general's office.

Rick Guida was back in the movie producer mode. I wasn't complaining either, because Carlisle was my hometown, 10 minutes from my home, and I like new carpet and sound systems, too.

Then Rick got the call that Dauphin County was making Courtroom 1 available for the Smith trial, and Guida got sick.

Cumberland County officials were not displeased with the "much-needed" improvements to the Victorian-era courtroom. Gary Hollinger, the Cumberland County Court Administrator, said the new sound system should improve the poor acoustics, and the tan carpet should muffle the creaking of the old wooden floor.

★ ★ ★

Skip and Nick and I worked day and night. We argued a lot, we fought over what meant what, but we worked as a team. We all agreed that with the pieces of the puzzle we were given by the Commonwealth, we were coming up with a different picture than the prosecution's. Our picture was consistent with Smith's innocence.

"Or they're holding out on us, Bill," Skip cautioned.

"You mean those guys would do something like that, keep pieces of the puzzle out of the box and then spring them on us at trial!" Nick said, taunting Skip, feigning astonishment.

"Quit busting my ass," Skip snapped.

Rick Guida did represent to the court that he had "an open-file policy" in the case, which meant we could see whatever he had by simply asking for it, but there are a lot of tricky little ways around that.

Though the trial is not a game in the eyes of the law, but a sacred institution to ferret out truth, winning is important to guys like Guida and Holtz. It's also important to guys like Costopoulos and Gochenour and Ressetar. There's nothing wrong with wanting to win, just as there's nothing wrong with loving publicity—as long as you don't sell your soul and compromise the truth.

Sometimes in a high-profile case the need to win, or the fear of losing, can take you over. The Jay Smith case would put us all to the test legally, ethically, and morally, and also put our reputations and character on the line.

On the legal front, Nick prepared a well-researched and flawless omnibus pretrial motion. We wanted a change of venue because of the massive amount of trial publicity that Bradfield got in Harrisburg. Harrisburg is only so big, and the Bradfield trial was one of the most sensationalized trials in Pennsylvania's history. The newspapers in Dauphin County also sensationalized Smith's arrest and his preliminary hearing, with photo spreads of Smith in handcuffs and shackles leaving the magistrate's office, with quotes from Martray and Montione, and references to Smith's missing daughter and son-in-law. The television broadcasts did their own hammering with live footage in vivid color of Smith being pulled in and out of the sheriff's car. The radio stations put their spin on Smith's upcoming trial, and suffice it to say, it was not sympathetic.

Our first pretrial motion (filed in November 1985) was to get a jury outside of Dauphin County because of all the prejudicial publicity.

The court denied our motion for change of venue.

We then moved for a sequestered jury, and the court denied that.

We moved for separate juries to determine the degree of guilt, and if necessary, the penalty to be imposed.

Denied. There would be one jury.

We moved to preclude the imposition of the death penalty on the grounds that Pennsylvania's death penalty law was unconstitutional on its face.

Denied. Pennsylvania's death penalty law was constitutional.

We challenged the validity of the searches.

Denied. There would be no suppression of evidence.

The Commonwealth agreed not to mention during the trial that Jay Smith's daughter and son-in-law had been missing since 1978. The Commonwealth also agreed to keep out certain taped conversations between Martray and Smith when they discussed future armed robberies. However, the court ruled that their taped conversations about an escape plan and their talk about maybe killing some sheriffs and guards to effectuate Smith's escape was coming in.

All in all, at the pretrial maneuvering stage, we lost every bloody round. Skip and I blamed Nick, and Nick got mad and slammed the door as he stormed out of my office.

Skip and I laughed. The truth is, we expected every one of those pretrial losses.

★ ★ ★

On the fact-gathering front—Skip's department—we were making a lot of progress. Skip had prepared enormous blue notebooks with an index system that would put a witness's entire history, every previous statement given by that witness, in front of me with a flip of the finger. Skip and Nick went through the room full of boxes at the attorney general's office item by item. They gave me inventory lists in alphabetical or chronological order. Skip lined up some expert witnesses to blow the Commonwealth's one hair and red fiber evidence out of the water and into oblivion, which is where *that* evidence belonged.

The testimony given by Susan Myers, Chris Pappas, Vincent Valaitis, and Wendy Zeigler—that is, their testimony according to Bradfield—had been admissible in the Bradfield trial because Bradfield was the defendant. I was pretty sure that their testimony according to Bradfield would not be allowed in Smith's trial because it was classic, textbook, prejudicial hearsay. If the Commonwealth wanted to convict Smith in a death penalty case on what Bradfield had to say, then the Commonwealth would have to produce Bradfield himself. I looked forward to that day.

As I said, I was pretty sure the hearsay wasn't coming in.

The more Nick researched, the more Skip investigated, the more we interviewed Jay Smith, the more doubts we had about his guilt. Like everybody else, we had presumed him guilty when we started. His past was just awful, with Brink's guard uniforms, guns, knives, chains, acid, and pornography in his home. He even looked guilty, with his spooky-looking eyes, especially in his handcuffs and shackles; and to add to our problems (and my bouts of depression), Skip and Nick both felt that we could never call Smith as a witness.

"You can't put him on the witness stand, Bill," Skip said.

"I agree," Nick added.

I knew what they were saying, and they weren't giving their advice lightly. A jury *always* wants to hear from the defendant in a criminal case.

The presumption of innocence and his right to remain silent in a court of law don't mean a damn thing in a murder case.

"You guys are fucking nuts," was all I said to them about that.

"Bill," Skip pressed, "I talked to him. You talked to him. You know the problem. He'll deny he committed the Brink's jobs. He'll deny he possessed drugs. He'll deny he possessed guns. He'll deny he possessed pornography. Whatever you ask him, he'll deny it."

Jay Smith was a piece of work. We couldn't get around *that*.

★ ★ ★

It was a tough case to defend, and Smith's possible innocence was no defense. You can never confuse innocence with a winnable case. The grade school pictures of Michael and Karen alone were going to kill us. The depiction of Susan Reinert's battered and abused nude body in the fetal position was going to infuriate any jury. The evidence against Smith as the one responsible for their senseless deaths just wasn't there, but somebody had to answer for it, and that was our problem.

Why would the attorney general's office and the Pennsylvania State Police arrest somebody if that person wasn't guilty? That's how most people think. That was another problem—*for us*.

We couldn't rely on the weakness of the Commonwealth's case either. That may be the law, but it's not the reality of the courtroom. We would have to prove Smith's innocence with clear and convincing physical evidence. It was not going to be easy, but we decided to take the offensive.

"Look at this, Bill," Skip said. "This note came out of Susan Reinert's car when they searched it at the Host Inn. It's a note in Susan Reinert's handwriting with specific directions to Cape May. Actually, if you follow the directions on the note, you end up a little north of Cape May, but you're still within striking distance of Bill Bradfield and his friends."

"The directions to Cape May were in Reinert's car?"

"Right."

"Let me ask you something else, Skip, that's been bothering me."

"Go ahead, Bill."

"When did Sue Myers turn over to Holtz and DiSantis the 'Bradfield stuff' she got out of their apartment?"

"Not until July of 1980, which was 13 months after the Reinert murders."

"Those dumb asses."

"You got it."

"Did Holtz and DiSantis ever search Bradfield's apartment?"

"Not that I know of, Bill."

"Damn, Skip, they really did have their heads up their asses."

"I agree, but they were all hung up on Bradfield's alibi."

"Well, I'm not hung up on Bradfield's alibi. I'm not sure I believe any of them. Show me that report, Skip, the one that deals with the grocery store receipt found in Bradfield's apartment."

"The report itself?"

"Right."

There was a grocery store receipt found in Bill Bradfield's apartment that came from an A&P supermarket in the Phoenixville-Kimberton Mall on Route 23. That market was minutes from Bill Bradfield's place. The date 23 June 1979/6:18 p.m. was stamped on the register tape.

However, on that exact date, Bradfield, Myers, Pappas, and Valaitis were supposed to be in Cape May, New Jersey. June 23rd was *that* Saturday.

On July 21, 1980, Trooper John Holtz and Lou DiSantis drove over to the A&P supermarket on Route 23 with the register tape dated 23 June 1979. They met with John Williams, who was the store manager in charge of the cash registers. Williams confirmed that the register tape in Holtz's possession came from their store in the Phoenixville-Kimberton Mall. He made it clear that the tape in their possession was authentic and accurate.

"Somebody was in our store, gentlemen, that Saturday night, June 23, 1979 at 6:18 p.m. This stamped date and time on the register tape is not a mistake. That's all I can tell you," Williams said emphatically.

Sue Myers couldn't explain it. Bill Bradfield couldn't explain it. Vincent Valaitis couldn't explain it. Chris Pappas couldn't explain it. Holtz and DiSantis didn't even try to.

And I wasn't sure I believed Bill Bradfield, or his friends and lovers, about their whereabouts or lack of involvement. Joanne Aitken's police reports were a joke. I still don't know why Bradfield's friends were presumed to be telling the truth and given a free ride. That was absolute bullshit.

I personally called Rick Guida about the tape. It was going to fit very nicely into the defense that we were shaping up. I wanted it.

"We lost it," was all Rick said.

★ ★ ★

"You talked to John Balshy?" I asked.

"Yes," Skip answered.

"Recently?"

"Yes."

"Run that conversation by me again. Where was it? How did it come about? What exactly did he say?" I asked. Finally we had something to work with that would put Susan Reinert down at the shore with compelling physical evidence.

• 13 •

CAPE FEAR

It was time to try the case.

Rick Guida and Jack Holtz had set up their command post for the Smith trial at the Holiday Inn in downtown Harrisburg, one short block from the Dauphin County Courthouse and four short blocks from Guida's office. The command post was a luxury suite of rooms, equipped with WATS lines, radio communications, and security systems. Boxes and boxes of files were neatly stacked in the corner, and more than 100 exhibits were carefully marked by Guida and Holtz to ensure a smooth presentation.

Room service was a phone call away. The dining room and bar was four floors down. The indoor swimming pool was there if needed.

And contiguous to the command post Guida and Holtz rented an entire wing of rooms to accommodate and entertain the 100-plus witnesses scheduled to appear for the Commonwealth. Bradfield's lovers, Bradfield's friends, Martray, Montione. They would all be there.

Joseph Wambaugh also moved in.

Even before jury selection, Holtz told Guida that Joseph Wambaugh was coming in to cover the trial for the purpose of writing his third non-fiction book.

Guida and Holtz were excited about that, and as Holtz predicted, Guida got the call. Wambaugh was calling from a downstairs phone asking if they could meet. Holtz and DiSantis and a number of investigators from the attorney general's office were present in the command suite when the call came.

"Come right up," Guida said, smiling at Holtz and DiSantis.

"That was Joseph Wambaugh himself," Guida told his boys after he hung up. And everybody gave Wambaugh a hero's welcome when he joined them.

Joe Wambaugh was a charming, charismatic guy and would have been that if he'd never written a book or produced a movie. He must have been deadly as a sergeant for the Los Angeles Police Department. He was proud to have been a law enforcement officer; even his business card as an author had his sergeant's badge emblazoned on it in gold—badge number 178. My guess is that he schmoozed a lot of defendants into telling him everything they knew.

Wambaugh became a best-selling author and movie producer by capturing the police experience as no author before him had done. His cop protagonists, though often plagued with self-doubts and personal problems, would always get their man. His formula worked time and time again for him, and with his unique, witty writing style and his past successes, he became a wealthy mogul in his own right.

Joseph Wambaugh was a power broker. Joseph Wambaugh had influence. Joseph Wambaugh could make you a star.

The command suite was buzzing with excitement.

★ ★ ★

Date: March 31, 1986
Time: 9:30 a.m.
Place: Dauphin County Courthouse, Harrisburg, Pennsylvania
Case: *Commonwealth v. Jay C. Smith*
Charge: Murder

Courtroom 1 at the Dauphin County Courthouse was built to do battle. When I was a young district attorney, I prosecuted a lot of defendants in that courtroom, and for the past 14 years I had defended quite a few. It was one of my favorite legal arenas because of the towering green marble behind a massive carved bench. All the walls had raised walnut paneling adorned with sconces and oil paintings of jurists long past, and the high ceiling had a skylight that provided the courtroom with a steady stream of natural sunlight.

It was a big courtroom with church-like pews behind the well of the courtroom floor that could accommodate at least 200 spectators. Every day the courtroom was filled to an overflow capacity, and observers who could not be seated were allowed to stand along the walls and in the back. To maintain some semblance of order and to minimize disturbances and shuffling, the media was allowed to sit in the jury box that was directly across from the main jury box.

But picking a jury "uninfluenced by anything they may have seen, read, or heard" was almost impossible. The pool was from downtown Harrisburg and the surrounding conservative, religious, suburban communities. I hired Dr. Arthur Paterson, a forensic psychologist from Penn State, who specialized in the dynamics of selecting and analyzing juries. Art was a friend of mine from past, similar dealings, and he had drawn up an elaborate questionnaire for me to work from to determine the "proneness" of prospective jurors. As I asked my prepared questions of the candidates, he checked out their clothing, how they walked into the courtroom and onto the witness stand, and how they responded and reacted to death penalty questions.

Most of them looked at us like we were nuts. It was an eerie feeling.

And the way most of them responded indicated a willingness to hang Smith without any further delay.

That made the prosecution's job of picking the jury easy.

It took six, long, boring days to pick a jury and four alternates. We had rejected 90 good people and had kept 16. Among the ones we okayed were a sewing machine operator, an electrician, a retired steel worker, an aviator, a mechanic, and a bank teller. There was only one black on the jury, and he was a distinguished-looking gentleman from a working-class background.

Finally, they were sworn in, and it was time to get down to the business at hand.

It literally looked like two juries were passing judgment on Smith throughout the entire month-long trial. On the right, facing the witness stand, was the main jury, attentive, somber. They were not allowed to take notes or even have notebooks. On the left was a media panel of at least 20 men and women. They were always very animated, scratching on pads and doing artist sketches of everybody, including the jury across from them.

I thought it was kind of neat at the time.

★ ★ ★

The Honorable William W. Lipsitt was the presiding judge. He had just turned 70, was a graduate of Harvard College and Harvard Law, and was a good man and a sensitive human being. I had always admired and respected Judge Lipsitt, and I was very fond of him and his wife on a personal level. She said I looked exactly like Bert Reynolds, and I kind of liked that, too.

Judge Lipsitt never tried to intimidate anybody with his position of authority. He had a great sense of humor and a wonderful laugh, but in the courtroom he was all business—in a gentle sort of way. The only complaint I had about Judge Lipsitt, and I've told him on more than one occasion, is that he was too trusting of the Office of the Attorney General. He never believed for one second that the Commonwealth was capable of intentionally misleading him, let alone deceiving him.

Rick Guida's strategy in the Smith case included taking full advantage of the court's trust, patience, and belief in how the system was supposed to work.

★ ★ ★

Guida's opening statement was tentative. He couldn't make too many promises to the jury because of all the unanswered questions in the case. He did tell the jury that for the first two weeks Smith wasn't going to be mentioned too much because the Commonwealth was going to try and convict William Bradfield all over again.

"You, ladies and gentlemen, are going to be looking at me saying, 'What are we doing here?' but it is necessary that I show you the first half before I show you the second. These cases are intricately linked together and without showing you the connection, I can't prove to you my case."

At times, Rick Guida seemed to be apologetic in his opening. It was not his finest hour, but he had plenty of time left in which to shine.

The defense has the option of opening at the conclusion of the prosecutor's opening, or the defense can "reserve," which means waiting until the prosecution rests its entire case.

Never reserve. Maybe in a civil tax case, but not in a criminal case, especially a murder case, unless you don't know what your defense is going to be until the prosecution commits.

I knew exactly what our defense was going to be. Smith did not do it. Bradfield *and others* did. Not only did Bradfield and others do it, but we had evidence and reason to believe that Susan Reinert was at the shore on the weekend in question.

As I approached the jury to make my opening statement, I was plenty nervous, but I had been preparing this opening in my mind and heart for months. My tempo would be paced, and my tone would be firm.

"Ladies and gentlemen of the jury, Jay C. Smith has been charged with three counts of murder, and he is not responsible for *any* of them. This is not just a murder trial. This is a high-profile media event in which a man's life is at stake for something he did not do."

I stepped aside to let the jury look directly across the well of the courtroom at the event I was talking about. Directly across from them was an identical jury box filled with reporters.

"What happened in August of 1978 also resulted in Smith being targeted by a man who was *very, very* good at deception, not as good as he thought he was, but good. Ladies and gentlemen, I am talking about none other than William Bradfield. The Bradfield accomplices are an interesting group. Yes, I call them accomplices. I call them a group. A book author might call them a cult. You, ladies and gentlemen, might call them co-conspirators. They slept with him. They gave him sexual favors. They lied for him. They practiced killing Susan Reinert with him. This group had possession and control of the instrumentalities of crime consistent with Susan Reinert's death. Their names were Susan Myers, Wendy Zeigler, Vincent Valaitis, Chris Pappas, and Joanne Aitken."

Guida and Holtz sat straight up when they realized we were going to take the offensive. They had taken a lot of notes during my opening statement. They may have suspected it before, but they now knew I was not simply accepting the testimony of Bradfield or his lovers and friends the way they did. Guida knew from my opening statement that I intended to put Susan Reinert at the shore on the weekend in question.

Guida and Holtz just didn't know how.

I glanced at them and enjoyed watching them squirm.

When finally I went to the defense table to sit down, my opening *felt* right. I had tried enough cases in my time to know when I did okay. I did okay. I felt good about it. I felt that the jury was willing to hear me out.

Skip winked so only I could see. I tapped Smith on the arm and whispered, "How did I do, Doc?"

He leaned over and whispered back to me, "C+."

"Damn," I said almost audibly, "you're a tough grader."

"I can be a little more objective than you in matters of this nature," he said, and sounded exactly like a high school principal. I could tell that he wanted to smile but didn't, and I was glad about that. We didn't want the jury to take any of this lightly. None of us were.

That night all of us—Skip, Nick, Dave Foster, Leslie Fields, and Charles Rector from my office, and my wife Jill—went to an upstairs nightclub one block from the courthouse. The newly decorated art deco club with dim lights and stained glass, a light oak bar, and plush mauve furniture was owned and operated by my 42-year-old cousin, Gus Giannaris. Gus speaks both English and Greek fluently, but I could never understand him in either language, and though my Greek isn't too good, I speak pretty good English. Gus is a real funny guy, especially when he talks fast. He was waiting for us with hors d'oeuvres and drinks.

I drank ice tea because I don't drink.

"Nice opening, Bill," Foster said, and meant it.

"Thanks."

"It's going to get ugly," Skip noted.

"I thought it went great," Jill said, toasting me. She lifted her glass playfully, and I loved her for it.

"I did too," Nick added.

"Who was that nice-looking man in the second row of the media box?" Jill asked. "The one next to the end."

"Which one was that?" I asked.

"The one with the short, dark hair over by the blonde news reporter . . . kind of tall, slender of build, in the sport coat, mid to late forties."

"I know who you mean," I answered, "but I don't know who he is."

"Don't you guys know who that is?" Skip asked in that all-knowing tone of his. He waited until he had everyone's attention before he explained. "That guy is Joseph Wambaugh, the famous author. You know, *The Onion Field*, *The New Centurians*. I told you, Bill that he was supposed to be coming."

"What's he doing here?" I asked jokingly, but inside I knew exactly what he was doing.

"You know damn well what he's doing here, Bill," Skip replied. "He's writing a book."

"Who's going to be the hero?" I asked, smiling.

"Not you, asshole," he said loudly. Everyone laughed.

★ ★ ★

For the first two days of the trial nothing happened. It was all very interesting to the jury and gallery, because this was their first time around with it. Rick Guida methodically called his well-prepared police witnesses, including Holtz and DiSantis, to tell the jury graphically about the car being found at the Host Inn. The jury was visibly shocked at the description of Susan Reinert's nude, mutilated body bent over in the trunk of her own car. Rick paraded the uniformed state troopers onto the stand to give every gory, uncontested detail of the crime scene.

Dr. Robert Bear testified about the autopsy, which had been performed at the Community General Osteopathic Hospital for the purpose of determining the cause of death. Dr. Bear also identified, for the jury, many of the state troopers in attendance at the autopsy, and Guida called them to tell the jury what they had been doing there.

One took pictures. One was an evidence officer. Holtz said he was there examining the body with everybody else. Then Rick Guida called Trooper John Balshy to the witness stand.

Skip nudged me, as we listened to John Balshy taking that long walk from the back of the courtroom. My heart started to beat a little faster with excitement. John Balshy had been an expert witness for the Pennsylvania State Police for 27 years and had been called to attend the autopsy and try to lift fingerprints from Susan Reinert's nude body. If anybody could have done that, it would have been Trooper John Balshy.

"Yes," Balshy testified, "I used lifters on her body to try to lift prints. I got some partials but nothing identifiable."

I guess Guida was trying to impress the jury further with his extensive investigation, because Balshy certainly didn't add anything to the case—at least not yet.

"I have no further questions, Trooper Balshy. Thank you," Guida said in a rehearsed tone. He then looked over at me with that smug smile of his to cross-examine—that is, if I had anything to cross-examine about.

Up until that point we hadn't said a thing.

"Wake their fucking asses up," Skip whispered, and I had to pause for a moment to keep from laughing.

I did my cross-examination from my table, without standing. I knew his answers, though soft-spoken, were going to be powerful. In a courtroom moments like that are precious.

Costopoulos:	Mr. Balshy, did you examine the victim's feet?
Balshy:	Yes, I did.
Costopoulos:	Did you notice any debris on the feet?
Balshy:	I did . . . I did in checking the feet . . . I checked between her toes.
Costopoulos:	What did you find?

Rick Guida started objecting like crazy, raising his voice, drawing a lot of attention to himself and the witness. He didn't even know what I was going to ask, but he knew he didn't like it. Holtz was also on the edge of his seat; so were DiSantis and the rest of their army of pin-striped assistants.

Guida:	I'm going to object. I don't think he's qualified

	to make an identification just from looking at something.
The Court:	I think it's relevant and important.
Guida:	Your Honor, he's outside the scope of direct.
The Court:	I'm going to overrule the objection.
Costopoulos:	Did you lift some foreign matter between the toes of Susan Reinert, or didn't you, Mr. Balshy?
Balshy:	Yes, sir, I did.
Costopoulos:	Did it look like sand?
Balshy:	It could have been.
Costopoulos:	Could it have been *beach* sand?
Guida:	Objection! We're taking something he looks at, and now we've got him on the beach.
The Court:	He's on cross examination.
Guida:	He hasn't been qualified.
The Court:	He certainly can tell whether something looked like sand. Even I can tell that. Objection overruled.
Costopoulos:	Thank you, Your Honor. Did it look like sand on her feet, Trooper Balshy, or didn't it?
Balshy:	Yes, it did.
Costopoulos:	I have no further questions.

Rick Guida was furious. He lost all composure. He was so stunned that he forgot how to cross-examine and rather than continue to try his case, he declared war on John Balshy and the entire defense team.

I put a little sand in the case, and he started to bring it into the courtroom in wheelbarrows. I wanted to put Susan Reinert at the shore on the weekend in question. Between the directions to Cape May found in her car and the beach sand on her feet I was well on my way.

But Rick Guida didn't want Susan Reinert anywhere near the shore. That was going to blow the alibi defense of Bradfield, and Guida put on the brakes of his case and made a quick U-turn back to the Philadelphia area. The friends and lovers of Bill Bradfield, who were out in the hallway waiting their turn, were just going to have to wait another day or two.

First Guida called Trooper Thomas Dacheaux, the evidence officer at the autopsy, who testified that Corporal Balshy had never called his attention to any sand on Susan Reinert's feet. There were no rubber lifters at the autopsy either, according to Dacheaux.

Guida:	Trooper Dacheaux, did Corporal Balshy submit to you any rubber lifters or material which he said he found between the toes of Susan Reinert?
Dacheaux:	He did not.
Guida:	Is there anything at all in your records or anything in your memory that shows that anything at all was

found between the toes of Susan Reinert or on her
feet?

Dacheaux: There was not.

Guida: Thank you. No further questions.

Guida then called Trooper Ronald F. Colyer, who was also present at the
autopsy, and he testified under oath that Balshy did not tell him about sand
between Reinert's toes, and in addition, he had not seen any rubber lifters
used to collect any sand from her feet or toes. So two Pennsylvania State
Police officers in a row testified under oath that John Balshy didn't use rubber lifters.

The case was getting stranger by the minute, as the prosecution of John
Balshy continued. I couldn't believe these guys were calling Corporal Balshy, who had been with them for 27 years, an outright liar. On the other
hand, anything goes, I guess, in a high-profile case when the rules break
down.

Jay Smith just sat there, expressionless, motionless.

Trooper Holtz was next. Holtz couldn't wait to get back on the witness
stand to call Balshy a liar. He was standing up ready to take the witness
stand before Rick even called out his name. Holtz, like Guida, viewed the
testimony of Balshy as treason. Guida and Holtz both felt threatened. They
did not want Susan Reinert anywhere near the shore on the weekend in
question. They were now in bed with Bradfield's friends and lovers.

Guida: Now, Trooper Holtz, were you—did you also attend
              the autopsy of Susan Reinert at the Osteopathic
              Hospital on June 25, 1979?

Holtz: I did.

Guida: While you were there, did you observe the feet of
              Mrs. Reinert?

Holtz: I did.

Guida: Did anything unusual strike you concerning the
              condition of Mrs. Reinert's feet?

Holtz: Yes, sir.

Guida: What was that?

Holtz: The bottom of her feet seemed extremely clean.

Guida's prosecution of Corporal John Balshy in front of the Smith jury
was having a twofold effect. First, Guida had convinced the jury that there
was no sand on the feet of Susan Reinert, or between her toes, and therefore the defense theory that she was at the shore was blown out of that
ocean water; and secondly, since there were no rubber lifters either, Balshy
was not only mistaken, he was also a liar, and only the defense team could
have put him up to such lies.

It was getting ugly.

The jurors and media in their respective boxes sat in stunned silence as they witnessed Guida's claim of perjury by the defense.

Guida then asked for a sidebar, and the two of us went up to Judge Lipsitt's bench. Guida represented to Lipsitt that the Pennsylvania State Troopers were instructed not to contact Balshy because "he may have perjured himself yesterday," and therefore, if they were to contact him, or if he were to contact them for any reason, Corporal Balshy would be read his rights.

"What's Judge Lipsitt have to do with that threat, Rick?" I asked Guida, now getting furious myself.

"I just want the court to know that," Guida answered in a threatening tone.

"Rick, you're out of control, that's what I think. What's the matter with you anyhow?" I asked, disgusted with his theatrics.

"Don't tell me I'm out of control!" he said, loud enough for the jury to hear.

The next day, Guida was still reeling from the thought that Reinert might have had sand on her feet and might have been at the shore, and he fired off a scathing memorandum to Robert Keuch, the executive deputy attorney general who was Guida's superior, requesting that an immediate investigation be undertaken to determine whether Corporal Balshy had committed perjury. That memorandum was also pointing the finger at me for putting him up to it. According to Mr. Guida's memorandum:

> On April 9, 1986, I called to the witness stand in the Jay Smith murder trial former Corporal John Balshy, Pennsylvania State Police. Ex-Corporal Balshy is now a private investigator and is employed by the private investigating firm which is assisting the defense in this matter. Mr. Balshy was called by the Commonwealth for the specific purpose of confirming an attempted lift of a fingerprint from the body of Susan Reinert and to chain blood samples from the PSP Lab to the toxicologist who analyzed the blood and found morphine in Mrs. Reinert's system.
>
> On cross-examination, Mr. Balshy was asked a number of questions outside the scope of direct examination. I objected but Judge Lipsitt allowed the questioning. With obvious knowledge, defense attorney William Costopoulos asked Corporal Balshy if he had found any debris on the feet or between the toes of Mrs. Reinert. Balshy immediately volunteered that he had observed some type of granular substance between her toes and had lifted the material with a rubber lifter at the autopsy. It is obvious from Costopoulos' tactics thus far that he will attempt to establish that Mrs. Reinert was killed at the shore in Cape May, New Jersey by William Bradfield, Chris Pappas, and Susan Myers. The sand, therefore, is extremely material to the defense case.

"It is clear to me that John Balshy perjured himself," Guida concluded, and demanded an immediate perjury investigation into Balshy and the defense team.

★ ★ ★

April 8, 1986.

It was 10:30 p.m. This trial was only into its first week and was already getting ugly.

Outside, a slow, drizzling rain continued to drench the east and west shore, causing the banks of the Susquehanna River to swell. Outside of my office, Market Street, which is the main street in Lemoyne, was desolate. The only parked cars on that street were mine and Skip's and Nick's and Charlie Rector's. Everybody else had gone home to their children and families and private lives.

It had been a long, grueling day in Courtroom 1, and I was livid. I've learned over the years to control my emotions in the courtroom, even if it gets personal—and often it does. But sometimes in the privacy of my office or with those that I trust, I just lose my composure.

Skip and Nick and Charlie just let me go.

"The son-of-a-bitch calls a sidebar, tells Judge Lipsitt that if Balshy tries to talk to any of his former fellow officers, they're going to read him his fucking rights!

"I knew it was going to get ugly, but this, this is getting personal. They've gone after us in front of Smith's jury. Normally I wouldn't give a shit. In front of a death penalty jury, when a guy's life is at stake for something he didn't do—that's bullshit.

"Let me tell you something else. I've known Guida for years. He's changed. He's not himself. He's so hyper I can't talk to him. The guy is completely out of control."

"Bill," Skip said when I finally gave him a chance, but only after he smoked up my office and adjoining conference room with a cherry-blend tobacco in his hand-carved bone pipe, "Guida wants to win this one. He can't afford to lose this one. The Pennsylvania State Police can't afford to lose this one. The attorney general's office can't afford to lose this one. I heard that Joseph Wambaugh has been hanging out in their command suite at the Holiday Inn since he got here."

"I want to win this one too, Skip," I said interrupting, and meant it. "We all do, but it's getting damn crazy in that courtroom. That's all I'm saying. Where in the hell are the lifters anyhow?"

No one could answer that. The room was filled with tension. My heart was filled with tension.

"Balshy said the procedure was to turn them over to an evidence officer at the autopsy. He didn't stick them in his pocket or up his ass. He turned them over to somebody!" I ranted angrily, continuing my tirade.

"Let me put it this way, you guys. Those sand lifters are more important to the case *now* than they were before. Before, they were our physical evidence that Susan Reinert had been at the shore. Sand on her feet is good evidence of that. And if there was sand on her feet, there's sand on those lifters!"

"But now, the very existence of those lifters will determine who is telling the truth, us or them, and in a case like this, where there is very little evidence of guilt or innocence, credibility will determine who wins. That's how I see it!"

"I agree with you," Charlie said with conviction.

"So do I," Nick added with equal conviction. "They've made the existence of those lifters pivotal."

"Is Balshy in any kind of trouble?" Charlie asked.

"Without those lifters, Balshy's in trouble. We're in trouble, and Smith's dead," I answered.

· 14 ·

RAILROAD

Rick Guida was constantly asking to go to sidebar. He was having a lot of success there because of Judge Lipsitt's trust in the attorney general's office.

Often, if a prosecutor doesn't have a good case, he can still win it with critical rulings from the bench, or in the judge's chambers, thus allowing irrelevant and highly prejudicial evidence into the proceedings. Many cases are won and lost outside the presence of the jury.

A good case doesn't require a whole lot of sidebars and risky rulings. But that's the train we were on in the Smith case, and Guida kept stoking the engine. He really didn't have the proof that Smith murdered Reinert or her children, but he could still put Smith to death with what he did have, which was Smith's past and bizarre behavior.

I was feeling the heat from that engine. Smith's past was so atrocious, he was such a strange individual. I just knew the jury was going to hate him, past and present.

"Your Honor," Guida said at another sidebar conference he requested, "at this time I'm going to retry the St. David's Sears robbery that took place in 1978. I intend to call the eyewitness to that crime; introduce the evidence of the Brink's guard uniform, the phony ID with Smith's picture on it; and I'm going to put the prosecutor on the stand from Bucks County, who convicted Smith in that case, to read Bradfield's alibi testimony into the record."

Judge Lipsitt just shook his head as Guida continued. He really did not want to give him this ruling. It would delay the proceedings, and it seemed extraneous and prejudicial.

"It is relevant, Your Honor, to show a relationship between Bradfield and Smith, which I don't have otherwise," Guida persisted. "It's my argument for motive."

"I object, Your Honor," I noted strenuously for the record. "This is irrelevant, prejudicial, and inflammatory."

"No, Your Honor," Guide said frantically. "The position of the attorney general's office is that it's proper procedure. It won't take that long, Your Honor. I can do it with just a couple of witnesses."

"Okay, okay, okay," Judge Lipsitt said reluctantly. "Your objection, Mr. Costopoulos, is noted for the record."

The retrial of Smith on the St. David's Brink's case dragged on. Guida put the Sears employee on the witness stand to again identify Smith as the bogus Brink's courier. Then the phony ID was introduced and shown to the jury. Then in dramatic fashion, Guida reenacted the Bradfield testimony by pretending that he was Smith's attorney and having Jackson Stewart, Smith's prosecutor in Bucks County, take the witness stand and pretend he was Bradfield.

It was a real sideshow, but the damage was effective in the presence of Smith's jury, which was what Guida wanted. And suddenly, it was Smith's possible innocence of those three murders that was fast becoming irrelevant.

"What do you think, Mr. Costopoulos?" a swarm of reporters asked me in the hallway at the next recess.

"I think they have an excellent case of theft by deception," I answered jokingly.

The reporters laughed out loud, because they knew exactly what I was saying. I shook my head and laughed with them, but inside I felt sick.

★ ★ ★

The days passed slowly as the parade of Guida's witnesses kept taking the stand, saying nothing to incriminate Smith but doing a lot of damage before they left the courtroom. Ken Reinert, the grieving father of Michael and Karen, testified he had not seen or heard from his children since that fateful Friday night. He identified their grade school pictures and Guida showed them to the jury every time there was a lull in his case. And every time the jury looked at those photographs, they winced and shook their heads in disgust and looked over at Smith with disdain. And every time, Smith whispered to me that he had nothing to do with the death of Susan Reinert or those two children, as if I needed reassurance.

Smith continued to sit expressionless, emotionless.

I believed Smith more and more as the days went on.

The reason? The evidence that he had done it just wasn't there. I did not believe that Jay Smith had outsmarted every law enforcement agency in this country with their unlimited resources and sophistication and that they had come up with nothing over six years, except Martray. Maybe I also wanted to believe in Smith's innocence. Maybe I needed to believe him. Maybe I was just losing my mind.

Guida's rote voice and movement toward the bench brought me back to the task at hand, which required more than my thoughts and feelings about my client.

It was back to the battle on the courtroom floor.

"May we approach the bench, Your Honor?" Guida asked again, standing up with his hands on his hips. It had gotten to the point that whenever Guida asked for a sidebar we just walked up to the bench. The most Judge Lipsitt did was give a look like "Is this necessary?"

"Your Honor," Guida said with authority. "I intend at this time to call Vincent Valaitis."

As soon as Guida mentioned Vincent Valaitis, I knew what was coming. He wanted all of Bradfield's lovers and friends—Vincent Valaitis, Chris Pappas, Sue Myers, Wendy Zeigler, and Joanne Aitken—to testify all the things Bradfield had told them about Smith. I just shook my head as the stenographer took down Guida's position. No, Guida wasn't calling Bill Bradfield to confront Smith. Yes, he was calling Bradfield's accomplices to say what Bradfield had told them about Smith.

I grimaced. I silently prayed that Judge Lipsitt would call this one right.

The judge had a lot of trouble with that proffer. It sounded like prejudicial hearsay to him. It was the kind of ruling that could cause a retrial, which Judge Lipsitt did not want. If there was one ruling that really bothered Judge Lipsitt in the Smith trial, one ruling that concerned him the most, it was this one.

"Mr. Guida," the judge said sternly. "I don't want to try this case again. This sure sounds like hearsay to me that could rise to the level of material error."

"No, Your Honor," Guida insisted. "This isn't hearsay . . . this is not being offered to prove the truth of the matter asserted. We agree that most of the things Bradfield said about Smith were false. This testimony is just being offered to show a relationship between Bradfield and Smith. The Attorney General's Office of Pennsylvania has researched this matter, and I have a memo for you, and this testimony is essential to my case."

"I don't like it," Judge Lipsitt said, shaking his head in distress. "I hope you know what you're doing because I don't want to retry this case."

"Your Honor, I need this testimony," Guida pressed. "The attorney general's office has researched it and . . ."

"Okay," Lipsitt said, reluctantly, interrupting Guida. "Mr. Costopoulos, I know you feel very strongly about this, but I'm going to let him do it, and I note your objection for the record."

I just shook my head. I couldn't believe it. This trial was completely out of control.

And they all took the witness stand—every one of Bradfield's friends and lovers—demurely dressed in new suits, soft-spoken, well-mannered, and well-prepared. They looked like such nice people, educators of our children.

Smith's train to death kept rolling.

One by one Sue Myers, Chris Pappas, and Vincent Valaitis—the Bradfield contingent—testified to outrageous statements made by Bradfield to them on different occasions regarding Smith.

"Bradfield said that Smith was a screened hit man for the Mafia and wanted to kill a number of people, including Susan Reinert."

"Bradfield said Smith gave him a gun with a silencer."

"Bradfield said that Smith knew how to take an ordinary household item and kill anyone with it."

"Bradfield said that Smith said the best time to commit murders would be during holidays."

"Bradfield said on the way to the shore that Smith was going to kill Susan Reinert that weekend."

"Bradfield said that Smith committed many crimes in the past."

"Bradfield said that Smith intended to kill Susan Reinert over a holiday weekend."

"Bradfield said that Smith was mentally unstable and that he intended to kill Susan Reinert and, furthermore, had a hit list which included Susan Myers."

"Bradfield said that Smith wanted to kill the judge, the people leading the investigations, and people who were remotely associated with the investigation."

"Bradfield said that Smith wanted to kill a number of teachers, including Susan Reinert."

"Bradfield said that Smith liked using chains, small locks, tape, a ski mask, a .357 magnum handgun, a .22 with a silencer, and acid."

Jeff Olsen, an acquaintance of Bill Bradfield's, testified that one day after Susan Reinert had been found dead, Bradfield had walked in and told him and his wife, "Smith killed that goddamned woman."

Vincent Valaitis testified that he met with Bradfield in the fall of 1979 and tried to challenge him about his involvement with the Reinert murder.

"Well, Bradfield was upset," Valaitis testified, and continued as he looked at the jury. "And then Bradfield said, 'All right, if I'm going to be blamed for this, I'll admit to it,' and he took a piece of white paper, and he drew a square on it, and he drew a line and he said, 'All right, I took the kids and I gave them to Smith,' and then I said, 'Don't do that,' and I grabbed the paper from him, and I said, 'Don't make things up' and I threw it away."

That was the first time *ever* that Valaitis recalled Bradfield saying, '*All right, I took the kids and I gave them to Smith.*' It seemed that Valaitis's memory improved that day and was inconsistent with every prior sworn statement he had ever given.

As to Vincent Valaitis, I don't know what refreshed his recollection during the Smith trial, but I had my suspicions, and they all started with Holtz's need to win. That recollection of his coming during the Smith trial ranked right up there with Bradfield dreaming about his alibi.

This was the craziest case I ever tried. Smith's right to confront his accuser was out the window. It was absurd. William Bradfield was putting Smith to death without even entering the courtroom. This was a star chamber. I felt as if I were in another country.

* * *

Jill had spent all day at home preparing stuffed pork chops, parsley potatoes, Greek salad with feta cheese, and a chocolate mousse cake. She had bought fresh flowers for the dining room table and red and white wine. Dinner would be by candlelight, and she had a fire going in the den when I got home that night.

"Is Wambaugh with you?" Jill asked when I walked in.

"No," I answered. "He'll be up shortly with Skip."

"What do you think?" Jill asked, pointing to the dining room.

"I think *you* look great," I answered, looking at her. Jill had her blonde hair swept back, showing diamond earrings that matched her necklace. Her dark blue silk dress opened in the back, revealing the loveliness of her skin, and her high heels completed the picture of perfection.

"I want in the book too," she said jokingly.

Downstairs, our mahogany bar was stocked with whiskey, vodka, gin, ice, and mixers. The refrigerator was chilling Budweiser, Miller, and Heineken. I had no idea what Joe Wambaugh drank, but I heard that he was a drinker, and I wanted to be ready for his arrival because I wanted to be in his book too.

Joe Wambaugh was a lot of fun. He arrived on time, at 7 p.m., dressed casually, with my buddy Skip. Joe was a good listener with a great sense of humor. He had a lot of funny war stories, and Jill fell in love with him. I could see why, because he was a charming, unassuming, smooth-talking guy, a ladies' man and a man's man. Skip liked him too.

After dinner, we went downstairs and talked about the Smith case together. I told him how Smith kept grading me on my courtroom skills. C+ for my opening, B- for cross-examination, C for my objections, D for my sidebar performance. Dr. Smith was a tough grader, and we all laughed at the ongoing evaluation by the strict teacher.

We also talked about Bradfield, his lovers and friends, the witnesses, and each other. I asked Wambaugh whether I should call Smith to the witness stand, and he was intrigued by our dilemma. His many years of police experience made him worth listening to, and I could tell the savvy street cop was still in him.

Wambaugh personally would have loved to see Jay Smith on the witness stand.

We agreed to stay in touch. I wanted him to meet Nick and the other lawyers in my office.

★ ★ ★

The next morning.

By far, the most memorable witness of them all was Joanne Aitken, the mystery woman whose loyalty to Bill Bradfield at any cost and whose ability to carry it off to the end fascinated the entire courtroom for an entire afternoon.

I, too, was fascinated.

When Joanne Aitken took the stand, everybody in the courtroom watched her, especially the women, and she did not lose anybody's interest for one second. She wore a long, black skirt with a matching jacket and a blouse with a tiny, black necktie. Flat shoes. No jewelry. No makeup. Her chestnut hair was very straight and shoulder-length. She moved and dressed and looked impenetrable.

Predictably, she added nothing to Guida's case. She made him phrase his questions carefully before she would answer them. I enjoyed watching him suffer and waited my turn.

"No, I never met Susan Reinert."

"Yes, I registered at a downtown hotel in Philadelphia as Mr. & Mrs. Bradfield."

"Yes, I stayed there for three weeks, but I might be slightly off on that."

"I left that hotel on a Tuesday morning. I'm sure you could fill me in on the date."

Guida: The testimony up until this time, Ms. Aitken, has been that Mr. Bradfield was in Cape May for the entire weekend. What were you doing over the weekend when Mr. Bradfield was away?

Aitken: I was looking at architecture in Philadelphia. Getting to know the city.

That was her explanation. That was it!

No, nobody could verify her whereabouts on the weekend in question.

Yes, she drove Bradfield's car to New Mexico for him.

Yes, she still had a "romantic interest" in Bill Bradfield and that hadn't changed even though he had been in prison since 1983.

"You may cross-examine the witness," Guida said, frustrated, realizing it was hopeless.

"Are you ready for this?" I whispered to Skip, jesting.

"No fucking way," Skip whispered back, looking down at his hands, clutching his fists to hold back his laugh.

My cross-examination of Joanne Aitken was done from the defense table. Normally, I would cross-examine standing up, approaching the witness in flourishes, but not this time. I wanted all eyes on her without any distractions.

Q. Ms. Aitken, because of your romantic interest that has continued with William Bradfield until this day, is it fair to say that you communicate with him now that he is in prison?

A. Yes.

Q. And how frequently do you communicate?

A. I see him probably twice a month and talk maybe twice a month on the telephone.

Q. Have you always kept him advised of the investigation that was going on in this matter?

A. Meaning?

Q. When the police would come to talk to you, would you report that to him?

A. I would say probably. I probably talked to him about it, yes.

Q. And in fact, you'd tell him *exactly* what you were being asked about, wouldn't you?

A. There's a possibility. I don't remember specifically trying to tell him *everything* I'd been asked about.

Q. Do you remember resisting any cooperation with law enforcement after the weekend in question?

A. Resisting?

Q. Not cooperating?

A. Not by *my* definition.

The jury was on the edge of their seats, riveted by the mystery woman's coolness. The media representatives were sketching and writing frantically. Even Judge Lipsitt, who was normally laid back in his oversized, black leather throne with wheels, was peering at Joanne over his glasses.

Q. When was the last time you talked to Bradfield before coming here today?

A. I spoke with him on the telephone last night or the night before.

Q. Did you tell him you were under subpoena?

A. Oh, yes. He knew that.

Q. When did you first learn that Bradfield was having a romantic relationship with Susan Reinert?

A. I don't believe he *was* having a romantic relationship with Susan Reinert.

Q. You don't believe that to this day?

A. That's correct.

Q. When did you find out that he was having a romantic relationship with Sue Myers?

A. Since I've known him, he *hasn't* had a romantic relationship with Sue Myers.

Q. All right, just so I'm clear, we're not having a definitional problem about a romantic relationship, are we?

A. I don't think so.

Q. Did he ever tell you that he was the named beneficiary to the tune of $730,000 in life insurance?

A. No.

Q. He never told you that?

A. No, he didn't.

Q. Did he tell you that he was the designated beneficiary of her estate by a will executed May 4, 1979?

A. No.

Q. Did you ever learn of those possible facts?

A. Well, I learned of those *possible facts*, as you put it, after the death of Susan Reinert.

Q. Did Bradfield tell you after her death that he was shocked that Reinert would name him as beneficiary in that insurance policy?

A. Yes, he did.

Q. Now, Ms. Aitken, when you say you were looking at architecture for the three weeks before the weekend in question, what is it that you would do?

A. Wander around in Philadelphia, go to see specific buildings, go to see neighborhoods in general.

I paused for a moment to let *her alibi* sink in for the jury. There are a lot of nice buildings in Philadelphia to look at, including the cracked Liberty Bell, but the jury was not impressed with Joanne's explanation that she was just wandering around the streets of Philadelphia for three weeks gazing at buildings and neighborhoods.

The jury was staring hard at Joanne Aitken throughout her testimony. She was lucky, I thought, that this wasn't *her* jury.

"Ask her if she had Reinert and the kids with her on the tour," Skip whispered to me, egging me on.

Jay Smith was impassive as ever, but listening very closely to *this* accuser.

Q. Do you recall where you were on June 22, 1979, in the evening hours?

A. June 22nd was a Friday, I understand, from what Mr. Guida has said.

Q. Yes?

A. No.

Q. You don't know. When was the first time you were asked that question by the authorities?

A. Probably the first time I spoke to them.

Q. Do you recall when that was?

A. No.

Q. The fact is, is it not, that on that Monday, June 25th, when the two of you were supposed to go to Santa Fe together, *that* was the day that [Bradfield] told you to drive because he was flying?

A. On that Monday?

Q. Yes, on that Monday, Ms. Aitken?

A. That probably was the day that the plans were eventually clear that he would fly and I would drive.

Q. How far is Santa Fe?

A. Approximately 2,000 miles.

Q. So, when he told you to drive 2,000 miles in his car with his belongings, you really didn't even question that, did you?

A. Question it what way?

Q. Would you consider your act of driving that car 2,000 miles an act of obedience?

A. I consider it an act of common sense.

Q. Would you consider it an act of loyalty?

A. No, we had to have the belongings and the car taken to New Mexico.

Q. How did you learn of Reinert's death?

A. When I was driving across the country, I spoke with [Bradfield] on the phone.

Q. When did he tell you about the children?

A. I don't remember if he had anything to say about them or not.

Q. Did you ever ask him what he might know about her death and their disappearance?

A. No, I did not.

Q. When the two of you left Santa Fe to go to Boston there was a certain typewriter that he left in your custody and control, wasn't there?

A. That's correct.

Q. The authorities were interested in that typewriter, weren't they?

A. Yes, that's correct.

Q. You refused to give it to them for a long period of time, didn't you?

A. No, that's not precisely correct.

Q. What *is* precisely correct?

A. There was, I believe, an FBI agent who came and asked for it. My lawyer in Philadelphia and I didn't think that I should give up something without a subpoena or warrant of some sort. I told him to contact my lawyer, that I wasn't going to give it to them. And I contacted my lawyer for instructions.

Q. And he told you to give it to them?

A. That's correct.

Q. And you of course had talked to Bradfield before you gave it to them, didn't you?

A. I don't recall whether I did or not.

Q. The typewriter that you gave them had a ball on it, didn't it?

A. An element, yes.

Q. Did you give them the *same* ball element that was on the typewriter when Bradfield left it in your custody and control?

A. Yes, as far as I know.

Q. As far as you *know*?

A. I turned over the typewriter, as it existed, to them.

Q. What else did they ask you to give them?

A. What? It seems to me that they never actually took the typewriter but took the ribbon and the element, what *you* call the ball, from the typewriter. If my memory is correct.

I had in my possession a document in code. On the reverse side was the deciphered message, which would be explained to the jury by an FBI cryptanalyst. I was really enjoying this part of the trial.

Q. After Susan Reinert was murdered, did you and Bill Bradfield develop a code system for communications?

A. No.

Q. What was the purpose of the Ezra Pound book?

A. I don't know what the purpose of the Ezra Pound book was.

Q. When did you receive immunity from the government?

A. I really don't recall the date. It was after that summer.

Q. Do you understand what immunity is?

A. I believe my lawyer explained it to me.

Q. Were you given immunity to the point where anything you said could *not* be used against you even if you had a role in the murder? Or was your immunity limited to anything you said, presupposing that you *didn't* have anything to do with the murder?

A. I don't really remember at this time.

Q. You've had how many years of schooling?

A. At that time?

Q. Today.

A. Nineteen and a half.

Q. And it was only after you got immunity that you gave any statements whatsoever, isn't that right?

A. I believe that's correct. Yes.

Q. When Bill Bradfield made a claim on the insurance policies and the estate of Susan Reinert, your relationship was a romantic one, correct?

A. Yes, I suppose so.

Q. And it was a romantic one on the weekend in question, right?

A. That's correct.

Q. Is it your testimony that there were *no* letters in your possession from Bill Bradfield while you were in Boston? In code?

A. Yes, there were *no* letters in code.

Q. Was there anything in code in your possession from William Bradfield while you were in Boston at Harvard?

A. No.

Q. What is cryptology?

A. Cryptology? That's the study of codes.

Q. Did you study codes?

A. No, I haven't studied codes.

Q. Was there a letter from Bradfield to you *congratulating* you for becoming an expert in cryptology?

A. No.

Q. Was there a letter while you were in Boston, in code, instructing you to destroy, burn, and scatter the ashes of the typewriter ball that was in your custody and control?

A. No.

Q. Do you understand enough about immunity that if you testify untruthfully under oath you could be charged with perjury?

A. Yes, I understand that.

I was fascinated by Joanne Aitken. I had the damn coded message in my hand. She was so cool about her testimony. She didn't care who believed her. Soon she was going home, whether we liked it or not, and then she was going to tell Bradfield on us.

Q. You don't remember *where* you were Friday night, June 22, 1979?
A. That's correct.
Q. Or Saturday, June 23, 1979? You don't remember?
A. Other than in Philadelphia, no.
Q. And of course you *don't* remember anything other than being in Philadelphia on Sunday, June 24, 1979, do you?
A. That's correct.
Q. And you don't remember your whereabouts or your activities that Monday, June 25, 1979?
A. Aside from being in Philadelphia, no.
Q. You don't remember whether you left the residence of Bradfield and Pappas when the authorities came down to Santa Fe in the early summer of 1979, do you?
A. No, I don't.
Q. You don't remember any coding system, and in fact you *deny* any coding system between you and Bradfield, don't you?
A. That's correct.
Q. And you don't remember that in Thanksgiving of 1978, Bradfield called Reinert's mother's house from where the two of *you* were staying, do you?
A. I don't remember. That's correct.
Q. Knowing Bradfield romantically for the years that you've known him, is there *anything* you can remember that would help the prosecution in their effort to learn anything about the murder of Susan Reinert and the disappearance of her two children?
A. I don't have anything to add.

"I bet," Smith whispered to me, and the two of us conferred briefly in hushed tones while Joanne Aitken remained on the witness stand, expressionless, patiently, with her hands folded properly on her lap.

"What do you think?" I asked Jay.

"I think she knows what happened to Susan Reinert and the children," Smith answered.

"You do, huh?"

"I have always believed that about her, especially her."

"Is there anything I should ask her?"

"No, let her hang there. Just let her hang there."

"I agree."

"By the way . . . "

"What?"

"Nice job, Bill."

"Thanks, Doc."

"B-"

"Oh great."

A cryptanalyst deciphers codes. The FBI had a document in code, to Joanne Aitken, based on a book about Confucius by Ezra Pound. When the cryptanalyst decoded the scrambled numbers and letters, the message was, "Immunity improbable. My danger conspiracy. Does FBI have typewriter? Does FBI know B has it? Have B remove ball and destroy, or better, claim whole thing stolen. Then get rid of it. FBI must not get it, especially ball."

On the reverse side of the coded message there was a letter that the FBI cryptanalyst had decoded. I read the entire letter to the jury.

> Miss you, Hon. Love you terribly. Love you so much. Hurt for you. Hope I can see you soon, but lawyer says going up there now could be grounds for unlawful flight to avoid prosecution. Lawyers warn there will be FBI plant near you soon. Car bugged. Chris has been subpoenaed for grand jury. He will say nothing much. He must maintain this all the way up through possible (probable) trial. Hand on Bible et cetera or be in perjury five to ten years.
>
> If you're in same position, you know practically nothing about case and nothing at all about Smith P of D. You must maintain this all the way up through trial hand on Bible forever. Did we mention Smith to Pappas? Try to remember. We can't be inconsistent about what we told them. Perhaps you could write them and warn them. Will be visited by FBI. If they haven't yet. Ask them exactly what they remember about what we said. Love you. Remember that we made it. Love you. Wish I were lying next to you and holding you.
>
> Destroy this and ashes. Congratulations, you're on way to becoming expert cryptologist. Can you take some more rules? Hope so. Lawyers assure us we are dealing with the best FBI has. So we better be fairly sophisticated, okay?
>
> When coding, use last number then first and so forth back and forth. Destroy messages after receiving them. Destroy them without being observed. Don't let anyone know you're receiving or destroying code. Repeat. Destroy completely. If ashes are left, destroy them also. Grind them underfoot or something.

Joanne Aitken ground the prosecution underfoot all right, or something. She left the courtroom as quietly and as mysteriously as she had entered. My guess is she went straight to Graterford to tell Bill Bradfield everything that was going on. It is also interesting to note that as of 1995—nine years after her testimony, 16 years after the weekend in question—Joanne Aitken is still visiting Bill Bradfield in prison.

★ ★ ★

Recently, in a celebrated case out of Los Angeles County, California, a jailed inmate came forward and admitted he routinely lied at many trials and put many innocent people behind bars by claiming that fellow inmates had confessed to him. These "jailhouse confessions" were in return for lenient treatment.

Our highest appellate courts—both the United States Supreme Court and the Pennsylvania Supreme Court—have made it clear that if a jailhouse informant is given a deal or any favorable consideration in exchange for that informant's confession from the defendant, the defense must be advised. This disclosure to the defense is mandatory, and if the prosecutor *forgets*, an immediate mistrial is the result if there is a conviction.

There are very few exceptions.

I watched the video from Smith's preliminary hearing one more time. I watched Raymond Martray deny having received any consideration from the Commonwealth in return for his cooperation and testimony. I watched Guida and Holtz sit there during the cross-examination of Martray at that hearing.

Q. Has anybody ever done anything for you from the law enforcement community?
A. No, sir.

I didn't believe that. I made it a point to ask Rick Guida at his office, face to face, on more than one occasion, whether Raymond Martray had been given any favorable consideration in exchange for his testimony. I have dealt with the Raymond Martrays of this world in the courtroom for 14 years, and I didn't believe for one second that a manipulative, once-convicted perjurer like Raymond Martray was a born-again Christian who was on a mission against all evil.

"Bill, there are no deals with Raymond Martray," Guida told me repeatedly.

"You're sure?" I asked, looking at Rick from the corner of my eye, wanting to believe him, but trusting my instincts.

"We have made him no deals," Guida said emphatically.

I should have factored in the stakes going into the Smith trial, especially when it became obvious as the trial progressed that the only direct evidence they had against Smith was in the hands of Raymond Martray. And Guida didn't seem like himself either. According to Wambaugh, "Rick Guida was so overloaded with nicotine he could have jump-started a DC–10."

Amid heavy security, Raymond Martray took the witness stand. He was dressed in a two-piece gray suit. Guida was successful at a sidebar conference in keeping out Martray's perjury conviction, and silenced the courtroom with his questioning of Martray.

Q. What did Smith tell you when the two of you were in prison together?
A. Smith said, 'I killed the fucking bitch.'

Now that's a confession. That's damaging testimony. Several jurors blanched.

In a court of law, where the search for truth is an endless maze, we must be careful with jailhouse informants, because no other single witness can make as great a mockery of the system. I personally believe jailhouse confessions have convicted more innocent people than any other corrupt source of information. Raymond Martray would add Jay Smith to that list.

Then the tapes and the videos on which Martray tried to trick Smith into making an incriminating statement were played for the jury.

Not once did Smith incriminate himself regarding the death of Susan Reinert or her two children. Not on tape. Not on film.

But Martray *did* get Smith to talk about escape plans on tape, and Martray *did* get Smith to talk about killing guards and sheriffs and cops if they had to in order for Smith to make his escape. It did not matter to the jury that Raymond Martray was doing all the talking and getting Jay Smith to say outrageous things. It did not matter to the jury that Martray was leading him on. It did not matter to the jury that what Smith said was unrelated to the murders.

Nor did it matter to the jury that on every single tape and film, Smith either said nothing about the murders because the Reinert killings weren't brought up by Martray, or Smith vehemently denied that he had anything to do with the Reinert killings when Martray touched on the subject at the insistence of his handlers.

The jurors were stunned at the things Smith *did* say and would be willing to hang him for those things alone.

"I'm in the cell alone," Smith said to Martray in one of the taped conversations, and continued, "I think the best time to get me out would be about 11:15 because everyone is up in court. If you could say that the sandwiches were ready, they might open the door for you."

"Okay," Martray answered.

"But also have a crowbar. I mean, when I'm down in that place I'm free. There are no handcuffs on me, and there is only one old guy."

"I got you."

"Get the key, Ray. Take your time. Open it, get me out, and lock him in, and we're gone. If they indict me with Bradfield testifying against me, you should go ahead. Of course, you definitely have to be armed. Now, the old guard in there is not armed, but he may have a young guy with him, and he will be armed. He's a deputy sheriff."

"Well, that's no problem," Martray answered. "If we've come this far, we might as well take it the whole way."

"Yeah, get him away from the phone and onto the floor and then into the cell. Exchange him with me and then we leave. It wouldn't be more than three to four minutes."

End of tape. The jury removed their headsets and stared hard at Jay Smith.

Then came a video, and the lights in the courtroom were lowered. A hugh TV screen was set up facing the jury. The prosecution had a TV of their own to watch. So did we. So did the gallery. So did Judge Lipsitt.

"Listen, man," Martray said, now on TV for the jury. "I don't want this Reinert thing coming up and kicking us in the ass. If you get screwed up, thrown back in jail, where am I?"

"Well, I don't know," Smith answered pensively, "but, see, the Reinert thing shouldn't come up with me."

"Okay," Martray answered. "But what if it does? What if it comes up and kicks you in the ass? Then what do we do?"

"We have to work it out somehow," Smith answered.

"All right," Martray said abruptly. "If he does anything, I'll take care of him."

"Who? Bradfield?" Smith asked.

"Yeah, you know, Bradfield could disappear and never show up again forever. You just get the word to me," Martray added, "and he's done. That sucker, I don't trust him."

"That's right," Smith said.

"I am not in the police eye right now," Martray continued, "but you know, soon I'm gonna be. I have been thinking about this very seriously. I could turn around and Bradfield could disappear. The motherfucker would never show up. What's everybody gonna think: 'He took off.' The heat is on, and he knows it. I'm just afraid he's gonna crack."

"Well, but you see, there's nothing they can do about me 'cause I had nothing to do with it."

"Well, okay, Jay, okay. Just remember what I said before. I'm putting all my eggs in one basket. What happens if they nail you for Reinert? Then what do we do? Where am I gonna be at?"

"You mean if they try me?"

"Yeah."

"And convict me?" Smith added. "Well, then they will probably send me to the electric chair."

"No shit," Martray said. "And look what that does to me."

"Yeah," Smith acknowledged, "it's a problem."

"Like I said before, it's a loose end. We got to get rid of loose ends."

"I guess if they were to arrest me with Reinert, the best thing for you to do is to go kill Bradfield and make him disappear," Smith said.

And the jury sat up.

"That's it," Martray bellowed. "You made the comment. That's it."

"But, see . . . ," Smith continued.

"You don't have to say anymore," Martray interrupted, cutting Smith off.

"But, see," Smith insisted, "that would be very hard."

"They would never suspect," Martray cut in again, "I'll go find my own information. I don't want you to tell me anymore about him than you already told me except one thing. Just in case . . . I get rid of Bradfield, do you, uh . . . " Martray paused. "Do you have any suggestions on how I could make sure he never shows up again? You know, just to help me. I'll do it even without the suggestion. But if you have something good so I can make sure he never shows up again."

"Well," Smith said, "I think your best bet is to get him back in your car, kill him, and take his body into the woods in Fayetteville or someplace, but nobody should know where his body is but you. You should never let anybody else know. Now, do you see the advantage of that?"

"Yeah," Martray answered. "If nobody knows, then who could ever tell on you?"

The jury slowly removed the headsets when the tapes stopped playing. The tapes, though they had nothing to do with the murders of Susan Reinert and her two children, instilled fear and anger in that jury. It was a good day for the prosecution.

★ ★ ★

I personally asked Raymond Martray on the witness stand the big question that Guida and Holtz knew the answer to.

Q. Did you at any time receive any preferential treatment with regard to any sentence that you served, any of your prison experience, anything at all from the police?
A. No, sir.

Martray testified that he was cooperating because he had children of his own. It sounded very much like Proctor Nowell's reason for coming forward.

Guida said no deals. Holtz said no deals. Martray said no deals.

And the train to death for Jay C. Smith was nearing its final destination. Next stop, death row.

· 15 ·

DEATH STOP

I was in my office, alone. I don't remember where Skip was, or Nick, or anybody else for that matter. I had never had a client sentenced to death, and the reality was setting in. I was sorry I had ever taken the case.

Jill was at home with our daughters, and I knew they were safe. Being in the business that I'm in, the safety of my loved ones is a constant concern. It's not paranoia, it's reality. I wanted to call them, but it was much too late. Then my phone rang.

Normally, I never answer the phones in my office, at any hour, for any reason. I just don't, but the ringing wouldn't let up, and it was almost midnight.

"Hello," I finally answered, hoping everything was okay at home.

"Is Mr. Cost . . . Mr. Costop . . . Mr. Costolpas . . . there?"

"Speaking," I answered.

"This is Proctor Nowell."

"Proctor Nowell?" I replied, my interest peaking. I knew exactly who Proctor Nowell was. I had never met him or talked to him, but I knew who Guida's jailhouse informant and star witness was in the Bradfield case.

"I . . . I have to talk to you, sir. It is very important . . . I have to talk to you," Nowell said with urgency in his voice.

"Where are you, Proctor," I asked, wanting to see him immediately. The midnight hour no longer mattered.

"In Philadelphia."

"When can you come in?"

"I . . . I don't know. I don't have any gas."

"I'll pay for your gas and your turnpike tolls. I want to see you. Okay?"

"Okay."

"When?"

"Tomorrow night."

★ ★ ★

Charles Montione followed on the heels of Martray. He had a trim goatee and a dark, blown hairdo and was dressed like the sport that he was.

Montione also told of Jay Smith's escape plans and said that Smith "smirked" when Montione asked him if he had killed Susan Reinert. I found Montione likable, and though I wasn't worried about Smith's "smirk," I was worried about the additional escape talk.

I couldn't get Proctor Nowell off my mind. Skip and Nick were on standby. I had said nothing to Jay Smith.

★ ★ ★

Rick Guida's case was winding down, but not without a dramatic impact.

Karen Reinert's former sixth grade classmates, who had made a museum field trip with Karen, were called in to testify. These were all nice kids—well-dressed and polite. They were seniors in high school when they appeared as witnesses for the Commonwealth. They brought their best recollections with them into the courtroom.

The first three kids from Karen's grade school, the Chestnutwold Elementary School, remembered going to the Philadelphia Museum of Art with her and that each got a green pin with a white "P" on it. The fourth kid had actually saved his, and it was shown to the jury for comparison. His green pin with a white "P" would be compared with the pin found in Jay Smith's car by Trooper Dove in 1980, and Rick would argue in his closing that Karen had lost her pin in Jay Smith's car.

I did not cross-examine those kids. I had nothing to ask them. I believed every one of them.

I could handle a similar pin found in Smith's car 14 months after the night in question. Smith was in prison the entire time and was a sitting duck for Bradfield, and others, who were out running around that entire time. Smith had also been to the Philadelphia Museum of Art on his own on more than one occasion.

Then Guida called Bethann Brooks, and I noticed Holtz sit up. I assumed that she was being called to testify that she and her grandmother, Mary Gove, saw Susan, Karen, and Michael leave the house on that stormy Friday night.

That's what Mary Gove had said under oath.

That's what Bethann Brooks had testified to at Bradfield's trial.

That's what Bethann Brooks had told the police when she was questioned in 1979, and I had those police reports in front of me. Bethann's description of what the kids had on that night was unclear, with very few specifics, but that was understandable. The visibility had been poor that night and Bethann was only 16 years old at the time.

"Bethann," Guida asked, "do you recall a hailstorm that evening?"

"Yes."

"And what happened after the hailstorm was over? What did you do?"

"My grandmother and I went out to the porch. Karen and Michael and Susan were coming out of their house. Michael went down, and he was picking up the hailstones. And he brought them to us, and he said, 'Oh gosh! Look how big they are!'"

Then Guida dropped another bomb, one that had been assembled and made during the Smith trial. The assembler was Holtz.

Q. Now, Bethann, how was Karen Reinert dressed that night while you
were out collecting hailstones?

A. She had on a white shirt with a scooped neck, a pair of shorts, and
sneakers.

Q. Did she have anything on that shirt that you remember?

A. She had on *the* pin.

Q. The green pin with the white P?

A. The cute green pin with the white P.

Q. I'm going to show you what has been marked as Commonwealth
Exhibit 110. Does that look familiar to you?

A. Yes, it does.

Q. And what is it similar to?

A. That's the pin Karen had on.

Q. Bethann, did you ever see Karen or Michael Reinert again after that
night at 9:00?

A. No, sir.

I had to be very careful with Bethann. She was only 16 at the time, but
her present description of Karen's clothing did not match the police reports. Never before did she mention anything about a pin.

"Bethann," I began with caution, because I did not know the answer to
my own question, and you never ask a question that you don't know the
answer to on cross-examination, *but I had to know.*

"When was the first time you were asked to recall if you saw a pin?"

"About four weeks ago," she answered.

"About four weeks ago?" I repeated. "Who asked you?"

"Mr. Holtz."

Just what I thought.

Holtz *refreshed* that child's memory during the Smith trial. I will never
believe that Bethann remembered that little pin on Karen Reinert six years
after the fact. She may have thought she remembered a pin after Holtz got
done talking to her, that I believe.

Police officers should also remember that it's not our personal welfare at
stake in a criminal trial, no matter how high the profile. A trial is a search
for the truth and what is at stake, always, is the fate of the accused and the
integrity of the system.

* * *

That night.

I didn't want to scare Proctor Nowell with too many white guys standing around in suits. It was a dangerous move on my part, but I decided to
talk to him alone when he finally arrived. I had asked Skip and Nick to
wait upstairs.

Proctor Nowell arrived at my office about 9 p.m. Guida was going to
rest his case the next morning. Nowell was very nervous as he sat across

from my desk, alone. He was a poor, illiterate—but not dumb—black kid from Chester County, Pennsylvania, who had been in and out of the prison system. I liked him immediately. There was a certain sensitivity about him. I found him credible, and he hadn't said a word.

"How was your trip, Proctor?"

"Okay."

"Are you all right?"

"Yes."

"Is that your girlfriend in the car?"

"My wife."

"Tell her to come in."

"No."

"What's up?"

"You know . . . I was in a cell with Bradfield?"

"Go on."

"He told me things in the cell."

"Go on."

"Well . . . I testified for the police a couple of years ago at Bradfield's trial."

"I know."

"I thought you might."

"Keep going."

"Bradfield told me things . . . told me something that I didn't testify to."

"Yeah?"

"Yeah."

"Like what?"

"He told me that he wasn't worried about gettin' convicted because . . . he said he wasn't worried because he was framing a guy for it . . . he said he was puttin' it on a principal."

My heart was racing a mile a minute. I actually thought God sent me this guy to keep an innocent man from being put to death. My excitement level went through the ceiling, because I couldn't wait to call *Guida's* witness. Guida's star witness in the Bradfield case, the star witness Holtz had found.

My case-in-chief was to start right after lunch the next day. I could see it all in my mind's eye. I would call Proctor Nowell as my first witness, and he would testify that while they were in jail together, William Bradfield had admitted to Nowell that he was framing Smith for the Reinert murders.

How could Guida call Proctor Nowell a liar? How could Holtz call Proctor Nowell a liar? This was the ultimate poetic justice, but Nowell wasn't done with me yet.

"Mr. Costoplis," Nowell asked, "do you have my gas money for me?"

"Sure, Proctor," I answered, willing to give him money for gas.

"I . . . I need some shoes . . . my . . ."

"I'll get you some shoes," I said. "Don't worry about it."

"Can they be sneakers?"

"Sure."

The ethical considerations were racing through my mind, but I was dismissing them as fast as I could. I didn't believe that the Pennsylvania Disciplinary Board would sanction me for buying a pair of sneakers for Proctor Nowell under the circumstances, or for a tank of gas.

But Nowell did not stop there.

And suddenly I felt threatened. I felt like I was getting set up. I wished I had Skip there.

"Mr. Costolopis . . . I . . . I have to ask you something."

"Sure, Proctor, what is it?"

"My woman . . . she . . . she's got sickle cell anemia . . . I have to help her."

My balloon was deflating fast. I didn't want to lose Proctor Nowell, but I could see what was coming. He needed money. I needed his testimony. I was fucked.

"I need $1,500. She needs medical attention, and I can't let her die," he said, pleading.

"I . . . I can't do that, Proctor. I just can't," I said, really upset, wanting to help him, knowing that I couldn't under the circumstances.

"If you help me out, I will help you out," he replied.

"Proctor . . . it's not that I don't want to help you, but I could go to jail for something like this," I said, hoping he would understand.

I honestly believed at the time that Nowell was sincere about his woman. Proctor and I talked at length, privately. I then got Skip, who was waiting in my outer office, to help me talk to him. We impressed upon him that an innocent man's life was at stake. He listened very carefully to that, and seemed to feel really bad, but he stuck to his gun.

"If you help me . . . I'll help you . . . I'll help Mr. Smith," Nowell said firmly.

"Proctor, please listen to us," Skip interjected, trying to help.

"No," Proctor interrupted angrily. "Don't lay that guilt shit on me, man. I'm not bullshiting you about what Bradfield said. I'm not bullshitting you about needing money either. No money, and I am out of here."

I made a last-ditch effort.

I talked Proctor into staying at the Penn Harris Motor Inn on the West Shore. I told him that I would see him in the morning to buy him and his woman breakfast. I promised him new sneakers. I paid him his gas money. I paid him for the flat tire he had gotten on his way in from Philadelphia. Finally, I gave him my unlisted home phone number if he wanted to talk. My parting words were "an innocent man's life is at stake here."

★ ★ ★

That night, I tossed and turned till dawn. I felt that everything I believed in about the system, which I had devoted my life to for the past 15 years, was a mockery and a sham.

There were several incidents during the trial that infuriated me. They made me crazy. The accusation that Balshy was a liar and the implication that I put him up to it was one.

Guida putting into evidence the blatant hearsay of Bradfield's friends and lovers was another. He didn't care if the appellate courts granted a new trial or not. He wanted the verdict at any cost.

Then there was the testimony of Vincent Valaitis that stunned me because of its outrageousness.

Then there was Bethann Brooks's recollection of the pin on Karen's shirt six years after the fact.

And I really resented Raymond Martray's orchestrated lies. Proctor Nowell was my vengeance and my chance to give the prosecution a taste of their own medicine.

★ ★ ★

The ringing of the phone in the early morning hours startled me. I grabbed the phone quickly, hoping Jill and our two-year-old daughter would sleep through it. I knew that our two teenage daughters would. It was Proctor Nowell.

"It's me, Proctor," he said, whispering.

"Are you all right?" I asked; I didn't want to sound annoyed.

"I'm calling from a pay phone. Nobody can hear us. Are you going to pay me that $1,500?"

I could hear that tape being played in front of a jury. I believed at the time that I was being set up. I was furious at the thought, but I wasn't taking any chances. The Smith case was already out of control.

"Proctor," I answered quickly, "if you've told me the truth about what Bradfield said, then I need your testimony real bad, but I can't pay for it. Do you understand me? I can't pay for it," I said, pleadingly.

"You don't understand me," Proctor said. "Bradfield told me he was framing Smith."

"I'll see you in the morning, Proctor. We'll talk again."

"Don't bother, man," Proctor said, and hung up.

Early the next morning, I drove to the Penn Harris Motor Inn looking for Proctor Nowell. He had already checked out.

★ ★ ★

I did not call Jay Smith to the witness stand. I knew I was in trouble with the jury, but I wasn't going to blow the appellate record. Jay Smith did not like that decision, but it was mine because Smith left it up to me, and trusted my judgment.

One dumb, unpredictable remark from him on the witness stand and my hearsay issue was out the window.

On the 29th of April, I would make my closing argument to the jury. I got up at 4 a.m. to work out in my basement gym, and between reps and exercises, I rehearsed stock phrases in front of the mirrors. I went over in my mind the hundreds of exhibits and witnesses, and by my last bench press, I convinced myself that I had a chance because they had no case.

My mother had called me the night before and told me she was coming to court. She was coming with my sister, and they wanted good seats. I promised them the best seats in the house, if they got there early enough; otherwise they would not be able to get in, because courtroom doors are locked once closing arguments begin.

Jill and I got to the courthouse early for them, and I grabbed an old tip-staff friend of mine. He would do me the favor. He promised me they could sit anywhere in the courtroom they wanted, and he would see to that. He had a badge.

The courtroom was packed an hour before closing arguments. When I looked around to see where my mother and my younger sister were, I saw them sitting behind Guida and Holtz!

My mother did not like Jay Smith.

All I can say is that it gets awfully lonely in that courtroom when you are defending high-profile defendants who have been charged with heinous crimes. I knew for years that I was not the darling child of the community, but it was still a shock to see my mother jump ship.

All eyes were on Judge Lipsitt:

Ladies and gentlemen of the jury, we have reached this final phase of the trial. Once the closings are finished, I will charge you on the law, and there-after you will retire to the jury room to render your verdict.

Let the record reflect that the defendant, Jay Smith, is present in the courtroom with counsel. Gentlemen, are you ready to proceed with closing arguments?

"Yes, Your Honor," I answered respectfully, standing up.

"Yes, Your Honor," Guida answered in like manner, also standing up.

I went first. The defense always goes first in a criminal case in Pennsylvania. I began my closing from the podium and had my notes and exhibits strategically placed to tie everything together and make it flow. I was nervous, but ready.

"May it please the court, Mr. Guida, Mr. Smith," I began.

"Ladies and gentlemen of the jury, very soon you will retire to deliberate the fate of Jay Smith, and in your hands lies the power of rendering the only appropriate verdict in this case based on the evidence, which is not guilty. In your hands lies the power of life and death. It is the gravest responsibility our country imposes on its citizenry.

"During the course of the trial, you've been patient, and you've seen a lot of interaction between the attorneys, and often intentionally or unintentionally we interject our egos into these proceedings. No matter what your verdict is, our egos will heal, but your verdict is forever."

I explained to the jury that in this country "beyond a reasonable doubt" means we don't convict on suspicion, conjecture, or surmise. We don't convict in this country on probabilities either. In other words, I stressed, "Even if you would decide that Jay Smith was probably responsible in some way, you must find him not guilty. Because in this country we would rather acquit nine guilty persons than convict one innocent man for something he didn't do. Let alone ask that he be put to death."

Then I went right to the sand testimony of John Balshy. I impressed upon the jury that Balshy was an honorable man, that he was a credible man, and that he had served the Commonwealth for almost 27 years. I told the jury, again, that he *saw* sand between the toes of Susan Reinert and removed that sand with lifters. I dovetailed Balshy's testimony with Susan Reinert's handwritten directions to Cape May, New Jersey, which were found in her car.

Destroying the Commonwealth's forensic evidence—the one hair, and the red fiber in her hair—was easy. *Our* experts demonstrated for the jury with slides and credible testimony how foolish the prosecution's actions were. I argued their forensic evidence was an act of desperation.

I held Holtz responsible for Bethann's belated testimony regarding the pin.

And I walked over to Jay Smith in the presence of the jury and put my hand on his shoulder and argued lack of motive.

"Motive? What motive did Jay Smith have to kill the woman and hurt her children? According to the Commonwealth's theory, Bradfield committed perjury for him. Well, that's Bradfield's problem, not Jay Smith's. Jay Smith didn't even testify at the St. David's trial. Motive. What motive? Are the two links going to hold together that Bradfield did in fact commit perjury, and in payment Jay Smith savagely and brutally assassinates a woman and two children on the weekend he's to report for sentencing?

"Use your common sense. Why in God's name would Jay Smith want the body to be left outside the Host Inn? In the very city within a mile or so of where he was to appear for sentencing? If there was any reason, you come up with it. I can't.

"And that woman wasn't just murdered for the purpose of collecting insurance proceeds. She was disgraced. She was left nude in the fetal position in the back of her car, and the hatchback was left up, three rows from the front door. Who, psychologically, had this character of disgracing and demeaning women? William Sydney Bradfield.

"And where was Joanne Aitken for 30 days prior to the murder? And Chris Pappas, ladies and gentlemen. I don't know where that guy's coming from. They practiced shooting silencers. They practiced tying each other up. Make no mistake about it, ladies and gentlemen, he knows more.

Joanne knows more. Sue Myers knows more, and if the prosecution would quit defending them they might find out what happened on that weekend.

"Does Smith have an airtight alibi for that weekend? Not even close. But neither do I. And neither do you."

Finally, I dealt with Raymond Martray. I argued to the jury how Martray went from knowing nothing to gradually, over time, giving the prosecution exactly what they wanted—a jailhouse confession—because without that confession, the prosecution had nothing! Except the blue comb found in the trunk of Susan Reinert's car. I picked up that comb for the jury to look at, the 79th USARCOM comb that Trooper Dove identified for them as Commonwealth Exhibit 7.

"You heard those tapes yourselves. Jay Smith talked to you, ladies and gentlemen, and you learned what he knew and didn't know about the death of Susan Reinert.

"I was worried about the fact that this crime was a savage one. Everybody gets angry, and it was an ugly crime, but my concern was never over the evidence against Jay Smith, because there isn't any. Once you get rid of Martray, that leaves them back where they were in 1980. With this new comb. What's that prove? Nothing."

Before I sat down, I reminded the jury of their awesome responsibility in this case. I urged them to return a verdict *based on the evidence*—uninfluenced by fear, sympathy, prejudice, or bias.

"Ladies and gentlemen, you have the power to render the only appropriate verdict in this case . . . and that is that Jay Smith is not guilty. It's in your hands. Thank you."

I felt good about my closing. I did not feel great about the case, but I had given it the best I had. I asked Jay Smith what he thought before we broke for lunch.

"The semester's not over yet," he reminded me.

★ ★ ★

Guida delivered a strong closing in the afternoon. My mother and sister were with him all the way.

"Four and a half years ago, I joined the office of the attorney general. My first assignment was this matter. Today, it's over. Today, all of the effort expended by the prosecutor, by the defense, by the FBI, all comes down to you."

Guida told the jury that we both agreed—and we did—that this was a case of first-degree murder, if there ever was one, or nothing. If Jay Smith took the life of Susan Reinert and her two children, it was first-degree murder. It was not vehicular homicide or accidental death.

Then Guida went after John Balshy and the defense. Guida was devastating in this part of his dramatic closing. I deeply resented Rick as I sat there taking the personal assault which went far beyond fair comment.

"Let's wrap up the defense case. During the first day of the case, a retired trooper took the stand. He worked for the defendant's private investigator. On cross-examination he suddenly talks about her feet, about some grains of sand. Mr. Costopoulos said it was like pulling teeth getting him to say it. It was more like pulling out dentures. A big smile came over Balshy's face. He said that gritty particles could have been sand.

"You found out that early in the investigation when the state police were exploring the possibility that Mrs. Reinert might have been to the shore, they called him to a meeting to determine that, and what did he say? Nothing. It's a sad commentary on what was a decent career with the state police.

"But the search for the dollar after you leave your police service does not include, nor does it allow you to commit, *perjury*."

Guida then dismissed the grocery store receipt from the Phoenixville market.

He dismissed it by saying that he couldn't explain it. He dismissed it by saying that Susan Reinert and Chris Pappas and Vincent Valaitis and Wendy Zeigler weren't capable of participating in such a shocking crime.

"And I ask you, ladies and gentlemen," Guida said, "did Vincent Valaitis and Sue Myers appear to be the kind of persons who would murder a child? Christopher Pappas was cut from the same cloth as Vincent Valaitis. Wendy Zeigler was 19 years old. Could she have cut up two children?"

Guida did not defend Joanne Aitken. He didn't dare do that, but on the other hand, he didn't prosecute her either.

Then Guida laid the barrage of devastating hearsay on the jury one more time. He reminded them of the testimony of Bradfield's friends—Sue Myers, Chris Pappas, Vincent Valaitis, Wendy Zeigler, and Joanne Aitken— as to what Bradfield told them Smith said. According to these witnesses, Bradfield told them that Smith said he was going to kill Susan Reinert, and that Bradfield said Smith *did* kill Susan Reinert.

And again, Guida told the jury that Martray had no deals, that Martray was given no favorable consideration. "Raymond Martray told you that the defendant said 'I killed the bitch' on two occasions. That, in and of itself, is sufficient to convict the defendant, if you believe it. The defense suggested that because Martray saw this was a big case he was going to come into this courtroom and perjure himself. What did Martray get? Nothing. Martray served his time. He got out on schedule. What did the Commonwealth do?"

Guida finished strong. Real strong. He told the jury that their investigation was over and now it was up to *them*.

★ ★ ★

Judge Lipsitt charged the jury on the law. It was a fair charge, to the point, and he instructed them not to infer guilt from the fact that Smith did not testify.

The tension was building. If there is one thing I hate about trying cases, it's waiting for a jury's verdict. Waiting for that phone to ring is unbearable. To ease that pain, I try to keep busy or surround myself with loved ones and friends.

Late that afternoon, April 29, 1986, at approximately 4:30 p.m., the 12 principal jurors retired to the jury room to render their verdict. I immediately went to Jay Smith's cell in the basement of the Dauphin County Courthouse to prepare him for the worst—a guilty verdict on all counts and the death penalty phase that would follow. While we were there, alone in that lockup, a young deputy sheriff brought Smith his dinner—a hamburger and some coffee.

"I'm going to call you to the witness stand," I said to Jay, after the deputy sheriff positioned himself by the outer door to maintain the heavy security.

"For what?" Jay asked.

"I want you to ask the jury to spare your life."

"I'm not going to do that," Jay said.

"Why not?"

"Because I'm not guilty, and I'm not kissing their ass."

That night, I waited at Skip's office with my staff and Jill, some news reporters, and Loretta Schwartz-Nobel, who was also writing a book. Loretta, a former investigative reporter for the *Philadelphia Inquirer* and *Philadelphia Magazine*, had landed a contract with Viking Penguin, a major publishing house in New York, to do the inside story of the Main Line murders. She had also been in the media box every day with Wambaugh, though there was no love between them.

Loretta kept asking me how I felt, and I told her that I was exhausted, that I had lost weight, that I had missed workouts, that my children didn't know me, that I hadn't slept, and would she please put her notebook down. I liked Loretta, but she was a child of the '60s who was holding onto an era long past. She was a sensitive human being, and I wanted to trust her with my feelings and thoughts, but I didn't.

My reason for not trusting her?

She was spending too much time with Holtz.

The phone rang at 10 p.m. My heart jumped, and I felt sick to my stomach. The jury, now sequestered, had not yet reached a verdict and was sent to the Holiday Inn. Jill drove me home for another sleepless night.

She was feeling the pressure, too. We had had no life together for the past five weeks. She remained supportive and upbeat, but the anxiety and stress were taking their toll on both of us.

By 11 a.m. the next morning, the jury had reached a verdict.

· 16 ·

BOTH BARRELS

April 30, 1986.

Outside, cameras were positioned on the Dauphin County Courthouse steps for live coverage to Harrisburg, Philadelphia, and Pittsburgh. The AP and UPI wire services already had their stories in print—all they needed was the conclusion.

The courtroom was packed, and those who couldn't get in waited in the corridors. Reporters. Spectators. Family. Friends. Courthouse personnel. They were all there. Word travels fast in a death penalty case.

I heard the jurors file in one by one. I did not look at them. I never do. I slid down in my chair and could feel my heart pounding. Jay Smith sat quietly in the defendant's chair, staring straight ahead.

The judge began:

Good morning, ladies and gentlemen. Let the record reflect that the defendant is present in court with his counsel. The court has been informed that the jury has reached a verdict. Would the foreperson please rise and hand the verdict forms to the clerk.

Waiting for any verdict is pure hell, especially in a death penalty case.

The clerk ceremoniously took the verdict slips from the foreperson, a woman juror, and handed them to Judge Lipsitt. He read them quickly and handed them back to the clerk for the formal reading by the foreperson of the jury. Judge Lipsitt now knew.

Dr. Jay Smith sat motionless, expressionless.

"All rise," the clerk said, and the entire jury stood up.

"In the case of *Commonwealth v. Jay C. Smith*, number 1677, the charge of murder, how do you find the defendant?" the clerk asked the forewoman.

"Guilty. Murder in the first degree," she said.

"In the case of *Commonwealth v. Jay C. Smith*, number 1677a, the charge of murder, how do you find the defendant?" the clerk asked again.

"Guilty. Murder in the first degree," the forewoman said again.

"In the case of *Commonwealth v. Jay C. Smith*, number 1677b, the charge of murder, how do you find the defendant?"

"Guilty. Murder in the first degree."

I stood up, badly shaken, and requested a poll of the jury. I was mentally prepared for this moment, but not emotionally, and I hated it. I then heard

133

"Guilty, murder in the first degree," 33 more times. I don't know why I do that.

Judge Lipsitt proceeded:

> Ladies and gentlemen, your verdict has been recorded. You will now retire to the jury room until further notification. You will then reconvene here, at which time an evidentiary hearing will take place, with arguments from counsel, and thereafter you will deliberate again to determine the sentence—life or death. Whether you sentence the defendant to life or death will depend upon whether the aggravating circumstances outweigh the mitigating circumstances in this case. Thank you.

As the jurors filed out, Guida and Holtz shook hands and slapped each other on the back. Many Guida supporters rushed forward from the back of the courtroom to congratulate them. Reporters rushed for the phones to meet their deadlines.

I looked over at Smith, who was still expressionless, as though he hadn't heard it. He twitched once, but that was about it.

Jay Smith then looked straight into my eyes. I felt like I had failed him. I looked to the back of the courtroom for my family. They were gone, even Jill, and the loneliness overwhelmed me.

★ ★ ★

I hated that jury. I hated being a trial lawyer. I hated myself.

This time, I called the sidebar. I told Judge Lipsitt that Judge Garb had precluded the penalty phase from going to the jury in Bradfield's case. I argued disparity in sentencing. Guida argued that Bradfield was a mere accomplice and that Smith was the actual killer. Guida won.

And the jury was back in the box for the final blow.

"Okay, Jay?" I whispered.

"You're the boss," he answered, like nothing unusual was going on.

"Then get up there," I said, feeling like I had no choice.

Jay Smith himself, erect, proud, undaunted, took the stand and made himself comfortable. You could have heard a pin drop in the packed courtroom.

Q. Mr. Smith, please state your full name for the record.
A. My name is Jay Charles Smith.
Q. Your age, sir?
A. I will be 58 on June fifth of this year.
Q. Where were you born?
A. I was actually born in Ridley Park, but lived all my life in Chester, Pennsylvania.
Q. Do you have any brothers or sisters?

A. I have three brothers living, one brother dead, and one sister.

Q. For how many years were you married before your wife passed away?

A. Twenty-eight years.

Q. When did your wife pass away?

A. On August 7, 1979.

I then asked Jay what he had done in prison from the date of his confinement. I was playing every card I had, but at that point, I didn't have a single face card, and I was down to my last chip.

Jay methodically testified that he considered himself a jailhouse counselor, not a jailhouse lawyer, because he helped inmates with their personal letters and personal problems. He had helped 15 Vietnam veterans with their Agent Orange cases. He had helped a large number of Hispanics who couldn't speak English. He taught inmates how to make out applications for jobs. He handled the Bible studies in prison, but his main activity was working on a criminal justice dictionary.

Then the Jay Smith I was worried about surfaced.

Q. How does the request for two back issues of *Penthouse* tie in with your dictionary?

A. I've found that *Black's Law Dictionary* and *Ballentine's* do not cover criminal justice definitions very well. I had inmates bring up words that they know. Then I went through about 50 or 60 sociology and criminology textbooks and began writing definitions in the criminal justice dictionary. There's nothing in *Black's Law Dictionary* about the Muslims. In prison the Black Muslims and the Muslim faith has grown tremendously. You have a great deal of trouble in the criminal justice system finding out about corrections, especially halfway houses, furloughs, leaves of absence. Most lawyers do not know very much about corrections. It's in that category, corrections . . . . The *Penthouse*. Let me answer how I got to the *Penthouse*. I found over the past five or six years a number of crimes involving battered wives and child abuse. If you look at those issues, you'll find that they have Yoko and John Lennon in there. John Lennon beat up Yoko. I was considering her as an example of a battered wife, because John Lennon is known throughout the world. Also John Lennon in the article kicked his child, Sean. Yoko thought he was going to kill him. This was a child abuse item.

I couldn't fucking believe it. I wanted Jay Smith to ask the jury to spare him his life, and he's talking about Yoko and John Lennon, that John Lennon beat up Yoko, that he considered Yoko a battered wife, that John Lennon kicked his child, and that was child abuse. It was incredible, and I've seen a lot in the courtroom over the years.

I quickly moved to another area and intended to control him this time. I couldn't afford another run like that.

Q. Mr. Smith, since your arrest for the death of Susan Reinert and the disappearance of her children, what have your living conditions been?
A. I've been kept in isolation ever since.
Q. Explain to the jury what that means.
A. I'm not allowed any communication or calls. I'm not allowed to visit with my relatives except one time every two weeks, when they're behind a screen. I get no religious activity whatever. It's the only place in the United States where you're not permitted to have any church services.
Q. Did you want to testify before this jury during this trial?
A. Yes. It was my feeling to testify, because I felt the jury was entitled to hear my side. You said if I didn't testify it couldn't work against me. I mentioned to you I didn't think they could bring up the previous conviction. That shows you how much of a jailhouse lawyer I am.
Q. Mr. Smith, if this jury would spare your life, are you aware that you will spend the rest of your natural life in the prison system of this Commonwealth?
A. I don't think there's any doubt about that.
Q. If this jury would spare you your life, what would you do within the prison system until your natural death?
A. I don't see any major changes. I would go on as I am, trying to help people when I could, trying to work as closely as possible with my family so they can get over the disgrace. Finish the criminal justice dictionary and work in the church. I guess I would complete the Agent Orange lawsuits against Dow Chemical. Probably I'd start teaching again. I volunteered to teach English and reading. I'm not permitted to teach subjects where they have a hired position, although that's what I could really do best.
Q. Mr. Smith, are you asking this jury to spare your life?
A. Absolutely. Of course.

Guida should have just let him go, but Smith and I were both down for the count, and with the crowd rooting for death in the back of the court-room, Guida went after him.

Actually, Smith did just fine under cross-examination. Smith didn't get excited, even though he was fighting for his life, and he didn't beg.

★ ★ ★

Guida stood up and screamed his first question, then yelled his second question, and the one after that. It was way overdone.

Q. Where are the bodies of Karen and Michael Reinert?!
A. I do not know.
Q. You do not know?!
A. I do not know.
Q. Where did you kill Susan Reinert?!
A. I did not kill Susan Reinert or her children. I had nothing to do with Susan Reinert.
Q. In other words, what you're telling this jury is that they made a terrible mistake, isn't that right?
A. All my life I've lived in the American system. I think they've made their decision honestly on the basis of what they were given. We accept their judgment. They say I'm guilty; I'm guilty. You asked me if I think I really did it? I didn't do it. I respect their judgment.
Q. I didn't ask you if you think you did it. Did you do it or didn't you?
A. I said I did not.

Guida then started arguing with Smith. He berated him for denying his guilt. Judge Lipsitt put an end to that in a hurry after I objected. The judge told Guida to just ask Smith relevant questions and to quit arguing with him.

I felt sorry for Smith. I was sorry I called him. He was right when he told me that it would be useless.

Q. Let me ask you this, Mr. Smith. Are you telling us that you are not upset, even though you've been unjustly convicted of three counts of murder in the first degree?
A. Yeah, I'm upset. But I'm not the kind who falls apart. I've had enough military training. I can take whatever happens to me.
Q. Where were you during the weekend of June 22, 1979, between 10 o'clock at night and noontime on June 24, 1979?

I objected. The answer to Guida's last question would have been a retrial of the case. The sole issue at this final hour was life or death, not guilt or innocence. Judge Lipsitt agreed and directed Guida to move on, and he went back to *Penthouse* magazine and dictionaries and movies.

I'm not sure Guida had ever put a man to death before. I felt that he was enjoying it too much, and I hated everything that was going on in my life at that moment.

Q. Mr. Smith, on direct examination, you indicated that you wanted issues of *Penthouse* so that you could write a legal dictionary. Is that correct?
A. I am writing a legal dictionary. Yes.
Q. What specific word did you define in your dictionary using the Yoko Ono article?

A. Battered wives. I'm not saying that I completed the total entry. Child abuse and battered wives are the two terms I was going after.

Q. How long an entry in your dictionary did you plan for battered wives?

A. I would say 25 words.

Q. In order to get 25 words for the dictionary to define the term battered wives, you ordered two copies of *Penthouse*, is that right?

A. That's correct.

Q. The prison library has a lot of books, doesn't it?

A. The prison library has very few books, Mr. Guida. I had purchased my own books. I had over 150 books in my cell, including a full encyclopedia set.

Q. You, of course, have a Ph.D. in education.

A. I'm a doctor of education.

Q. As part of that, you did extensive research both in your master's and your doctoral theses, did you not?

A. Correct.

Q. Are you saying that given your educational background, your knowledge of libraries and books, and the places to find information, that the best place for you to get a definition of 'battered wives' was in the issues of *Penthouse* magazine?

A. On those two celebrities, yes.

Q. In other words, your dictionary was going to include a list of famous cases. Is that right?

A. That's right.

Q. Were you also going to include the Ted Bundy case?

A. Absolutely.

Q. How about the Jeffrey MacDonald case from *Fatal Vision*?

A. I had those books in my cell.

Q. As a matter of fact, you had a lot of books on Ted Bundy.

A. I had three. I consider him to be the first major serial murderer.

Q. Also, *Fatal Vision*. Correct me if I'm wrong. That's the man who killed his wife and two children?

A. Yes.

Q. A woman and two children?

A. No. It was his wife and two children.

Q. She's still a woman, isn't she?

A. Of course, she's a woman.

That's how Guida ended his cross-examination. He wasn't getting anywhere with Jay Smith. Everybody had had enough, including the jury.

I had one final innocuous question. At least I thought it was innocuous. I was sorry that I asked it, because Jay Smith went back to lala land.

Q. Mr. Smith, is there anything else that you wish to tell this jury, your peers, before they pass judgment on life or death?

A. The only thing I wanted to mention was that comb. I spent 28 years in the Army reserves. Twenty-eight years. I spent every Wednesday night for 20 years doing reserve work. I'm the one who originated the idea for the comb.

We had trouble getting into schools to talk about recruiting, because it was very anti-military back in the '60s. There was a television program called "77 Sunset Strip." On that program there was a fellow who was a detective. He used to comb his hair. They had a song called "Kookie, Kookie, Lend Me Your Comb." That's where I got the idea to hand out combs with the 79th USARCOM decal inscribed on it. That comb now works against me.

I did not kill Susan Reinert. I never had anything to do with Susan Reinert. Nothing whatever. Nothing. Never saw her off school property at any time. Never saw her children.

Q. Nevertheless, you accept the judgment of your jury?

A. Of course. They're honest people. They made an honest decision. You accept it. That's the way it goes.

That was it for me. "Kookie, Kookie, Lend Me Your Comb"? Jesus!

★ ★ ★

"Mr. Costopoulos, are you ready to close to the jury?" Judge Lipsitt asked.

"Yes, Your Honor," I answered respectfully.

It was all happening so fast, too fast. It was a blur. I wasn't ready. The jury had already found against my client. They found "beyond a reasonable doubt" that Jay Smith had murdered Susan Reinert and her two children. There would be no mercy for such a defendant.

I felt that my credibility with the jury was at an all-time low. I was now reduced to a beggar. I would plead for mercy, when there was no mercy for Karen and Michael Reinert, when they were robbed of their youth, without even a grave where their loved ones could mourn. There was no mercy for Susan Reinert. Her death surmounted all horror. Did she witness her children's execution? Did they witness hers?

No, I wasn't ready to close to the jury.

"Ladies and gentlemen of the jury," I said. "I believe that this is the greatest system in the world. I cannot question your verdict now that you have reached it, and I must admit to you that I am frightened.

"Jay Smith has always maintained to me, as he has to you, that he did not murder Susan Reinert. He did not murder her two children—can you appreciate the frightening position that I am in?

"The Supreme Court of Pennsylvania has found capital punishment to be legal. Thus, in your deliberation on the question of punishment, you are to presume, if you sentence Jay Smith to death, that he will be executed.

"You are to presume, if you sentence Jay Smith to life imprisonment, that he will spend the rest of his life in prison. You will make no other presumptions.

"The life he will lead in prison is no life at all. For all practical purposes, he began his life term on June 25, 1979. Since his arrest for murder in 1985, the man has lived in a hole. He lives by himself. He's got minimal contact. They transport him in handcuffs and shackles.

"He has elected, between the two options of death and that kind of life, to die in our prison system. I'm asking you to let him do that. Thank you."

It was the worst closing that I had ever made in my life. I wanted to run, to get away from it all, from everybody, from everything I had devoted my life to.

Jay Smith continued to stare straight ahead, expressionless. He would not give the jury the satisfaction of looking at them.

★ ★ ★

Waiting for death is not easy. Everybody lingered in the courtroom and in the corridors and on the courthouse steps for that announcement. A lot of the followers had sandwiches and sodas as the hours ticked by. Some were in bars getting drunk. It took six hours to reach a verdict.

The jury returned to the courtroom at 8:15 that night.

By 8:18 p.m. they had said it all.

"Have you reached a verdict of life or death?" the clerk asked the jury.

"We have reached a verdict of death," the forewoman said.

"Ladies and gentlemen," the clerk said, "will you stand, please. Hearken to your verdict, as the court has it recorded. You say that Jay C. Smith should receive death. So say you all?"

"We do."

I stood up and requested a poll of the jury. It was automatic, like a soldier shot in battle making a last-ditch effort without hope. Maybe one juror would realize he made a mistake.

The forewoman said "death" three times.

Juror number two said "death" three times.

Juror number three said "death" three times.

Juror number four said "death" three times.

I heard "death" 36 times that night, and every utterance went through my heart. Jay Smith didn't flinch.

I resented the jubilation in the courtroom.

Judge Lipsitt ordered Jay Smith to the bench. We went together. Deputy sheriffs surrounded us as the judge explained to Smith his appellate rights, his right to counsel if he could not afford counsel, and that he would be brought back to court on a future date for the formal imposition of his sentence.

"Do you have any questions?" Judge Lipsitt asked Smith.

"No, Your Honor," Smith answered, then leaned over to whisper in my ear.

"You flunk," he said quietly, sounding like a high school principal who was not happy with his student.

· 17 ·

THE INFLUENCE

As the trial wore on, we all began to feel more pressure. Our murder case had received more massive publicity than any murder case in the history of Pennsylvania, and we were at the center of the story. We knew that newspaper stories are forgotten days after they are published, but books last forever. With Joe Wambaugh's skill and reputation, anything he wrote would certainly be a best seller, and whatever we did in April of 1986, would be laid bare for the world to see for a long time to come.

Rick Guida

June 1986.

Rick Guida was on top of the world when he got the Smith verdict. Within weeks of the death penalty sentence, he flew to Palm Springs, California to vacation with Wambaugh at his home. Joe picked up Guida at the Palm Springs Airport at noon in a 190 Mercedes Benz, and the two wined and dined at a bar before arriving at Wambaugh's home near dusk. For the next three days, Wambaugh was a gracious host, and the two of them played golf at various country clubs in the Palm Springs/Indian Wells community. Guida got to meet a lot of Joe's old police buddies who were the models for fictionalized characters in Wambaugh's books.

One night, the two of them went to Sonny Bono's restaurant and met Bono. Guida also enjoyed having dinner with Tony Puente, a detective with the San Diego Police Department, who is a character in Joe Wambaugh's previous nonfiction book, *Lines and Shadows*. It struck Guida that the bond between Tony and Joe was not one of author and subject, but one of two policemen.

While Guida had been vacationing with Joe Wambaugh in sunny California that summer, the two of them drove up to Wambaugh's beach condominium near San Diego. Wambaugh's beautiful wife, Dee, was waiting for them there, and Guida watched the ocean roll in from a balcony high on a cliff. The fresh salt air, the glowing red sunset, and the view overlooking the Pacific Ocean were magnificent.

The next morning, at 6:45 a.m., Guida was awakened in the rear guest room by burglar alarms and what felt like people picking up his bed and slamming it on the floor. Guida sat up startled, looking around, frightened.

There was no one in the room, but everything was moving, jumping, and pounding. Guida remembered a poltergeist movie he had seen on television and grabbed his shorts and ran through the house screaming for help. He almost knocked Dee over as she was exiting her bedroom.

Soon, the three of them—Joe, Dee, and Rick—were outside the condo standing on a cliff as the ocean roared loudly beneath them. They felt the ground trembling, and Guida feared the cliff would fall into the ocean and the three of them would plunge to a violent death.

He was sorry he had left Harrisburg.

It turned out to be a mild earthquake, so mild that the three of them laughed when it was over. Guida's only regret was that he did not buy one of the "I survived the earthquake" T-shirts being sold on every street corner by late that afternoon. Guida, however, would never forget those tremors.

They weren't the only tremors Guida was going to get.

★ ★ ★

The publication date for Joseph Wambaugh's book about the Reinert murder cases was nine months away. Wambaugh had originally planned to call the book *Blood Crimson*, but after talking with Jack Holtz and Guida, he decided to use a quote from an Ezra Pound poem, and he called the book *Echoes in the Darkness*.

Guida and Holtz couldn't wait. While Guida was vacationing in Palm Springs with Wambaugh, Jack Holtz had just bought a red Porsche and a vacation home in Nags Head, North Carolina. They were both on top of the world.

Smith was on death row.

★ ★ ★

"Get in there," a uniformed guard said to Smith, pushing him into his cell.

"Do you take my handcuffs and shackles off while I'm in this hole?" Smith asked politely, looking around, trying not to offend the cadre of guards who walked him down the long, dimly lit hallway to the restricted housing unit.

"Yeah," the guard answered with a smirk.

"Thanks," Smith said quietly.

"Now you can play with yourself, which is all you'll be able to do in *here*," another guard said, laughing, and they all chuckled as they slammed the steel door shut.

Once the jury had sentenced Smith to death in the Dauphin County Courthouse, he was immediately taken under heavy security to "the hole" at the Camp Hill State Correctional Institution. There he would be kept, like a caged, dangerous animal, until his Phase 1 paperwork was processed. That would take five months.

"The hole," as it is commonly known to correctional officers and inmates, is for criminals who have been sentenced to die. It is a 6- by 10-foot tomb of solid cinderblock with one steel door. Inside this cell there's a steel frame bolted to the wall, a spongy mattress, one blanket, and a toilet and sink.

Smith looked around his new environment. He had been in jail since June 25, 1979—six years and 10 months ago—before he was put in *this* death-status holding cell. He testified earlier that day that he could take anything, but Smith swallowed hard, realizing that this place was going to put him to the ultimate test.

No windows. No indirect sunlight. No exercise privileges. Nobody to talk to, but *that* was okay, because Smith knew that prisons were crawling with Martrays and Montiones waiting for a ticket out of there.

At least he was allowed his typewriter. He would write to Costopoulos, every day, to remind him of what he should be looking for with his appeals. He would write to his brother, William, and maybe his daughter, Sherri. He would read a lot, especially the Bible, to give him strength. If he was going to be put to death, he needed the Christian doctrine to hold onto. For six years and 10 months Smith worked out when he was in the general prison population. He looked around his new home trying to figure out a program that would keep him alive; he did not want to atrophy and die; not yet, he didn't.

Smith was 58 years old, and his right knee was causing him severe problems. They told him it was transient meningitis. It caused him a lot of pain, and he knew it wasn't getting any better. During his time in the hole, Smith put his right leg up on the waist-high sink, then down, then up again. He did that with each leg, 200 times a day. He called them "sink-ups."

He also did sit-ups, 50 at a time. Four times a day. To keep his mid-section strong.

The books and thick transcripts from previous proceedings served a purpose in his gym. On the first day, Smith put them on his blanket, all except the Bible, and tied them into a stork's baby pouch. Those books and manuscripts weighed approximately 30 pounds. He used that homemade bag to do curls, one arm at a time. He also did chin-up pulls and back pulls with his makeshift weight. It was better than nothing. In fact, it was a pretty good routine under the circumstances. If only he had a little more air in that cell.

Every day, Smith marched in place—faster and faster—to keep his heart in shape. Every day he would get his pained knee higher and higher. If he was going to be put to death, he wasn't going to go without a fight.

The guards down the hall could hear him in his cell, "One, two—one, two—one, two."

★ ★ ★

July 1986.

Sometime after Smith was sentenced to death, maybe two months, I got a mysterious call. The voice was that of a young male.

"Mr. Costopoulos?" the caller asked, distraught.

"Yes," I answered.

"Is this Mr. Costopoulos?"

"Yes."

"Sir . . . I followed the Smith trial. Maybe I should have called you before, but . . . I'm . . . I'm in a difficult position. My conscience. I'm a clerk with the Superior Court of Pennsylvania. Are you still there, Mr. Costopoulos?"

"Yes, I'm still here. Please continue," I answered very politely.

"I . . . I don't want to get involved. I haven't been out of law school that long and . . . "

"I understand," I said in a confidential tone, wanting to hear more. "I don't need your name."

"Well, the witness, Raymond Martray, was out of Fayette County."

"Right."

"Check him out. Check his record out. He got a deal."

"He what?!"

"He was taken care of."

"Where should I look?"

"Check the records."

"Out of Fayette County?"

"And the Superior Court."

The caller quickly hung up. I sat in deep thought. I then buzzed Nick.

★ ★ ★

September 1986.

Attorney General LeRoy Zimmerman had called a state-wide news conference. At the bottom of the white, winding marble steps on the ground floor of Pennsylvania's ornate state capitol building a cadre of reporters waited. The Italian marble staircase was modeled after the one in the Opera House of Paris and is a perfect setting for news conferences. Rows of metal chairs were set up for the capitol newsroom reporters, who included television, radio, and newspaper correspondents.

Pennsylvania's capitol is a magnificent architectural icon that commands a hill overlooking the Susquehanna River. It is strikingly similar in appearance to the nation's capitol in Washington, D.C. Whether you are seeing the state capitol for the first time or the hundredth, you are bound to be impressed. This Italian Renaissance structure, built in the early 1900s for $10 million, couldn't be matched today at any cost. Greco-Roman statues of men, women, and children flank the enormous bronze doorways representing family, work, and brotherhood.

The building itself covers more than three acres of ground and its one-half-mile circumference holds over 600 rooms, which include the Pennsylvania Supreme Court with its stained-glass dome. The recessed arches of the rotunda hold wonderful paintings by Pennsylvania artist Edwin Austin Abbey. They commemorate the spiritual, intellectual, and economic advances of the Commonwealth.

Visitors are welcomed at all of the buildings in the Capitol Complex. To make the most of your visit, you might like to pick up the explanatory literature at the capitol guide desk.

Roy Zimmerman was a master politician who made it in his hometown of Harrisburg, and the local media loved him. He was Pennsylvania's first elected attorney general with an eye toward becoming Pennsylvania's next governor. Everybody in Harrisburg would have loved that, including me.

This press conference, however, was no big deal. It started out without fanfare, and was a simple statement from the attorney general himself that he was adding more firepower to the ongoing drug war that had been declared by all law enforcement agencies at all levels of government. Zimmerman was asking the legislature for a series of stiff sentencing guidelines for anyone arrested for selling drugs to children or within designated school zones.

The questions from the media floor were routine enough, but then the general got stung.

Sandy Sterobin, KYW's radio reporter from Philadelphia, was lying in wait. Sandy was an aggressive reporter in his early thirties, and he had his notepad poised. He confronted Roy at that news conference while the cameras were still rolling and all "mikes" were on, "General Zimmerman," Sandy said in a strong tone, "are you aware that one of your top aides is using and distributing cocaine?"

"No," Roy answered, shocked.

Sterobin said he had confirmation from six sources.

Roy tried to handle the embarrassing allegation, but he had been nailed hard, and he fell against the ropes hoping for the bell to ring. The attorney general, flailing, said he would pursue it vigorously and had every intention of getting to the bottom of it immediately.

Three days later, Rick Guida—who had just been promoted and put in charge of all state criminal prosecutions, as well as the in-house drug testing in the attorney general's office—resigned after acknowledging that *he* was the subject of an investigation for possible cocaine use.

"Look at this," Nick said, and handed me the morning newspaper the minute I walked into our office.

"Let me get a cup of coffee first, will you?"

"No," Nick insisted, "read this."

Guida's picture was on the front page under the headline ZIMMER-MAN AIDE RESIGNS, ADMITS COCAINE INQUIRY, and Nick watched me while I sat at my desk and read the article with total concentration.

HARRISBURG – The official in charge of all criminal investigations resigned yesterday after acknowledging that he was the subject of an investigation for possible cocaine use.

Executive Deputy Attorney General Richard L. Guida, 39, who was recently appointed to head the Criminal Law Division, including the Bureau of Narcotic Investigations and Drug Control, said in a letter to Attorney General LeRoy S. Zimmerman that he does not use cocaine.

Guida wrote that he had submitted to a urinalysis at Harrisburg Hospital on Tuesday and that the results had turned up no evidence of cocaine use. "The results of that test clearly show that I do not use cocaine," Guida said.

"Unfortunately, the position of director of criminal law requires not only the confidence, but the trust, of the employees of the Criminal Law Division," he said. "Given the allegation in question, and my inability to defend against it, it is now impossible for me to fulfill my function as director of the Criminal Law Division."

The article mentioned that the most publicized investigation in Guida's career came as the chief prosecutor in the Susan Reinert murder case, which prompted one of the largest investigations in Pennsylvania's history, and that he had successfully prosecuted Jay C. Smith.

"It is unfortunate," Guida lamented, "that anyone who attempts to work in the public arena for proper motives is subject to this type of speculation."

"Okay, Nick, I read it," I said, throwing the paper down on my desk with mixed emotions.

"What do you think?" Nick asked, grinning.

"I . . . I don't know, Nick. I feel sorry for him."

"You're nuts. After how he treated you during the Smith trial. After how he *tried* the Smith case. Four months ago he put a guy to death that's innocent . . . and you feel *sorry* for him!"

"I know . . . I know," I said, irritated, interrupting Nick. "But this is different . . . this isn't related to that."

"Don't bet on it."

"Come on, Nick."

"Okay, okay."

"All I'm saying is I feel bad for him . . . anonymous sources for Christ's sake . . . I met his parents . . . I worked for Roy Zimmerman . . . I've known Rick Guida . . . "

"I know," Nick said, now interrupting me. "Fourteen years you've known him . . . you started your careers together . . . you two, and Rich Lewis; and now Lewis is the District Attorney of Dauphin County; and Roy Zimmerman is the Attorney General of Pennsylvania. You've told me that a thousand times . . . and I'm telling you, Bill, he tried to fuck you in the Smith case with that Balshy testimony, and I'm still not convinced *that's* over."

I thought about what Nick said. He was making a lot of sense. I wasn't sure what to think.

"Has anybody heard from Balshy?" I asked.

"Nobody, not a word."

"How are you making out with that Martray business?"

"I've got enough to show that Martray lied under oath . . . no deal, huh, no favorable consideration . . . that lying son-of-a-bitch."

"And you say Guida and Holtz knew it?"

"Knew it?! . . . I know you're a great trial lawyer, Bill, but sometimes I think you're naive. They not only knew it, they not only got him out of prison in exchange for his testimony, but they did it *illegally!*"

★ ★ ★

November 1986.

Within two months of Rick Guida's resignation, an in-house investigation cleared him of alleged drug use and distribution.

An exhaustive effort by the state attorney general's office where Guida worked found no evidence that he had used cocaine or any other drug.

"We believe there are no further leads to pursue and no basis for action by the attorney general," Deputy Attorney General Thomas G. Saylor, Jr. wrote to the Pennsylvania State Police. "We are, therefore, closing this matter."

Robert Gentzel, Zimmerman's spokesman, said he briefly talked to Guida by phone and reported that "Guida feels vindicated by the investigation's result."

Gentzel further told the press that about two dozen people were interviewed during the in-house probe and that the attorney general's investigation went further than an investigation of that type normally would.

In the meantime, Guida had disconnected the telephone at his Susquehanna Township home. He could not be reached for comment.

Murder Victim: Susan Reinert. *(AP/Wide World Photos)*

Susan Reinert's car at Host Inn parking lot, Harrisburg, PA. Her body was found nude and mutilated on June 25, 1979 in the car with the hatchback open. *(Philadelphia Daily News)*

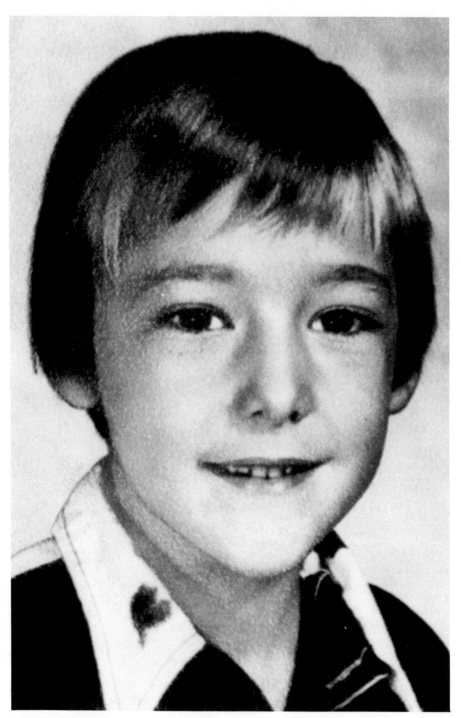

Murder Victim: Michael Reinert. *(AP/Wide World Photos)*

Murder Victim: Karen Reinert. *(AP/Wide World Photos)*

William Bradfield, former chairman of the English Department at Upper Merion High School, at the time of his arrest for the Reinert murders in April 1983. *(Stuart Leask, Allied Pix Service, Inc.)*

Jay Smith, former Principal of the Upper Merion High School, is escorted by state police into state police headquarters for processing in connection with the Reinert murders. *(AP LaserPhoto).*

Sgt. Joe VanNort, of the Pennsylvania State Police, was chief investigator of the Reinert murder case until late 1981. VanNort died of a heart attack on October 1, 1981 while at a police firing range. *(Pennsylvania State Police Yearbook, 1967).*

Trooper Jack Holtz worked the Reinert case full time for seven years; he was named chief investigator after VanNort's death. *(Stuart Leask, Allied Pix Service, Inc.)*

Judge William W. Lipsitt,
Dauphin County Senior Judge
who presided at the trial of
Jay C. Smith and at evidentiary hearings concerning
Raymond Martray and the
rubber lifters.

Exterior of Dauphin County Courthouse, Harrisburg, Pennsylvania.
(Timothy P. Keating)

Susan Myers leaves the Dauphin County Courthouse following her testimony at the Jay Smith murder trial, April 1986. A teacher at Upper Merion High School, she lived with William Bradfield for 20 years. *(AP LaserPhoto)*

Vincent Valaitis, an English teacher at Upper Merion High School, was a friend, associate, and neighbor of William Bradfield.
(UPI/Bettman)

Christopher Pappas, a substitute English teacher at Upper Merion High School, was part of Bradfield's circle of confidants.

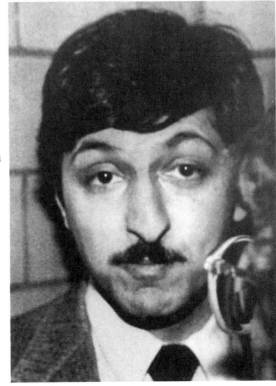

Wendy Zeigler, a former student who had a platonic relationship with Bradfield but wanted to marry him. *(Temple University Libraries Urban Archives)*

Raymond Martray, a former policeman convicted of operating a burglary ring in western Pennsylvania, testified that Smith confessed to him while he was a prison cellmate. *(AP LaserPhoto)*

Charles Montione, another inmate who testified that Jay Smith confessed to him. *(AP Laser/Photo)*

Proctor Nowell, an inmate who claimed that William Bradfield had confessed his guilt to him while in prison. Nowell was later convicted of murdering his girlfriend. He is shown accompanied by Trooper Louis DiSantis. *(Temple University Libraries Urban Archives)*

Trooper John Balshy, who testified at the Smith trial that he had found grains of sand on the feet of Susan Reinert during her autopsy.

Richard Guida, Chief Deputy Attorney General of Pennsylvania, was the main prosecutor in the Reinert murder case. He is shown with Joseph Wambaugh, author of a national best-seller about the murders, at a post-trial party in 1987.

Mark Hughes, who found the infamous box of damaging evidence in the home of Trooper Holtz. *(Stuart Leask, Allied Pix Service, Inc.)*

Jay Smith at his post-release press conference, September 1992. *(Stuart Leask, Allied Pix Service, Inc.)*

Jay Smith on the night of his release, September 18, 1992, along with his brother, William. *(Stuart Leask, Allied Pix Service, Inc.)*

William Bradfield in October 1993.

• 18 •

TREMORS

The trial of Jay Smith had lasted for five weeks. The post-trial effort of Jay Smith went on for seven, long, arduous years. I drained my law office financially and emotionally to an all-time low, but my entire staff—Bill Kollas, Dave Foster, Leslie Fields, Charles Rector, Allen Welch, Nick, Skip, all my secretaries—and my loved ones and friends hung in there with their patience and help all the way.

Nick had already filed 10 compelling reasons in support of a new trial and nine constitutional challenges in the hopes of vacating the death penalty. The appellate issues included, but were not limited to: the Bradfield hearsay issue; the allowing of the prosecution to retry the St. David's theft case, which included the physical reintroduction of a Brink's guard's uniform, phony identification cards, and eyewitness testimony; the allowing of testimony that Smith told Martray that he wanted two policemen killed; the allowing of testimony that Smith agreed to have Martray, the prosecution's informant, kill William Bradfield; the escape plans; the introduction of inflammatory and prejudicial tapes that had nothing to do with the deaths of Susan Reinert or her two children; the assertion by Guida that Balshy perjured himself during the trial and the implication that he was put up to it by the defense; and the impossibility of picking a fair and impartial jury in light of Bradfield's conviction in Dauphin County and the court's refusal to sequester the Smith jury.

Nick and I both agreed that our best issue for a new trial was the Bradfield hearsay. Nick's supporting brief in flowing legalese had been well researched, and the bottom line was that Bradfield's friends and lovers should not have been allowed to testify to what Bradfield had allegedly told them regarding Smith's past and murderous role, assuming that's what Bradfield had told them.

To me, the Bradfield hearsay issue was a sure winner, but there are no *sure* winners in the appellate courts, especially in a high-profile murder case where a woman and two children have been brutally murdered. I had to live with that gnawing anxiety for years.

Smith's appellate course would twist and turn and go in directions like no other appeal in American history. The first twist, resulting in an off-road, lengthy detour, started with the call from the anonymous clerk. That call meant filing more motions and more briefs, but only after days and days of additional testimony to bring out the truth.

It was no use calling the attorney general's office or the Pennsylvania State Police about Martray's deal or favorable consideration. They said there wasn't any, which meant we had to go looking for that suppressed evidence, and suppressed it was.

But we would have to do it. We had no choice. Jay Smith was on death row, and we believed he was innocent.

★ ★ ★

Smith heard the steel door to his living tomb creeping open. His one phone call a month, which he used to call our office, produced very little information. Nobody ever told him anything in there. It was not time for his weekly shower when he walked down the dark corridor in handcuffs and shackles with a towel wrapped around him. He had no idea what was going on.

"Mr. Smith, we're moving you to Huntingdon SCI. Your Phase I paperwork has been processed," a guard said nonchalantly as the leg irons and handcuffs were being strapped on.

"What month is this?" Jay asked politely.

"September."

"Thanks," Jay said.

Smith squinted when they took him out of the hole. He had been in that 6- by 10-foot holding cell for five months. He was being transferred to death row at Huntingdon, a two-hour drive north from Harrisburg.

Smith knew exactly what that meant. He had read a lot about the phases he would go through before execution.

There are three phases that a person with a death penalty sentence goes through in the state of Pennsylvania.

Phase I, pending appeals, is a holding cell where a person spends at least a year if the appellate process runs its normal course. Otherwise, the time is longer, meaning more solitary confinement. Isolation 24 hours a day. No windows. No sunlight. No air. The wardrobe on death row Phase I consists of two pairs of undershorts, one jumpsuit, and a towel.

Phase II is worse. It means all appeals have been exhausted and the Governor of Pennsylvania has signed the death warrant. The prisoner is taken to a small holding cell on the ground floor and stripped. In time a van picks up the doomed person and transports him to Rockview, the site of Pennsylvania's famous electric chair. The only nice thing about Phase II is that it only lasts about a day, long enough for the van to come get you.

Phase III is the hour-by-hour wait in a cell contiguous to the electric chair. It's here that the prisoner is given the last rites before being taken to the chair itself, strapped in, and electrocuted.

Jay Smith thought about life and death on his way to Huntingdon. Outside the leaves of fall were once again beginning their majestic turn, and soon the quiet snow would fall as another year ended. God's four seasons were very much like life itself, Jay thought, and wondered whether he would ever see spring again.

Normally, the ride north through Pennsylvania's rolling mountain ranges to Huntingdon would have been a pleasant break for Jay Smith, who had been in the hole for five months. He thought it was five months. He wasn't sure, but this ride to Phase I was a grim reminder of what was coming. Smith was in the back of the prison van, a two-seat cage, and his companion was a prison guard with a single-barrel shotgun resting menacingly on his lap.

"Do you want to hear a quote from a book I read?" Smith asked the guard, to break up the silence.

"Sure," the guard said, smiling.

"In addition to shaving him, they had put diapers on him. The surge of electricity would convulse his body, would wrench his every muscle, including the sphincter muscles that would empty his bowels. The disposable diapers peeked above his hips, forcing a smile at the ludicrous situation in which he found himself. A grown man, diapered, shaved, stripped of his dignity in preparation for his killing. In order to kill him, the state was transforming him to an expendable infant, bald and diapered. A disposable man in disposable diapers."

"Shut-up," the guard said angrily, interrupting Smith.

★ ★ ★

The official publication date for *Echoes in the Darkness* was February 23, 1987, but Guida and Holtz couldn't wait. Through a connection that Guida had, he obtained the galley proofs, and by the time the book hit the stores in hardback, the two of them had already read *their* story twice. Guida and Holtz were very pleased. They liked how Joe Wambaugh described them and loved their heroic roles. Guida told everybody that Wambaugh's descriptions of the people in the book were flawless. Holtz agreed that his description as an Adonis was also flawless.

Echoes in the Darkness, in true Wambaugh style, became an immediate best-seller. It was on the *New York Times* best-seller list for weeks.

I read Joe Wambaugh's book. He is a great writer.

I have been asked time and time again whether the book accurately reflects what happened. I believe the book accurately reflects Wambaugh's imagination based on what he was told.

I did like the way Joe Wambaugh treated me in the book. He said that I was known as a "magician." He said I had the "muscular good looks of the Greek islanders, tailored to fit his courtroom image." He said I had "a leonine head and a rugged jaw decorated with a salt and pepper Venetian goatee that made you think he would make a great Iago if he could act." He also said that I could.

Maybe Guida was right about Wambaugh's "flawless" descriptions.

Jay Smith also read *Echoes in the Darkness*, and he had a different opinion about Joseph Wambaugh's descriptions. So different that while on death row, he wrote in tiny but legible cursive, a 21-page complaint suing Wambaugh and his publishers in the Court of Common Pleas of Huntingdon County for everything from libel, to slander, to outright fraud.

Smith was suing the mogul himself and one of the biggest publishers in the industry, from death row.

Smith resented Wambaugh's treatment and description of him. Maintaining his innocence throughout the complaint, Smith challenged Wambaugh's assertion that "He frequented Plato's Retreat, a notorious night club and brothel catering to sexual perversions, including mate swapping, group sex, sodomy, frottage, etc."

Smith challenged Wambaugh's assertion that "he had killed a pair of Dobermans that were found months earlier with their sex organs mutilated."

That "a tipster told of seeing Jay Smith kill cats by dousing them with nitric acid and driving their bodies towards Valley Forge Park."

That "a janitor saw him strolling out of his office on the way to the lavatory in his underwear."

That "he had shit on the corridor floors, making piles of guano for the janitor."

That "at night he was a sadist who indulged in porno, drugs, and weapons."

That "he had incestuous relations with his daughter."

That "according to a letter, in the hands of the local police, he was said to have induced cancer in his wife by putting toxic substances in her food."

That "Jay Smith admitted he killed a couple of people in King of Prussia, probably prostitutes."

That "he chopped up some bodies and put them in trash cans around the school."

That "he had demonic powers, owned a devil's costume and some weird dildos, and must be some special kind of party animal."

Jay Smith's lawsuit demanded injunctive relief, compensatory damages, and punitive damages. Smith's motion to plead gave Joe Wambaugh and his publishers 20 days to get their high-powered, mega-firm lawyers to answer his complaint; otherwise he was going to enter a default judgment against all of them, and they could lose "their money or property or other rights important to them."

I read Jay Smith's lawsuit against Wambaugh, William Morrow Publishing, and Bantam Books. Even the local rules of procedure were complied with by Smith. His lawsuit would have scared the hell out of me.

Jay Smith had style. That's what I loved about him. Maybe the state was going to put him to death, but he didn't want his reputation ruined in the meantime. He wanted to die with a good reputation, even though he was living in a concrete tomb, by himself, with no one to talk to.

★ ★ ★

I had filed our post-trial motions in a timely manner. They were argued before the Dauphin County Court on November 26, 1986. All of the Dauphin County judges sat for the oral argument in the very courtroom where Smith had been tried and sentenced to death. This time, however, though open to the public, Courtroom 1 was almost empty. It was eerie arguing for Smith's life before five black-robed jurists sitting high above me.

No jury.

No media.

No authors.

No onlookers.

No Smith.

Not even Guida was there because he had resigned from the attorney general's office the month before.

As expected, in the months that followed, Judge Lipsitt refused to grant Jay Smith a new trial. The judge wrote his own 17-page opinion refusing to admit he had made a mistake with the Bradfield hearsay, refusing to reverse himself, refusing every argument we made.

Judge John C. Dowling, however, a fellow jurist of Lipsitt's for 20 years, refused to go along with the lower court. Dowling was considered a hanging judge in Dauphin County and had earned the reputation of being the toughest sentencing judge on the bench. He was known throughout the state as "Blackjack Dowling."

At the time, Judge Dowling was 65 years old. Five years before that, there had been a 10,000-meter run, known as the Kipona Run, over Labor Day weekend in downtown Harrisburg. I had trained hard for that race and I ran it somewhere in the middle of the pack. With 100 yards to the finish line, Judge Dowling passed me like I was standing still. It was his 60th birthday.

I really admired John Dowling.

Outside the courtroom, he was one of my favorite people.

For 15 years, however, I did what I could to stay out of his courtroom, because of his sentencing record. Dowling admitted that he was a tough sentencing judge. He believed that tough criminals should be dealt with harshly, and some should get death.

But before Dowling passed sentence, he gave the accused a fair trial. He believed in a fair trial for everybody; and that included Jay Smith.

Dowling sent a tremor through the halls of the attorney general's office and the Pennsylvania State Police, and through the heart of Rick Guida and Jack Holtz, when he wrote in the Smith case:

> I dissent for the reason that the trial court admitted evidence which, though of some relevancy, was outweighed by its overwhelming prejudicial nature.
> How could the jury who had heard from various persons, quoting Bradfield, that "Smith killed that goddamn woman" . . . "I took the kids and

gave them to Smith" . . . "I am afraid this is the night Smith is going to kill Susan Reinert" . . . "I followed him. He circled her house 14 times" . . . "He told me he took the kids and gave them to Smith," do the legal gymnastics necessary to put these statements in their proper perspective?

Whoever was directly involved in these dastardly crimes should suffer the extreme penalty, and it may well have been Jay Smith. However, in convicting him the jury should only consider legally admissible evidence.

While no trial can be expected to be perfect, the highest standards should be observed and the utmost caution taken when one is on trial for his life.

Since it has not been established to my satisfaction that the evidence was admissible, I am constrained to agree with the defense that a new trial is in order.

Coming from "Blackjack Dowling," this opinion was a big win for the defense. It would not be the last.

· 19 ·

HOLLYWOOD

Guida got the call he was waiting for, six months after he resigned from the attorney general's office. He was told that he would be appearing on NBC's *Today Show* with Joseph Wambaugh for the purpose of promoting *Echoes in the Darkness*. Guida met Wambaugh at the Omni Berkshire in Manhattan at about 4 p.m. on March 19, 1987. Later that evening they had a candlelight dinner with Wambaugh's editor and her husband.

Guida had learned, the week before, that Wambaugh had already completed a screenplay for New World Television, a production company, to produce a two-part mini-series to be aired some time in the fall of 1987. Filming was to take place in Toronto, Canada, that summer. Casting for the major roles had already begun.

Early the next morning, a sleek, polished, black limousine picked up Wambaugh and Guida in front of the Omni to take them to the NBC studio. After coffee and donuts and casual conversation with some of NBC's personnel, Guida was taken to the makeup room for some finishing touches.

The Today Show and their joint promotional effort for *Echoes in the Darkness* went extremely well.

Within weeks after that national appearance in New York, Rick Guida and Jack Holtz were sent copies of Joe Wambaugh's screenplay for New World Television, and they were asked to read the material for accuracy. Guida and Holtz each read the screenplay once privately and then together at Guida's home, page by page, so they wouldn't miss anything. There were changes Guida and Holtz thought should be made and Wambaugh agreed to almost all of them.

Joe Wambaugh also asked Guida to contact various people who were to be depicted in the CBS movie to sign "character depiction waivers" (releases provided by New World Television), but Wambaugh and Guida agreed that such releases really weren't necessary, because the actions of most of the characters depicted were a matter of public record. The few people Guida did call about the "character depiction waivers" signed immediately and willingly.

Just as Guida was impressed with Wambaugh's "flawless descriptions" in his book, he boasted that Wambaugh had a unique talent in casting the central figures. The fact that the young and handsome Treat Williams was going to play Guida, and that Gary Cole, who had starred in *Fatal Vision,* was going to play Jack Holtz may have had something to do with it.

155

Guida and Holtz regretted the decision by Glenn Jordan, the director of *Echoes in the Darkness*, not to have any of the major characters meet and talk with the real people they were portraying.

Then Guida and Holtz got their second showbiz setback. The two of them had originally been scheduled to be on-site technical advisors for the movie. But after they had gone out and bought their sunglasses and directors' chairs, Joe called and told them that Glenn Jordan was killing that idea, too.

Guida and Holtz were heartsick. That damn Glenn Jordan. They had been going around telling everybody they were going to be movie consultants, and now they couldn't even do that. Instead, the attorney general's office and the Pennsylvania State Police sent other representatives from their departments to help in the production.

Guida would not give up so easily, however, and he called his travel agent and bought a ticket to Toronto without anybody's authorization. He decided that he would never again be blessed with such an opportunity. He was going whether Glenn Jordan wanted him there or not.

Jack Holtz called Joe Wambaugh's home in California to make sure it was okay for him to simply show up. He planned to go with Guida, but when Holtz failed to reach Wambaugh, he decided not to go. Wambaugh was making himself scarce when it came to Guida and Holtz.

But Rick Guida would find him.

★ ★ ★

March 1987.

Throughout the nation, the buying public was grabbing *Echoes in the Darkness* off the bookshelves for the book depicted Jay Smith as a psychotic, deranged, kinky, and calculating murderer.

Guida was wining and dining in New York with Wambaugh, promoting his book, proofreading his screenplay, and working his way into a cameo appearance in the upcoming film shoot.

Jack Holtz was depressed that the director of the movie would not allow him to be an on-site consultant, but he got over his depression quickly with his new red Porsche and recently acquired vacation home in Nags Head, North Carolina.

And I was stuck in the smallest courtroom in Dauphin County—Courtroom 6—with Nick, with Skip, with Jay Smith fighting for his life, calling witness after witness to surface Martray's deal—the deal Martray and Guida and Holtz had withheld during the trial. Our position was that the deal was *intentionally withheld*, that it was prosecutorial misconduct, and that Jay Smith should be given a new trial.

Deputy Attorney General Robert Graci came to court with his superior, Paul Yatron, a middle-aged veteran administrator and former district attorney from a northern, rural Pennsylvania county. They had plenty of backup staff with them. These guys always had a show of strength, with or without a jury, to remind Judge Lipsitt that they were still the highest law enforcement agency in the Commonwealth. They were still the attorney general's office. My first encounter with Graci was on March 3, 1987.

Bob Graci was a short, feisty, up-and-coming pain in the ass. From thereon out, Graci was going to quarterback the Commonwealth's position in the Smith case. He had been handpicked by the newly elected attorney general, Ernest Preate, to do just that because of Graci's past experience on the playing field. Graci was not a big playmaker or a crowd-pleaser like Guida, but he was the most persistent, plodding guy I ever dealt with in the courtroom.

He looked a lot like Nick, with his thick, black hair combed neatly to the side and his meticulously trimmed beard, which gave them both the look of young, learned scholars. In the courtroom, they stuck to dark, two-piece, pin-striped suits. Graci could have passed for Nick's older brother, but they never got close to each other.

"How . . . uh, how long is this hearing going to take, Mr. Costopoulos?" Judge Lipsitt asked me in chambers.

"My best guess, Your Honor, is three or four days," I answered respectfully.

"Darn," he said, shaking his head, obviously getting sick of this case.

"Yes, Your Honor."

Judge Lipsitt was back on the bench; no jury; a curious media following; and a new, fiery, deputy attorney general that drove me crazy with his objections and relentless personal barbs.

Within hours of testimony on that day of the hearing, in Courtroom 6 in the Dauphin County Courthouse, we convinced everybody in the stadium that we weren't fooling around—everybody, that is, except Lipsitt. Our first big witness to prove Martray lied when he had said "no deals, no favorable consideration," and to attest that Guida and Holtz knew Martray was lying, was Martray's lawyer, Anthony S. Dedola, Jr.

He was out of Fayette County, Pennsylvania, where he had practiced law since he was admitted to the Bar in 1979. Fayette County is where Martray was from—where he was sentenced by two tough sentencing judges for masterminding a burglary ring, while he was a police officer in that county, and for committing perjury in the presence of the Fayette County jury.

Dedola looked like a young Greg Lougannis in his prime. He was a sole practitioner, with a general practice of law, and he just wanted to do the right thing—to tell the truth. He had no intentions of covering up for anybody. Not the police. Not Martray.

Martray had been sentenced to three and a half to seven years for the perjury conviction by Judge Cicchetti in Fayette County. He got four to eight years for the burglary convictions from Judge Adams. Those sentences were to run *consecutively*, which meant he got a total of seven and a half to 15 years, commencing March 20, 1979. They don't fool around in Fayette

County with police officers who burglarize the citizenry they were sworn to protect or with convicted perjurers.

And when Martray's first lawyer had asked for bail, pending appeals to the Superior Court of Pennsylvania, both sentencing judges had said no.

My questioning of Mr. Dedola, in front of Judge Lipsitt, was to create a record for the appellate courts. I came right to the point. His answers were crystal clear.

> Q. Mr. Dedola, you were court-appointed to represent Mr. Martray?
> A. Yes.
> Q. He had already been convicted of the burglary counts when you were asked to represent him?
> A. Yes. He had pled guilty to the burglary counts.
> Q. Had he already been convicted of the perjury counts by a jury in Fayette County?
> A. Yes.
> Q. So, it's not as though you tried the case before the jury or you entered the pleas on his behalf?
> A. Right. Both were post-conviction petitions that I was asked to see him through.

That meant Martray's direct appeals were either waived or exhausted. That meant that Dedola's appointment was for a last-ditch effort—known as a PCHA, which is a post-conviction, post-appeal effort—and bail isn't even *legal* pending PCHAs.

Martray had been in jail since March 20, 1979. Dedola testified that he learned Martray was "cooperating" with the state police in the case involving Jay Smith, and that Jack Holtz wanted to help Martray get out of jail.

> Q. Who wanted Ray out?
> A. Basically, Jack Holtz. He was the state trooper involved, and the one I talked with most of the time.

Yes, Dedola also had some contact with the attorney general's office, specifically with one Paul Tressler. The attorney general's office was also interested in Martray's perjury conviction because, as long as that conviction was on the record, Martray was an *incompetent* witness. He could not testify in a courtroom ever again.

Yes, Dedola said the state police and the attorney general's office wanted Martray out of jail. They felt he would be more effective if he was out, and they asked Dedola if he would petition the court for bond.

> Q. Who made the request?
> A. Again, I believe it was Jack Holtz. He was the one I dealt with throughout.

So Dedola, according to his testimony, with two district attorneys from Fayette County and Jack Holtz, went to the sentencing judges to see if they would let Martray out on bail. Both sentencing judges from Fayette County said no.

Q. Judge Adams said no?
A. Correct.
Q. Judge Cicchetti said no?
A. Correct.
Q. Denied?
A. Equally adamant.
Q. They did not want Martray out pending the PCHA?
A. Right.

Then Dedola's testimony got *real* interesting. According to Dedola, he was instructed—not asked, *instructed*—by either Holtz or Paul Tressler to prepare a petition for bail for the Superior Court of Pennsylvania. Dedola thought that was a little unusual, but he did it. I would have done the same thing on behalf of a client who was hopelessly lost in the prison system and would have asked no questions.

Q. Continue.
A. Trooper Holtz asked me if I would go down to the superior court with them that day because they had made arrangements for bond for Mr. Martray.
Q. Who told you that the arrangements were already made to bail out Raymond Martray?
A. Jack Holtz.
Q. Did you have anything to do with the arrangements that were made with the superior court?
A. No.

Dedola testified that Jack Holtz and Lou DiSantis had picked him up in an unmarked state police car. It was the Thursday before Easter, Holy Thursday. Dedola specifically remembered that they wanted to get Ray out for Easter, so he could be with his family. Martray apparently cooperated with them a good bit, according to Dedola, and they wanted to do this favor for him. They picked up Dedola and took him to the superior court in downtown Pittsburgh.

Judge Lipsitt was paying close attention to Dedola, who was testifying about maneuverings in the superior court. Graci and Yatron sat at their table, starring straight ahead, knowing the truth was about to come out. There was no stopping it now, and they knew it.

According to Dedola, Holtz and DiSantis took him up to the eighth floor of the City-County Building in downtown Pittsburgh. In a conference room, the three of them met with one of the superior court judges who explained that *he* couldn't sign the prepared order to release Martray. He obviously knew why they were there, however, because he talked about the Smith investigation. Dedola believed that the superior court judge was Judge Hester, but he wasn't sure.

So from the City-County Building in Pittsburgh, the three of them immediately went to Judge Popovich's office in McKeesport, Pennsylvania. Judge Popovich was the motions court judge, and apparently everything was prearranged with him.

Q. Did Holtz and DiSantis drive you?
A. Yes.
Q. You went into Judge Popovich's chambers?
A. Yes.
Q. What happened there?
A. Not much happened then. We went in to see the judge and it was all three of us. Myself, Jack Holtz, and Lou DiSantis. He didn't say much. He reviewed the petition, made sort of a funny remark about how I had the order phrased, and he signed it, and that was it. We were only in there for a matter of a few minutes.

Somebody higher up had made arrangements with the superior court to get Martray released on bail pending PCHA appeals, something unheard of, especially since the sentencing judges had said no. There were two bail orders signed by Judge Popovich: one was to release Martray on the burglary convictions until his PCHA appeal was exhausted; the other was to release him on his perjury conviction until his PCHA appeal was exhausted.

Martray was a very lucky man. He was released on bail by the superior court. He then beat his perjury conviction before the superior court on December 31, 1984. That win made him a competent witness against Jay Smith before the investigating grand jury on April 1, 1985, and a competent witness at Smith's trial a year later in April 1986.

Q. Now, Mr. Dedola, at some point in time did you on behalf of Ray Martray vacate his perjury conviction?
A. Right.
Q. You won before the superior court?
A. Right.
Q. Were there any congratulatory calls once the perjury conviction was vacated?
A. I can remember receiving a call from Jack Holtz congratulating me, and I'm not sure if Paul Tressler called me or not. I think he may have called to congratulate me.
Q. You know as Ray Martray's attorney that the Commonwealth did not appeal *that* order to the supreme court?

A. Right.

Martray's "luck" did not stop there. Though he lost his burglary appeal to the superior court on March 1, 1984, which meant he should have gone back to jail to serve out his four- to eight-year sentence, he never returned to the prison system. That's right, Martray owed the Commonwealth hard time in a state correctional institution, but he walked away from it in exchange for his testimony.

As the testimony unfolded, exposing Martray's deal with the Commonwealth, the fury in my heart raged. I had been lied to for years. Due process for Jay Smith had become a travesty. The system had been abused.

★ ★ ★

Bob Graci may have been quarterbacking this hearing for the Commonwealth, but I don't believe that he was calling the plays. Instead of acknowledging Martray's *arrangement* with the Commonwealth and letting the supreme court deal with it, we were forced into three more days of hearings to prove that they were still withholding the truth in a death penalty case.

I didn't know how much more I could take.

On March 16, 1987, I was back in court, and this time I called an assistant district attorney from Fayette County to confirm Dedola's testimony. Assistant District Attorney Ralph C. Warman did exactly that.

On April 21, 1987, I was in court again, and this time I called Lou DiSantis and Jack Holtz back to back. To get the truth out of those two regarding Martray's deal was going to take some serious drilling.

DiSantis denied that *he* was the one who had gone to see Judge Adams and Judge Cicchetti on behalf of Martray to get him released. He could not deny, however, that he and Holtz drove Dedola to the superior court to get Martray out.

Q. How did you know where to take the defense attorney to get the bail application signed?
A. Jack told me he got a call to take Tony down.
Q. Did Jack tell you who he got the call from?
A. I don't remember who made the phone call, sir.

Of course, he didn't remember. Nor did he remember who made Martray's arrangement in exchange for his testimony. Maybe it was somebody who had something to do with the Democratic party, according to DiSantis, but DiSantis wasn't sure.

I didn't waste a whole lot of time with DiSantis. This was the third day in court for me, trying to get the truth out of those guys, and they were still stonewalling. Their credibility with me had run out a long time ago, a year ago to be exact, because one year before, in April, we had been in front of the Smith jury.

I called Jack Holtz. He looked tired. Maybe he was up all night reading Wambaugh's screenplay. I was tired of fooling around with him.

Q. Let's go right to the bail question, Mr. Holtz. You went into chambers in the Fayette County Court of Common Pleas, did you not?

A. I do not recall, sir.

Q. Do you ever recall going into a judge's chambers on behalf of Raymond Martray at the lower court level?

A. I could have. I could not have. I do not recall.

Now how's that for an answer from someone sworn to uphold the law?

He said his reason for picking Dedola up was "to transport him to Pittsburgh." He testified, "I transported Mr. Dedola to the superior court in Pittsburgh. I believe he was going to file some type of petition."

After a lot of cute answers from Holtz—Judge Lipsitt kept telling him to keep his voice up, and Graci kept objecting to everything I asked—I finally got him squirming, nervous, sweating on the witness stand. I wanted the Supreme Court of Pennsylvania to know who made the arrangement with the Superior Court of Pennsylvania to get Martray out of jail.

Q. Who is Fred Lebder?

A. I believe he is the Democratic chairman for Fayette County.

Q. He may have called you and requested that you and DiSantis drive the defense attorney to get the bail petitions signed?

A. Yes, sir.

Q. If the Democratic chairman of my county would call you and ask you to drive me to the superior court for some bail pieces, would you do that?

Graci: Objection.

Costopoulos: I will withdraw the question.

I couldn't help it. I liked poking Holtz in the ass. I was now convinced that Smith had been right all along about him—Jack Holtz was holding out on us, and he was not to be trusted.

Q. When did you have dinner with Lebder?

A. I had dinner with him several times.

Q. Did it have anything to do with this investigation?

A. The purpose for the dinner?

Q. Yes.

A. No, sir.

Q. Did you talk about this investigation?

A. Oh, yes.

Q. Did you talk about Raymond Martray?
A. We could have. I remember most of the conversation dealt with the children.
Q. Did you talk about wanting Raymond Martray out?
A. Quite possibly.
Q. Did you want Martray out?
A. Yes, I did.

Either Mr. Lebder made the arrangements with the superior court to get Martray out of jail at Holtz's request, or somebody from the attorney general's office made the arrangements with the superior court to get Martray out of jail. It would have taken that kind of "pull," because guys like Martray don't get out on bail pending PCHA appeals, not by a superior court judge they don't.

But I didn't care whether Martray got his walking papers arranged by a Democratic chairman or by the Office of the Attorney General. I didn't even care if it was improper to contact a superior court judge to do it, assuming it was, which I believed. What I *did* care about were the lengths that the prosecution had gone to for Martray in exchange for his testimony.

Because I was entitled to that information as a matter of law, and my having been denied it gave Smith grounds for a new trial.

Because if I had had that information when Smith was tried, it would have blown Martray's credibility to hell and back; and Martray's "confession from Smith" would have been exposed for what it was—an arranged, bargained-for lie.

Q. Trooper Holtz, you were working this case full time and he was an important Commonwealth witness?
A. He was a—he was not a Commonwealth witness at that time, no, sir.
Q. He eventually became one?
A. Became one in 1985.
Q. You got him out for the purpose of determining whether he would become one?
Graci: Objection.
The Court: Overruled. Let's hear what he has to say.
A. I was glad that he got out. I was glad that he eventually became a Commonwealth witness.
Q. As a matter of fact, did you call up Dedola and congratulate Dedola when Martray's perjury conviction was vacated?
A. It is possible that I did.

When Holtz finally got off the witness stand this time, he was not smiling. We exchanged glances. There was no lost love between us, none whatsoever.

★ ★ ★

That afternoon, Graci called Rick Guida as a witness. Guida had gone to the attorney general's office from private practice to oversee this prosecution. He had lived with this case, day in and day out, for years. He knew everything about the case, every known fact, and for as long as I had known him, at that time 15 years, he had never called a witness without knowing everything about that witness.

No, Guida testified, *he* had nothing to do with Mr. Martray getting bail.

Yes, Guida testified, he was aware of Mr. Martray's perjury appeal.

Yes, Guida testified, he was aware that Martray won his perjury appeal because that made him a competent witness.

No, Guida testified, he wasn't aware of Mr. Martray's appeal from his burglary convictions.

No, Guida testified, he didn't know that Martray's burglary convictions were upheld on March 1, 1984, that Martray was to go back to jail.

No, Guida testified, he didn't know that Martray was a free man, when he should have been in jail during Smith's trial.

Q. During your closing argument, Mr. Guida, in the trial of Mr. Smith, you stated and I quote:

> What did Martray get? Nothing. Martray served his time. He got out on schedule, and he is on parole. What did the Commonwealth do? Well, why would Ray Martray walk into the courtroom and try to sentence a man to death? Because it is fun? Because it is fun to get in front of all these people? He didn't get a single thing.

A. Correct.

★ ★ ★

On May 15, 1987, I was back in court again, this time for the final testimony in what would be known as "the Martray hearings."

Q. Please state your full name for the record.
A. Allen James Beegle.
Q. How old are you?
A. I will be 55 in July.

Beegle had known Raymond Martray for 13 or 14 years. He was very good friends with Martray's father, Frank. Beegle lived approximately half a mile from Frank Martray's residence.

No, he did not know Jay Smith; never met him; never talked to him; owed him nothing.

Q. Mr. Beegle, did you ever have an opportunity to talk to Raymond Martray once he was released on bail in 1982?

A. Yes, I talked to him up until about four or five months ago.

Q. When he got out on bail in '82, where did you see him and where did you talk to him?

A. Up at his dad's place.

Q. Which was about half a mile from where you lived?

A. Right.

Q. What did he tell you about how he got out and what arrangements he had with the police, if any?

Graci: Objection!

A. He . . .

The Court: Well, that's the heart of this proceeding, Mr. Graci.

Q. The question, Mr. Beegle, is you already testified that you knew Raymond Martray, you knew the family, and you had a conversation with Raymond Martray after he got out on bail in '82, is that right?

A. Right.

Q. When you talked to him, did he say anything to you about what deal he had with the police, what arrangements . . .

Graci: Objection. Now he is leading the witness, Your Honor, and that's completely improper. We have had a lot of leading through this hearing. This is clearly this man's witness, and he cannot lead his witness, and I ask that he move to another area.

The Court: He cannot lead a witness, and I think Mr. Costopoulos recognizes that.

Q. What did Martray tell you, Mr. Beegle?

A. We sat and talked at his dad's house or the place he was supposed to be living, which was . . .

The Court: You dropped your voice and unfortunately you are projecting your voice away from me.

A. We started bullshitting at his dad's place or at the garage where he was supposed to be living. They have a little apartment there, and we started talking because I knew Ray before, Ray Martray. I asked him how he got out of this and so on, and he said he had a deal going with the police and some other people in high places, that he wasn't going to pull anything, any more time that is. That if he gets what he needs, he will be right out.

Q. What?

A. He will be out.

Q. That he won't have to pull any more time?

A. Right.

Mr. Beegle brought the Commonwealth full circle. The Commonwealth got Martray out on bail by pulling strings with the Superior Court of Pennsylvania. The Commonwealth did not appeal when his perjury conviction was vacated. Martray had told Beegle that he had a deal with the police and some other people in high places, and that he wasn't going to pull any more time, *and he didn't.*

No deal for Ray Martray, huh? No favorable consideration for Ray Martray? He came up with a jailhouse confession because he had children of his own?

My ass. Maybe in Hollywood.

I couldn't wait to tell the Supreme Court of Pennsylvania what we now knew.

★ ★ ★

It was a beautiful sunny day in early June 1987, and Guida was elated to be there. Three major U.S. film productions were nearing completion in Toronto, Canada, and *Echoes in the Darkness* was one of them.

Lights!

Camera!

Action!

Rick rode over to the final location shoot with Glenn Jordan from the Four Seasons Hotel. This particular scene was in a small dry-cleaning establishment run by a middle-aged Greek immigrant who didn't speak very good English.

Outside the dry cleaners, a crowd of ethnic neighbors watched in awe as the large tractor-trailer rigs pulled in, parking at various angles, for the shoot. There was a make-up trailer, a wardrobe trailer, props, cameras, lights, catered food, and a portable electric generating system.

The setup, the filming, and the move to the next location took four hours. The scene itself, Guida picking up clothes at the dry cleaners, dressed in a plaid shirt and a pair of dark, pleated pants, would take six seconds of national air time, on camera, in focus. This was Guida's cameo appearance in a $10 million production.

Everybody was happy after the fourth take. Guida got to keep his wardrobe from the trailer. He was happy that Joe Wambaugh had talked Glenn Jordan into letting him do it.

Little did Guida know that *Echoes in the Darkness* was an unfinished story.

· 20 ·

THE HOURGLASS

I had heard Jay Smith sentenced to death 36 times in Courtroom 1 by a jury of his peers. I never talked about it, except to Jill, but I heard that verdict—"Death," "Death," "Death"—in a recurring dream. Every pronouncement in my dream got louder and louder, and the voices were coming from Hell, echoing in my head, with a blurred vision of Jay Smith crying out his innocence. And the dream always ended with high-voltage electricity going through my body, which would startle me awake.

In Pennsylvania, a defendant who is sentenced to death by a jury is once again sentenced to death by the trial judge after the post-trial motions are denied by the lower court. This formal sentencing usually takes months, if not years, after the jury has spoken. The jury had sentenced Jay Smith to death on April 30, 1986.

And now, September 8, 1987, I was back in Courtroom 1 with Jay Smith beside me for the formal imposition of sentence by Judge Lipsitt. The jury box to my right was empty. The media box to my left was empty. The back of the vast courtroom had a few curiosity seekers, mostly local media.

There was plenty of security.

Bob Graci was there for the Commonwealth.

Standing there, with Jay Smith to my immediate left about to be sentenced to death, I felt like I was also about to be sentenced to death. I felt that due process and fundamental fairness in our courtrooms had already been buried.

"Mr. Smith," Judge Lipsitt began from the bench with genuine concern in his voice, "do you have anything to say before I impose the sentence?"

"Yes, Your Honor," Jay Smith answered, with an obvious need to be heard.

"Certainly," Judge Lipsitt remarked politely, nodding his head for Smith to proceed.

"I know you have to sentence me, Your Honor, in accord with the jury's verdict, but I want you to know. I want Mr. Graci to know. I want everybody in this courtroom to know . . . in the world . . . that I had nothing to do with the death of Susan Reinert. I had nothing to do with the death of those two children. I did not kill them or harm them in any way." Jay Smith spoke, and his tone was so credible that it pained me.

"Objection, Your Honor!" Graci said loudly, interrupting Smith's remarks. "This is improper. This is utterly improper. The jury has spoken."

167

"Mr. Graci," Lipsitt said sternly, "Jay Smith has a right to say whatever he wants at this time."

"I just want my objection noted for the record, Your Honor," Graci responded, politely backing off.

"Go on, Mr. Smith."

"That's all, Your Honor."

"Mr. Costopoulos?"

"Nothing, Your Honor."

"Very well . . . in connection with the death of Susan Reinert, in accord with the jury's verdict, I direct that the sentence of death be carried out by electrocution.

"In connection with the . . . what are the children's names?"

"Michael and Karen," Graci said in a loud, clear voice.

"In connection with the death of Michael Reinert, in accord with the jury's verdict, I direct that the sentence of death be carried out by electrocution.

"In connection with the death of Karen Reinert, in accord with the jury's verdict, I direct that the sentence of death be carried out by electrocution.

"Anything else, Gentlemen?" Lipsitt asked in a judicial tone.

"That's it," Graci answered as he gathered up his papers.

I didn't even look over at Graci. I had nothing to say to him. I put my hand on Jay Smith's shoulder and told him what I felt. "Jay," I said, clearing my throat, "I'm sorry."

★ ★ ★

Five weeks later, I watched Jay Smith tried again, convicted again, and sentenced to death again, 36 *more* times, this time on national television over two nights.

The CBS mini-series *Echoes in the Darkness* was given a lot of promotional hype in the Harrisburg area. I read in the *TV Guide* that the handsome Treat Williams was playing Rick Guida; the enormously talented Gary Cole was playing Jack Holtz; Peter Coyote was playing William Bradfield; and Robert Loggia, one of my all-time favorite actors, was playing Jay Smith.

The *TV Guide* had in very small print that Chuck Samatos was playing me. I had to look for it to find it. I didn't know who in the hell he was, but I would just have to wait and see. I was hoping he was handsome, too, and articulate. Maybe he would have "the muscular good looks of the Greek islanders, tailored to fit his courtroom image." Maybe he would have "a leonine head and a rugged jaw decorated with a salt-and-pepper Venetian goatee that made you think he would make a great Iago if he could act."

According to the *New York Times* review, the public was going to see "probably the best film of this kind ever made for television . . . because the crimes involved indeed are horrendous, but the story is told more in sorrow than in anger, and with a distinct literary flare . . . a tribute to the gifted Joseph Wambaugh who adapted his own book for television."

I knew my mother would be watching it.

I knew my friends would be watching it all over the country. At least, I kept telling them to.

Because I didn't know what my role was going to be, or what I looked like, I hid at home with Jill, just in case there was a mistake.

Sunday night's segment detailed the background of the crimes, and the process offered a devastating portrayal of academia and its privileged, suffocating isolation. The true eccentricities of the characters were captured.

Coyote's portrayal of Bradfield was meticulous to a fault. I loved Loggia's acting and wrote him a letter to that effect, but it wasn't the Jay Smith I knew. Loggia was awfully strange in that scene where he was climbing the wall naked.

I was not portrayed at all on Sunday night. Neither was Guida, so I didn't feel so bad.

Guida showed up early Monday night as handsome as ever. Holtz was a hero, as was Guida, in true Wambaugh style. My character still hadn't made an entrance. Finally came the scene where Smith was being taken to court, and an actor playing me showed up with a briefcase. I went into immediate shock!

The guy was no Greek islander, not by a longshot. And he was certainly no orator; he could hardly speak English. The son-of-a-bitch was old enough to be my father.

I turned the TV off. I disconnected my phone. I didn't go to the office for two weeks. I vowed to get Smith a new trial, and his guilt or innocence had nothing to do with it.

The truth is I felt used.

★ ★ ★

Life went on at our law office. Personal injury cases, more homicide cases, big drug cases, small drug cases, routine criminal cases, domestic cases; but the Smith case hung over us like a dark cloud.

Not one week went by that something about Smith didn't come up. Every day, with rare exceptions, I would get a multi-page handwritten letter from him on death row. He would remind me about "Martray's lies," "Guida's deception," "Holtz's intentional and ongoing concealment of physical evidence that would demonstrate my innocence." Smith maintained in his letters a strong belief in "Americanism" but felt the criminal justice system had failed him miserably.

I agreed with him.

"My innocence," he wrote, "doesn't seem to matter anymore, not that it ever did. I don't want to be put to death for something I didn't do. I resent being confined like a leper in this tomb of hell, and if I am put to death, no one will care, for I will be forgotten in time. But the real tragedy of my execution will be the death of due process. My death will be like a cancerous tumor in the American justice system, because if it can happen to me, based on lies and fabrication at the hands of the Pennsylvania State Police and the attorney general's office, then it can happen to anyone."

Over the years, Smith sent me newspaper clippings, articles on forensic evidence, editorials on the Constitution, case law relevant to our appeals, and pamphlets on the death penalty and the electric chair.

Smith also sent carbon copies of his handwritten letters to Nick and to Skip. Sometimes Smith wrote directly to certain media representatives who were keeping a close watch on the developments in the case. He sent me carbon copies of the letters he had sent them.

Never, however, did he send a letter to me complaining of his failing health. He never gave any indication that he wasn't going to make it. I just didn't know how any man could live in a concrete tomb and keep going.

"I will hold on for as long as I can," he wrote. "I will fight to the bitter end. My innocence and my belief in you is my strength."

Then there was the "fan" mail we got. There wasn't much of *that*, but what little there was, represented a small segment of society that believed in Smith's innocence, and those writers usually prayed for us and urged us on.

The hate mail was also part of our "Smith diet," and there was plenty of *that*. Many of those letters were threatening, but I never took them seriously, because if I did I would live in perpetual fear, and I didn't want to do that.

Then there were letters from psychics who wrote me promising that *they* could find the kids. One needed Susan Reinert's ashes. One needed articles of the children's clothing. One needed to talk to Michael to find Karen, but he wrote that if he could talk to Karen, he would find Michael.

There were plenty of wackos out there!

One morning I got to my office before daylight, not unusual for me—I get up at 5 a.m., work out, and go—and there was a written message under the front door. It was printed neatly with a red magic marker. That was strange—in the way that everything else was strange in the Smith case.

First, it was delivered in the middle of the night. Second, the message was on the reverse side of a pornographic flyer. Third, it read, "If you want to know where the kids are, meet me tonight at the Nationwide Inn at 7 p.m. Don't be late."

The letter was signed "THE SLY FOX."

I called Skip at home. It was time to bring out the guns. It was time to go fox hunting.

For the past several days, the secretaries had been telling me about some "curly, redheaded, hobo-looking guy" who had been walking back and forth outside, across the street, looking into our office from behind a tree for hours.

"It sounds like a fox to me," Skip said, laughing, when I showed him the note on the day I got it.

"The son-of-a-bitch is nuts," I said, grinning, shaking my head.

"Yeah, who isn't in this case?" Skip remarked sarcastically.

"What are you going to do, Skip?"

"Well, apparently Josh Lock got one of these notes too."

"How do you know that?"

"Because Rick Guida called me wanting to know if we got one. He got one too."

"Guida?" I said, surprised.

"Yeah."

"So everybody is to meet tonight at 7:00 at the Nationwide Inn, and we aren't to be late?"

"You are not going," Skip said protectively.

"I wasn't planning on it," I said, laughing. "I live in the woods, Skip. I got bit in the ass by a fox one time."

"The guy could be planning to wipe out principal players in one shot; that's why he wants you guys together," Skip said, getting serious.

Skip always got serious when he thought danger was lurking. That's why he ran around with three guns on his person at all times. To me, he was a bit paranoid about everything, but I loved him for it.

"Call me if you need any help," I said, still joking.

"I won't need any help," Skip said with a wry grin, opening his coat to show me the two guns strapped to his upper body.

Leslie then came running into my office with tears in her eyes. Somebody had just killed her cat.

That afternoon at approximately 3:30, Skip pulled into the parking lot of the Nationwide Inn by himself. He walked through the lounge where the 7 o'clock meeting was to take place, looking for anything unusual, like a bag or a box that might contain a bomb. He checked under the tables. He then asked the bartender if he could look behind the bar, saying that it was official business. Then Skip went back to his car and waited, watching the only entrance to the lounge.

The debonair Charles Rector from my office was to show up later that afternoon. He would be a patron at the bar and watch for The Fox from that position. Skip watched Charlie walk in at exactly 4:10, right on time, in a full length cashmere coat, looking like one of Al Capone's boys.

At approximately 4:30, Skip spotted The Fox in his rearview mirror, sneaking from tree to tree along the riverbank, and then, just as quickly as he had appeared, The Fox vanished from sight.

Overhead, a Pennsylvania State Police helicopter made a pass.

By 5:30, Skip had seen three guys enter at different times. He recognized the heads, but not the bodies, of all three. They were Trooper Holtz and Trooper Lotwick and Rick Guida, and they were wearing so much body armor they had doubled their size. Not even a howitzer would have penetrated those guys.

At 6:45, Charlie was on his third soft drink at the bar. Holtz and Lotwick were also patrons at the bar, pretending not to know each other, or Charlie. Skip was in a booth, smoking his pipe. His free hand was on his guns. Guida was at a table, barely visible because of the smoke that surrounded him from the two packs of cigarettes he had just consumed.

Then The Fox walked in and sat at his own table.

Everybody converged on this lost soul, stood him up, turned him around, frisked him, and sat him back down. Then they all sat around him. Skip, Charlie, and the three fat guys, with Guida doing the talking.

"We got your note," Guida said like a tough guy.

"It looks like it," said The Fox, smiling politely.

"What is it you want?"

"I would like a soda."

"No, I mean, why did you call this meeting?"

"Well, I was hitchhiking in the New England states, and I went to a library to get warm. There I read a book about Reinert and the kids. You guys should read it. It's a good book. And then when I got to Philadelphia . . ."

"By hitchhiking?" Guida asked, bewildered.

"Yeah, that's how I travel. Anyhow, when I got to Philadelphia, I went to a library to get warm, and that's where I saw one of the kids."

"You did?" Guida asked.

"Yeah, it was Karen. I recognized her from her picture on the cover."

"You did?" Guida asked, incredulous.

"Right . . . but I didn't talk to her . . . but I did come here to tell you guys."

"Tell us what?" Guida asked.

"Check the library in Philadelphia."

"Didn't you guys check there?" Skip asked Holtz, laughing out loud, and Holtz became furious.

★ ★ ★

May 12, 1988.

The wheels of justice crept forward.

It had been over two years since Smith was convicted in Dauphin County. We had gone through the post-trial motions and arguments. We were delayed for months and months because of the Martray hearings. But finally, the day had come for me to argue Smith's case before the Pennsylvania Supreme Court.

The Pennsylvania Supreme Court is the highest court in our Commonwealth. It is the court of last resort in a death penalty case. Seven supreme jurists had the power vested in them by law to grant Smith a new trial and start the process over, or send his death warrants to the Governor of Pennsylvania.

The courtroom itself is breathtaking. It is in the dome of the capitol building, located in the east wing of the fourth floor. The solid mahogany fittings from Belize are the finest in the entire capitol. Below the stained glass dome by Van Ingen are four large chandeliers. In the center of each chandelier stands a small statue. The two Hebrew statues, Solomon and Moses, face the West, and the two Greek statues, Aristotle and Solon, face the East. The room itself is in the Greek Ionic style.

Sixteen panels by Violet Oakley, portraying the evolution of law through the ages, are displayed in this room of quiet dignity. The court crier orders absolute silence when the robed jurists make their grand entrance.

I was no stranger to the Supreme Court of Pennsylvania. I had argued before them in 1979, challenging the constitutionality of Pennsylvania's new Grand Jury Act. I had argued before them in 1984, challenging the constitutionality of Pennsylvania's new Drunk Driving Law. I had appeared before them time and time again seeking new trials in high-profile murder cases.

I lost some. I won some. I may have questioned their wisdom and judgment, but it would do no good. They were the Supreme Court of Pennsylvania.

The Supreme Court of Pennsylvania was my last hope. I had to believe in them.

Every seat in the courtroom was taken, and lawyers dressed in their finest were standing along the walls in the back. Twenty cases would be argued that day, and they too had waited ever so long for this chance.

The case of *Commonwealth v. Jay C. Smith*, however, would be argued first, and I was nervous and excited.

"Hear ye, hear ye, hear ye," the court crier announced. "All those having business before this Honorable Court, please rise."

The seven supreme court jurists—Justice Stout, Justice Zappala, Justice Flaherty, Chief Justice Nix, Justice Larsen, Justice McDermott, and Justice Papadakos—entered in their black robes and assumed the bench high above the courtroom floor.

The justices sat on the bench in the order in which they entered, with Chief Justice Nix in the middle.

When the Smith case was called, I walked directly to the podium. Graci went directly to the appellee's table, and Chief Justice Nix nodded to go ahead.

I had waited a long time for this moment. It was an opportunity to do something—for Jay Smith, for the system, and for myself. I felt the weight of the law on my shoulders, and the responsibility I carried in my heart.

The supreme courtroom may be a place of quiet dignity, but when the arguments start all hell breaks loose.

"May it please the court," I began in a rote voice. "My name is William Costopoulos, and I represent Jay Smith, who has been sentenced to death by a jury of his peers. I tried the case in the court below, in the Court of Common Pleas of Dauphin County, and the jury rendered its verdict on May 1, 1986, over two years ago."

"Jay Smith was the principal of the high school, and Susan Reinert was an English teacher?" Justice Nix asked.

"That's correct, Your Honor."

"Mr. Costopoulos," Justice Nix continued, "we have read the voluminous record. We are familiar with the facts. Please proceed with your legal arguments."

"Yes, Your Honor. I have set forth 10 reasons for a new trial in our brief, which is before you, and nine reasons to vacate the death penalty. I will restrict my argument to my first two issues for a new trial and submit the other eight on the brief itself."

"Thank you, Mr. Costopoulos," Justice Nix returned politely.

"I have been practicing law for 14 years. I've tried a lot of homicide cases. I have never tried a homicide case like this one where the testimony consisted primarily of hearsay, specifically, where a fellow schoolteacher by the name of Bradfield put Smith to death in that courtroom through the testimony of his lovers and friends."

"You're referring to the testimony of Vincent Valaitis, Chris Pappas, Sue Myers, and Wendy Zeigler?" Justice Zappala queried, with an obvious command of the facts.

"Primarily, Your Honor, yes."

"What were they allowed to testify to?" Zappala asked, very interested.

I was waiting for that question and I was ready. I had the quotes in front of me, but I knew them from memory. I knew the exact pages where they appeared in the record, just in case the court asked, because often they do.

"One witness, Your Honor, testified that Bradfield told him 'Smith killed that goddamn woman.' Vincent Valaitis testified that Bradfield told him that 'Smith was a screened hit man for the Mafia and wanted to kill a number of people including Susan Reinert,' that 'Smith knew how to take any ordinary household item and kill anyone with it and how to tape and immobilize a person very quickly.'"

"Very interesting," Justice Larsen interjected, and leaned slightly forward to hear more.

"Susan Myers testified that Bradfield told her that 'Smith had committed crimes of which he was guilty,' 'Bradfield said that Smith intended to kill Susan Reinert,' 'Bradfield said that Smith tended to kill on holidays.'

"Wendy Zeigler swore that Bradfield told her that 'Smith was mentally unstable,' that 'Smith intended to kill Susan Reinert and had a hit list that included Susan Myers.'

"Chris Pappas testified that Bradfield . . . "

"Mr. Costopoulos, are you telling this court that these witnesses were saying these things about Smith not from personal knowledge but because that's what Bradfield told these witnesses on previous occasions?" Justice Flaherty asked in an incredulous tone.

"That's exactly what I'm saying, Your Honor," I answered, getting excited, "and we don't even know whether Bradfield told these witnesses these things in the first place, but even if Bradfield did it would still be in-admissible."

"This is crazy," Justice Papadakos said. "What about Smith's right to con-front his accusers?"

"Exactly, Your Honor," I replied.

"How did that testimony get in?" Justice Flaherty asked, fascinated.

"The prosecutor told Judge Lipsitt that the attorney general's office re-searched it," I answered jokingly.

"Mr. Guida?" Justice McDermott asked, to clarify.

"Yes, Your Honor."

"Tell us about this Martray witness, Mr. Costopoulos," Justice Larsen asked.

"I will be happy to, Your Honor," I answered, looking directly at Justice Larsen. "At the preliminary hearing, under oath, Raymond Martray testi-fied he got no deal, that he was given no favorable consideration, none whatsoever."

"Where was the prosecutor and the trooper?"

"They were the ones that called him."

"Sitting right there."

"That's right."

"I personally asked the prosecutor, Your Honor, whether Martray had been given any deals. He told me no . . . no deals whatsoever . . . no favor-able consideration . . . nothing whatsoever. That's what he said.

"And at trial, this Martray witness testified again under oath, on direct examination, that he was given no deals, that he was given nothing, that he was doing it because he had children of his own."

"He testified that Smith confessed?" Justice Zappala asked, incredulous.

"That's what he said and that he got nothing for that testimony. He was helping the Commonwealth for free, so to speak."

"Well, maybe Mr. Graci can explain *that falsehood*, one that a representa-tive from their office maintained throughout the trial," Justice Larsen re-marked, leaning back in his chair and looking up at the stained glass ceil-ing, obviously disgusted with the prosecution.

"He can't explain it, Your Honor, but I would request that you ask him."

"Was the jury sequestered, Mr. Costopoulos?" Justice Nix asked.

"No, Your Honor, it wasn't."

Normally, a party has 15 minutes before the Supreme Court of Pennsyl-vania. The court let me go on for almost an hour. They truly were inter-ested. They truly understood. They had obviously read the record and were very concerned about the fairness of the proceeding in the court below.

I felt great. I felt like the system I devoted my life to was finally working.

The minute Graci stood up to defend the conviction and to ask the supreme court to affirm the death penalty, I knew that he was in trouble. Graci started out with his voice loud and clear, but it dropped quickly when Justice Papadakos hit from the far left side of the bench.

"If you throw out the hearsay, Mr. Graci, and from the record I've read that's all there seems to be in this case, what's left?"

"There's a confession, Your Honor."

"To a convicted perjurer or a one-time convicted perjurer, isn't that right?" Justice Larsen asked testily.

"That conviction was vacated, Your Honor," Graci answered defensively.

"Well let me ask you this, counselor," Justice Zappala said, leaning forward. "Didn't the prosecutor tell the jury in his closing that Martray got *absolutely nothing* in exchange for his testimony?"

"Yes, but . . . ," Graci answered, wavering in his resolve.

"Well, what do you do when the prosecutor makes a statement that was *absolutely false*," Zappala asked, cutting off Graci.

"It was a mistake. It was . . . "

"What *do* you do with that falsehood?" Larsen asked angrily, again cutting off Graci.

I was getting more excited with every question from the bench. Finally, I thought, the attorney general's office was being put in their place by somebody bigger than they—the Supreme Court of Pennsylvania, the law of the land.

Those at the back of the courtroom, mostly lawyers, watched in stunned silence. Most of them were just glad they weren't Graci. They didn't mind waiting respectfully for their turn or watching the supreme court in one of its thunderbolt-hurling moods.

"And why, Mr. Graci, did the Commonwealth call Bradfield's friends to say those outrageous things about Smith, outrageous things according to Bradfield, I might add?" Justice Nix asked, looking at his fellow jurists on the bench to his left and right.

"Because, Your Honor, Mr. Costopoulos said in his opening statement that they were somehow, or might have been, involved at the beach," Graci answered, looking at me.

"Wait a second, counselor," Justice Papadakos intervened angrily. "Those witnesses were on the prosecution's witness list before the trial ever started."

"Yes, Your Honor, but . . . "

Graci tried to explain his *new* theory of admissibility, but Justice Papadakos wasn't buying it and didn't let him finish.

"Mr. Costopoulos had nothing to do with that *tactic*, counselor; you couldn't have known what the defense was going to say. Why don't you just put me on the witness stand to say I read in the *Pittsburgh Post-Gazette* that Smith committed the murders?"

"We understand your position, Mr. Graci," Justice Nix said sympathetically.

"One final short remark," Mr. Graci intoned, asking for more time.

"Keep it short," Justice Nix ordered.

"Yes, Your Honor," Graci responded, now talking quickly. He was getting desperate. "The position of the Commonwealth is that we want the death penalty upheld."

"We understand *that* position," Justice Zappala snapped.

"You didn't try this case in the court below, did you?" Justice Flaherty asked, giving Graci his final out.

"Oh no, Your Honor," Graci answered with some relief.

I felt the argument before the Supreme Court of Pennsylvania could not have gone better. But justice has its own pace, like sand that trickles ever so slowly through the hourglass of time, an hourglass that Jay Smith would have to keep watching from death row.

· 21 ·

SECRETS

June 1988.

Outside a pleasant warm breeze swept across the riding pen, a plank-board oval arena perched on a hill near our house. The floor of the pen was thick, soft sand. At one end of the arena were 20 head of young black angus cattle in a herd.

"Watch this," I said to Jill and our three daughters—Kara, Khristina, and Callista. Kara and Khristina were blond-haired, green-eyed, tall, beautiful teenagers whom I loved to death. They both thought they were 10 years older than they were, like a great many teens. Callista, my youngest, was four, with curly brown hair; a smart, fearless, spirited kid who meant the world to me. We were all on horseback holding herd, turning back. I was about to show what my young mare could do, and I was the one riding this controlled bronco.

The sorrel quarter horse moved quietly into the herd of black cattle at one end of the pen. Without disturbing them, we carefully separated a bald-faced yearling from the rest. The calf's instinct was to return to the safety of the group.

"Watch her melt this bald-faced calf right into the ground," I shouted, excited. Miss Jackpot Whiz, my spirited cutting horse, was about to explode.

"Don't fall off!" Jill yelled, laughing.

The horse mirrored the cow's every move in a dance of unusual grace, beauty, and excitement. It is a one-on-one performance, like ballet in the dirt, but explosive and fast, commingled with the sweet-sour smells of cattle and horses, saddle leather, sweat, and perfume.

The mare danced with the calf in flawless motion for 30 seconds, when I proudly took a hold of her. The little calf ran back to the herd behind us, and I gave my family the thumbs-up.

To me, cutting cattle at home with my wife and daughters is a cowboy fantasy come true. I love it.

Even more so, I love the laughter of my daughters when they try it.

"That was pretty good, Dad," Callista yelled, having fun holding herd for me.

"You're such a show-off," said Khristina from her palomino, putting me back in my humble status at home.

"Yeah, Dad," Kara said, perched safely on her aged, chestnut gelding, concurring in Khristina's assessment.

"Now, girls, give your father a break, will ya?" Jill shouted, laughing, loping her nervous bay mare over to Callista's side.

I felt safe up there with my wife and daughters, away from it all. The deaths of the two young Reinert children haunted me, however, and that pain would strike at any time, especially when I watched my own children—so full of life and love.

I also suffered a great deal knowing that Jay Smith was on death row, awaiting execution for murders that I believed he did not commit. I felt responsible for letting him down. It was as though I couldn't get his blood off my hands.

The argument before the Supreme Court of Pennsylvania was behind me. I felt good about that effort, and I had hope, something I hadn't had from the day I first got into the case. Though there are no sure winners on appeal, for the first time in a long while I could relax, at least for a bit.

The *normal* appellate course would have been to wait for the supreme court to render a written opinion. My hope and prayer was for a new trial and that the supreme court would not uphold the death penalty. My best guess was that I would know something within six to 12 months.

Until then, I intended to spend as much time with my wife and growing family as I could. I had neglected them much too long because of the Smith case, and I promised to make it up to them.

★ ★ ★

Only two months had gone by since I had argued the Smith case before the Supreme Court of Pennsylvania on May 12, 1988.

At that time, Jay Smith had been in solitary confinement for about two years.

On July 12, 1988, I went to the office early in the morning to wrap up some unfinished business before going to the shore with Jill and the kids. We were going to hook up with my parents, brothers and sister, and their families at the Acropolis in Wildwood, New Jersey. The kids were really excited, and Jill was looking forward to it.

Around 10 a.m., Nick came into my office, and he was obviously shaken. He shut the door behind him and locked it.

"Bill," Nick said, with a sense of urgency, "I don't want us to be interrupted, for *any* reason, until I tell you what's going on."

"What's the big deal?" I asked.

"Bill, this is *unbelievable!*"

"It must be," I said to Nick, "you're as white as a ghost. What is it?"

"I just talked to Gary Lysaght."

"Yeah?"

"You know Gary."

"Of course I know Gary. He works here. What's the matter with you, anyway?"

"He kids a lot."

"Yeah."

"Well, he's not kidding about what he told me."

"Yeah?"

"Well," Nick said, talking faster, "Gary has this personal friend in the attorney general's office. They're just good friends. She told him there's a letter on Graci's desk, and Gary asked me if you got it yet."

"What the fuck are you talking about, Nick?" I asked, growing concerned.

"Bill, the attorney general's office has Balshy's lifters with the sand on them, the same lifters Balshy was accused of perjuring himself about . . . the same lifters the Commonwealth had claimed didn't exist as recently as two months ago during oral argument before the Pennsylvania Supreme Court. They've had them all along. They had them *during* the Smith trial!"

"Come on, Nick," I said angrily, thinking this was a bad joke.

"Bill . . . I . . . I swear to God . . . Gary wasn't kidding . . . it's all laid out in the letter from Graci to you."

"Nick, Graci just argued two months ago before the Supreme Court of Pennsylvania. He asked them to uphold Smith's death penalty. There's no way Bob Graci . . . "

"You're right," Nick said, interrupting. "Graci didn't know about those lifters either until two months ago. He just found out."

No, I hadn't received any letter from Bob Graci. No, Bob Graci hadn't called me either.

Yes, I was stunned, and furious—at Holtz, at Guida, at the attorney general's office, at the Pennsylvania State Police, at the world—but I recovered quickly, and when I did, I started barking orders left and right.

"Nobody outside this office is to know a thing. Tammy, call Skip and get him over here. Gary, call your friend and ask her if she knows anything else. Everybody get in here. We've got to decide what our next step is."

I was reeling.

It was a delicate decision. Do we alert the attorney general's office to the discovery? Do we simply wait for the mail and see if the letter arrives? How will this affect the pending supreme court appeal? When do we tell Smith?

There were also considerations of a more personal nature. Would Gary's friend be exposed? Would she be fired? Would Gary himself be compromised in any way?

When the early afternoon mail arrived, no Bob Graci letter was in it. Because of the shoddy treatment the defense had gotten over the years, we weren't so sure that the letter would ever be sent or that we would ever be informed. After all, it was only a draft version and probably needed high-ranking approval. A unanimous option was agreed to—call Graci and catch them all off guard. We had to let them know that we knew, and since we knew, it was only a matter of time before the press knew.

"Tammy, get me Graci on the phone right away," I told her, and she knew from my tone it was urgent.

"Where is he?" she asked.

"Call him at the attorney general's office. If he's not there, tell them it's an emergency. Find him!"

Graci wasn't in. He was at one of those prosecutors' conferences so favored by public servants, the kind held at exclusive country clubs and *always* paid for by Pennsylvania taxpayers. I insisted that he be reached. It was an absolute emergency. Within minutes, Graci was on the phone, probably from the pro shop where he was summoned off the golf course of the plush Toftrees Resort outside State College.

"Bill, what can I do for you?" Bob said politely, totally unaware he was about to get cold-cocked.

"Bob, I want them, and I want them now," I answered, seething, controlling my anger and outrage as the tone in my voice betrayed me.

Everybody in my office was standing there, waiting for *that* call to be placed—Nick, Skip, Gary, Charlie, Dave, Leslie, and Tammy. They listened to my end, with nervous anticipation, at what would be the beginning of the end, for somebody.

"I . . . I'm not sure what you mean, Bill," Bob said nervously, politely.

"Bob, you know *exactly* what I mean. I now know it all, and I want them right now, including the letter."

"The letter? . . . I'll . . . I'll get back to you, Bill . . . in about two hours," Bob said, a slight tremor in his voice, buying some time.

"Bob, my friend, you don't seem to understand . . . I want the lifters . . . I want the letter *now* . . . you get back to me within 20 minutes, or I'm going over to Strawberry Square and all hell is going to break loose . . . I might even bring a couple of TV stations along for backup," I added impatiently, threatening.

"All right, Bill, I'll get right back to you," Graci said, trying to stay calm.

When I hung up the phone, everybody in my office exploded into a mixture of laughter, amazement, self-confidence, and outrage.

"I told you, I told you, I told you," Skip said, fired up and ready to fight. "Those lying sons-of-bitches had those sand lifters all along. They had them before the trial. They were lying . . . they . . . "

"Calm down, Skip," Leslie said, laughing but nervous, and lit up a cigarette from her second pack of the day.

"Calm down, my ass. You tell Smith to calm down. He's been on death row for over two years because of this bullshit, and don't forget, Bill, they said *we* were the ones that committed perjury." By then Skip was clenching his fists and pounding my desk with rage.

"Bill, how did Bob Graci sound? What did he say?" Charlie asked, excited.

Then the phone rang, and everybody froze into silence. We just looked at each other and wondered what the next move was going to be.

True to his word, Bob Graci met the deadline and was calling back.

"Bill," he said, "I've spoken to my superiors, and you can send someone over to pick up the letter at my office. I wanted to make some typographical corrections . . . I . . . "

"When?" I asked, not letting up the pressure.

"This afternoon."

"Okay." Then I paused. "Bob?"

"Yeah?"

"I know you had nothing to do with this. At least, I believe that," I told him in a friendlier tone.

"Thanks," Bob said, appreciatively.

Bob Graci had been kept in the dark by his own office for over two years. He had nothing to do with the intentional concealment of the sand lifters, which we are sure would have acquitted Jay Smith two years previously. I believe that.

But now it was time to come out of the darkness.

"No more echoes," Nick said mockingly.

"No more echoes," Charlie said, shaking his head in disbelief.

There was no going back. The story of widespread intrigue and deception was on the verge of going public with unpredictable consequences for our client's fate.

I could feel the adrenaline rushing through me and my heart racing faster. It was time to strike back with a vengeance, to get the criminal justice system back on track, and maybe, just maybe, vindicate Jay Smith.

★ ★ ★

That afternoon I made a call from my office to Jill, who was at home, and told her that I would not be going to the shore with her and the kids. I dreaded making that call, hoping she would understand, knowing it would hurt her.

"What do you mean, Bill?" Jill said with a lot of pain in her voice.

"I'll . . . I'll call you tonight at the Acropolis. I'm really sorry, Jill, but I'm waiting for Nick to bring me the letter."

"The kids won't understand."

"I know . . . but . . . I'll try to make it down in a day or so."

"Please try, Bill, okay?" Jill said, pleading.

"Okay," I answered, feeling awful.

I didn't think Nick would ever get back. We joked at the office that they took him hostage, or maybe he got lost or stopped at the Locust Café to get schnockered.

They didn't take him hostage, and he didn't get lost, and he didn't stop at the Locust Café. They made him wait until certain "changes" were made in the letter before it was released.

Nick ceremoniously put it on my desk like it was the Magna Carta or the Constitution, and I read it word-for-word and between the lines three times, with Leslie and Skip breathing down my neck the whole time, before I passed it around. It read:

Last week I learned of the following information related to the testimony of former State Police Corporal John Balshy. At trial, Balshy testified, on cross-examination, that while he was examining Susan Reinert's body he used "lifters" to remove particles from between her toes. In response to one of your questions, he said that the substance could have been sand.

Balshy's claim was disputed by the testimony of other witnesses who said, in essence, that they knew and/or remembered nothing about the existence of these "lifters" or the removal of any debris from between Susan Reinert's toes.

During his closing arguments, former Chief Deputy Attorney General Guida contended, based upon his recollection of this testimony, that Balshy had lied about this information. You asked the trial court for an instruction concerning this argument. You argued that the facts of record were different from Guida's recollection. The judge instructed the jury to rely on its recollection of the facts as it differed from anything either counsel recalled. You claimed that the judge's failure to address Guida's comments in his instruction was an error warranting a new trial in your post-verdict motion and in your presently pending appeal before the Supreme Court.

Last week, I learned that during the last full week of the trial in this case, Trooper Victor Dove found an envelope containing "lifters" in an evidence drawer. The envelope indicated that these had been used to swab the areas between Mrs. Reinert's toes. Trooper Dove gave this envelope to Trooper Holtz on May 1, 1986, the day after the trial concluded. I have no reason to believe that Trooper Holtz or anyone other than Trooper Dove knew of the existence of these "lifters" before the conclusion of the trial.

Trooper Holtz received the envelope containing the "lifters" on May 1, 1986. He gave them to an agent of the Bureau of Criminal Investigation of this office on May 2, 1986. I have no information that Mr. Guida knew of the existence of these "lifters" before they were turned over to Trooper Holtz.

This Office forwarded all of the "lifters" to the FBI for examination. On November 25, 1986, the Assistant Director of the Bureau of Criminal Investigation was verbally informed that the material on the "lifters" was "dust." This Office received a formal, written report from the FBI dated January 20, 1987. That report states that a particle of quartz was found on two of the "lifters" submitted for examination.

I do not know the importance of this information. I provide it to you pursuant to my ethical obligation as a prosecutor since much was made at trial of the existence of these "lifters" and the testimony concerning sand provided by Balshy for the first time at Smith's trial.

The letter was dated July 11, 1988, and signed Robert A. Graci, Chief Deputy Attorney General, Appeals & Legal Services Section.

"What do you think?" I asked Bill Kollas, the most senior partner in our office. Kollas and I had been partners since 1972. In fact, it was the two of us who had originated the firm, and we had worked alone for many years. Bill Kollas, 56, was a brilliant, highly respected lawyer in the Harrisburg community, who made millions in real estate and looked like a Greek Rock Hudson.

My parents got married in Bill's parents' home when he was four years old, and they made him the ring-bearer. Bill's father, "Charlie," was my godfather, and 30 years later Bill Kollas became the godfather of my first-born daughter, Kara.

Kollas consulted with me throughout the Smith trial, and when everybody else was bouncing off the walls, including me, I always looked to him for the answers. He never lost his calm or ability to be rational.

"The letter is very carefully worded, Bill," Kollas observed. "It is very well-written, and it's obvious to me they're laying all the blame on Trooper Dove to cover their asses. I believe Graci didn't know about those lifters until last week, just like he said. I don't believe for one second that Dove sat on those sand lifters throughout the trial and didn't tell anybody, especially Holtz."

I grimaced at the thought that they were going to cover Holtz's ass. "And when Dove told Holtz, Holtz told Guida, but I'm not sure of that," I said, thinking out loud.

"I am sure that this guarantees Smith a new trial, pretty sure," Kollas said, shaking his head.

"I know," I put in, holding my hand up. "There are no *sure* winners on appeal, ever, especially in a high-profile death penalty case."

"That's right," Kollas said gravely. "I can tell you this concealment is *very* serious."

"Where do we go with it from here?" I asked him, my mind racing, wanting some help.

"We have to let the supreme court know about this. I'm just not sure how," Kollas mused in a rational tone.

"Smith's in solitary confinement. He's been on death row for over two years. This means another delay, at least months, and I don't know how much more Smith can take," I said, sighing.

"We have no choice," Dave repeated, echoing Kollas's view.

"Damn," Nick said, getting sick at the thought.

★ ★ ★

In the meantime.

Jay Smith lay on his bunk, staring at the ceiling, wondering if the supreme court argument had gone as well as I said it had. What else was there to think about? Was the supreme court going to give him a new trial? Were they going to uphold his death penalty?

Nobody ever told him anything in there. The two-month-old *Philadelphia Inquirer* among the papers under his steel bed headlined "Justices Critical of State Tactics in Smith Trial" and stated that "The supreme court members strongly criticized the tactics used by the prosecution in winning a 1986 murder conviction against former Upper Merion High School Principal Jay C. Smith."

But that was two months ago.

And the *Philadelphia Inquirer* and I didn't go into chambers with those guys after the argument was over. We had no idea what those justices would do in the final analysis, and I was always trying to put things in a favorable light.

So far, Smith wasn't doing so good.

The cell had just a little light coming into it from the food slot in the steel door. He had no idea whether it was night or day, let alone what time it was—not that it mattered. He wasn't going anywhere.

Smith's naked body was dripping with sweat. His death row cell—of two-foot-thick concrete walls with no windows or ventilation—got unbearably hot in the summer with temperatures that rose to over 110 degrees. It was sweltering in there, especially in July.

Jay looked at the dark, slime-green concrete walls that seemed to be moving in on him, closer and closer with each passing day. He wasn't even allowed to put a religious picture on them to help him get through his living hell. Jay wondered how much more he could take and believed he was dying. He prayed he was not. Jay had gone from 220 pounds to 165 and looked like he had cancer, even though he worked out every day. His teeth had completely rotted out. His hair was thinner and had turned white. His eyes were weakening, too, but at least he could still read and write with his strong glasses.

Reading the Bible seemed to help.

Despair and depression plagued him day and night. Sometimes he sat on the edge of his bed for hours, unable to move. His body would become rigid, and his eyes fixed into a blank stare, seeing nothing. Once a guard reported him dead.

"Jay!" a guard yelled, pounding on his steel door, startling him and causing his heart to race. "Your Greek lawyer called and left word for you to call him. He said it's an emergency!"

"When can I call him back?" Jay asked, shouting to make sure he was heard.

"Your next scheduled phone call is in two weeks," the guard answered.

• 22 •

DESPERATE

July 1988.

Graci just sat back and listened. Paul Yatron was his boss. The two of them sat in Yatron's office, which used to be Guida's, except now it was adorned with Yatron's diplomas and certificates of achievement. Our emergency petition, filed with the Supreme Court of Pennsylvania asking for Jay Smith's release, was on Yatron's desk.

Paul Yatron had been with the attorney general's office long before Graci had arrived and had assumed Guida's position of Chief Deputy of the Criminal Division when Guida resigned because of the drug scandal in '86. Yatron got stuck with this whole mess after Guida left, and he resented the position he was in.

"That's your fucking friend Costopoulos for you," Yatron said, shaking his head.

"He's not my friend, Paul," Graci answered, throwing his hands up defensively.

"He's not going to have any friends when we're done with him. Within 10 days of your letter, the son-of-a-bitch petitions the Supreme Court of Pennsylvania alleging intentional prosecutorial misconduct by our office and by the Pennsylvania State Police. Then he holds a statewide news conference telling the media that we *fixed* the goddamned Smith case!" Yatron said angrily.

Poor Yatron.

First, immediately after the Smith verdict, he heard about the Balshy lifters being found *during* the Smith trial. That was Guida's case, so he stayed the hell out of it. He heard that Holtz gave the lifters to Guida or showed them to Guida, and after that they were locked up in a desk someplace in the attorney general's office. That summer after the Smith verdict was when Guida was vacationing with Wambaugh in California, and nobody seemed to be worried about the lifters then.

When Guida resigned, Yatron got stuck with the damn things. He was told to keep investigating Balshy. That's when he decided to send the lifters to the FBI in Washington, D.C. to determine what was on them. Was he ever sorry he did that.

The lifters were examined by Agent Christopher Fiedler, a forensic geologist assigned to the materials analysis unit. Fiedler got the lifters on November 7, 1986, and it didn't take him very long. He wrote a report for the boys in Pennsylvania that there was *quartz* on two of the five lifters. Quartz is *sand*!

Since the investigation by Yatron was a perjury investigation into Balshy's testimony, and this cleared Balshy, Yatron closed the file, quietly and quickly, in November 1986.

No, those granules of truth were not turned over to the defense, even after it had been determined scientifically that they were sand.

Not even the new quarterback of the Smith case, Bob Graci, was told until two years later, after he argued before the Supreme Court of Pennsylvania. It seems that a young assistant to Guida ended up telling Graci, finally, because *that* seemed like the right thing to do at the time. It also seemed that too many people were buzzing in the attorney general's office once "their tactics" became a media event triggered by the questioning of the supreme court justices.

"I had to tell him," Graci said, reminding Yatron of his legal and ethical obligations.

"Yeah," Yatron answered, disgusted, "I guess."

"I did, Paul."

"I said yeah."

"We knew what Costopoulos would do."

"He's not done yet," Yatron said angrily, picking up the petition on his desk and reading the stinging averments again, word-for-word.

★ ★ ★

The media hammered with all guns pointed at the attorney general's office and the Pennsylvania State Police. The state police had found the lifters and given them to the attorney general's office; that was their official position and they had no intention of accepting any responsibility for this fuckup. Their honor was on the line, and they were going to take down whomever they had to.

They had some strategic problems, however. Trooper Dove found the lifters during the trial. He told Trooper Colyer. He also told Trooper Holtz, who was the affiant, and all three of them were Pennsylvania State Police officers.

Maybe there was a reason they didn't tell me. That was Guida's job anyhow.

What if they were planted by the defense?

Maybe some of Balshy's friends planted them in the evidence locker to kill the perjury investigation of Balshy.

Maybe the Pennsylvania State Police and the attorney general's office should expand on the "planting theory" and leak it to the media, while the lifters were sent back to Washington, D.C. for a little follow-up.

And that's exactly what they did.

The hope and prayer of the attorney general's office and of the Pennsylvania State Police was that the lifters weren't *real*. The autopsy of Susan Reinert was on June 25, 1979. If the lifters weren't manufactured until after 1979, then they weren't real. If the handwriting on the lifters was done with ink that was manufactured after 1979, then somebody wrote on the lifters after the fact to fabricate the scenario the defense wanted.

The lifters were then sent to Agent Robert F. Webb, a polymer materials analyst and expert. He got all five lifters purportedly used on Susan Reinert's feet. He examined them microscopically and did a chemical analysis of the component parts of each lifter to determine when they were manufactured. He used a transform-infrared spectrophotometer.

Webb was also given the lifters used at the autopsy to take hair and fiber samples from Susan Reinert's body to compare to Balshy's lifters.

All lifters were exactly the same!

Then the lifters were sent to Agent Ronald Duncan, an ink examiner and specialist for over 17 years. He couldn't tell how long the ink was on the lifters, but he confirmed that it was '79 ink.

Agent Christopher Fiedler was staying out of this one. He was afraid they might ask him if it was '79 sand.

Now, the attorney general's office was going to have to argue that whoever planted the lifters was pretty damn clever. The "guilty planter" in 1986 got '79 lifters and '79 ink and '79 sand, put them all together, and stuck them in the state police evidence locker.

I don't know who in the attorney general's office or the Pennsylvania State Police came up with that wild, scurrilous planting theory, but it was Bob Graci who had been told to run with it.

I couldn't wait for that ludicrous argument to be made in open court.

* * *

The state police put the crosshairs on the heads of Trooper Dove and Trooper Colyer with their internal investigation. They would have to be sacrificed.

That way Holtz, the PSP star of *Echoes in the Darkness*, would live to ride again.

That way, maybe, they could also save the Smith verdict.

Two top guns from the Bureau of Professional Responsibility, Internal Affairs Central Section—Captain Shimko and Corporal Clancy—were assigned to investigate "any allegations involving members of the Pennsylvania State Police with respect to the finding of certain rubber lifters on April 24, 1986."

Shimko and Clancy got their marching orders, not in April 1986, or in May or June, or even in 1987, but in late July 1988, after the petition was filed with the Pennsylvania Supreme Court alleging prosecutorial misconduct and the intentional concealment of critical physical evidence.

That investigation was unbelievable.

This is how that investigation was conducted.

First, the internal boys went to Trooper Dove, who had found the lifters during the trial. Trooper Dove told them that he found them on April 24, 1986, *which was during the trial*, before the Commonwealth rested their case. Dove told them that he informed Corporal Colyer right away, realizing that he had found "a hot potato," and that Colyer told him, "You've got to turn them over."

Costopoulos:	All right, Corporal Clancy, did Dove tell you on more than one occasion that the same day he found them he told Trooper Holtz?
Clancy:	Yes, sir.
Costopoulos:	Now, did you go to Trooper Holtz and determine whether Holtz got a receipt from Trooper Dove to confirm the date that Holtz says he got them?
Clancy:	Yes, I believe we asked him about that.
Costopoulos:	And did Trooper Holtz provide you with a receipt acknowledging when he physically got the lifters?
Clancy:	No, sir.
Costopoulos:	Did you at any time read Trooper Holtz his rights?
Clancy:	No, sir.
The Court::	Would you like some water?
Clancy:	Yes, sir.

Trooper Dove had been with the Pennsylvania State Police for over 20 years. He had been on the Reinert murder case from the day Susan Reinert's body was found. He was a team player all the way, and he knew exactly when he gave those lifters to Trooper Holtz.

After they had questioned Trooper Dove, Captain Shimko and Corporal Clancy went to Trooper Holtz. Holtz told them he got the lifters from Dove the day *after* Smith had been sentenced to death by the jury. That's when Holtz said he told Guida.

Since Holtz's version protected Holtz, the internal boys had some work to do on the memories of Dove and Colyer. By the time Clancy and Shimko were done, Dove didn't remember when he gave those lifters to Holtz; and at one point, he forgot when he found them.

And poor Colyer, because his handwriting was on the lifters—and it was, because he received the evidence from Balshy at the autopsy—Clancy and Shimko threatened to charge him with "planting" those lifters, or with perjury, conspiracy to commit perjury, and fabrication of or tampering with evidence.

Costopoulos:	Did you have any discussion with Corporal Colyer with respect to the investigation and what it might mean to him?

Clancy:	Yes, sir.
Costopoulos:	And who else was present during that conversation?
Clancy:	His attorney.
Costopoulos:	And were you responding to any questions by his attorney?
Clancy:	Yes, I was.
Costopoulos:	And what question was posed to you?
Clancy:	I don't know the exact words, but it was something to the effect where is this investigation leading to, are we looking at criminal charges in this particular investigation.
Costopoulos:	And what was your response?
Clancy:	I said yes, sir, we are looking at particular charges and then I enumerated the charges that we were looking at.
Costopoulos:	And what were those charges?
Clancy:	I believe at the time I indicated perjury, conspiracy to commit perjury, and the fabrication or tampering with evidence.

Poor Colyer. He had nothing to do with those lifters being concealed from the defense. All he did was tell Dove to turn them over after Dove found them during the trial.

Those internal boys play rough.

They should have stuck with the truth, which was stuck on those lifters.

★ ★ ★

Late summer, 1988.

Corporal John Balshy sat across the desk from Bob Keys at the young lawyer's office in the small town of Lebanon, Pennsylvania, and the smoke was streaming from his pipe and ears. Balshy had been retired for seven years, and nobody ever told him that he was being investigated for perjury, not until Captain Shimko called him in the summer of '88 to question him about the sand-lifters.

The mere suggestion by Captain Shimko that Balshy may have done something wrong outraged him. He gave the Pennsylvania State Police 27 years of his life and not only retired with honors and commendations but had never had a disciplinary write-up. Now he finds out that they want to question him about perjury and planting evidence in the Smith case. Maybe it was time to put down his fishing rod and books and come out of retirement swinging.

John Balshy never got over the murder of Susan Reinert or the disappearance of her children. In 1982 he discussed the sand on Reinert's feet with Dr. Herbert L. MacDonell, who was one of the nation's top consulting criminalists out of Corning, New York. VanNort and Holtz had also consulted with Dr. MacDonell in 1981 about the Reinert case before any arrests were made.

Dr. MacDonell was not able to help any of them with what they had, but his personal notes confirmed that Balshy talked to him about sand in 1982.

"Bob," Balshy said angrily, "this is bullshit."

"I don't know what to say," Keys responded.

Bob Keys had known John Balshy personally for six years and was horrified by what they were doing to him. Bob knew how proud Balshy was of his career and reputation and could see John's anger and hurt. Bob knew Balshy's wife, Rita, and how protective they were of their grown children. Now, Bob—single, never married, a sole practitioner with a small office on the second floor of a storefront building in the heart of the Dutchland— was feeling a little overwhelmed at the thought of protecting a legend like Corporal John Balshy. Though Balshy was a big guy, a former baseball catcher, and forever a tough cop, he was also a very gentle human being who hurt easily.

"The foreign matter between her toes sparkled like little diamonds and fluoresced when the ultraviolet light was directed on her feet. I thought it was sand at the time but didn't know, and I removed those particles with lifters and handed the lifters to Trooper Colyer," Balshy explained, briefing Keys, reliving the experience of the autopsy in 1979, and agonizing over having to go through this again.

"What are lifters, John?" Keys asked, his curiosity aroused.

"Lifters look like sticky tire patches, and they are used to gather debris, hair, fibers, foreign material—stuff like that, off of surfaces, like bodies. And in this particular instance, I used them between her toes to get the sand, or what I thought was sand," Balshy answered patiently.

"Did you ever see those lifters after that?" Bob asked, fascinated.

"One time," John answered, and continued. "The next day, the day after the autopsy . . . I think it was the next day . . . VanNort had them, and the two of us went to the chemistry section, where they were examined under a microscope. The guy examining them told us both that it was sand, but he couldn't tell where it came from by just looking at it under a microscope. That's the last time *I* saw the lifters."

"Do you remember who was working the microscope, John?"

"No."

"Anything else?"

"Yeah," Balshy said, and relit his pipe.

In addition, before the lifters were turned over to the defense and all hell broke lose, John Balshy was examining the inside of a Volkswagen, like the one Bradfield took to the shore with his friends.

"Susan Reinert, Bob," Balshy continued, "had a postmortem lividity mark on the left side of her body that puzzled me for a long time. The mark was white, while the surrounding area was a magenta color. The white area is where something was in contact with her skin after her death.

I'm telling you, Bob, that lividity imprint came from the hand brake between the front seats of a Volkswagen. The imprint was *exact!*"

"Unbelievable," Keys said, shaking his head, astonished.

"I immediately went to see Guida in Harrisburg."

"What did Guida say?"

"He said he was in private practice, said he was glad to see me, and then he started telling me that Treat Williams was getting an Academy Award or something like that for portraying him in the movie. I couldn't get him to stop talking about Treat Williams for one second, and I was really upset when I left there."

"I'll bet," Keys said.

"I spent years looking for a break and got one, and all Guida wanted to talk about was Treat Williams and the movie, so I went straight to the attorney general's office with a companion, and they told me that if they were interested, they would contact me," Balshy said, shaking his head.

No, nobody ever contacted John Balshy about *that!*

The only contact that the state police and the attorney general's office made with him was the call from Captain Shimko.

Later that same day, Shimko and Corporal Clancy—by prearranged appointment—showed up at Bob Keys's office and read Balshy his Miranda rights.

Balshy went nuts and Bob Keys did the right thing: he threw them both the hell out.

★ ★ ★

One gnawing aspect of this case that kept eating at me was whether Jay Smith could continue to hold on, to wait it out in solitary confinement. He was almost 60 years old and had been on death row for three years. I needed some psychological input from a qualified forensic psychologist, and late one night in the winter of '89 I called one.

Ritchi Morris was my old, good friend from White Plains, New York. We met in 1962 as freshmen at Dickinson College in Carlisle, Pennsylvania; and from day one, we bonded. We were both into lifting weights back then, competitive collegiate wrestling—I wrestled 177; he was our heavyweight because of his fat ass—and big motorcycles, beautiful women, and cutting classes.

"Hey, Bousti," I said over the phone, when I called my old friend Dr. Ritchi Morris from my home late that night.

"Hey, Malaka," he answered jokingly in our favorite Greek terms of endearment.

"How's the lifting going?"

"I can still kick your ass."

"Like hell you can."

He was built like a big fire hydrant. He looked like Odd Job in the movie *Goldfinger*, with long, silky black hair and a short and powerful body. His nickname was "Animal." Some people called him "Bear," and both were appropriate.

I went on to law school when we graduated, side-by-side, from Dickinson in 1966. He went on to get multiple doctorates in clinical psychology, but only after we both did a two-year tour of duty in the Army.

For over 20 years Ritchi had been a loyal friend to me, and never said no.

"I need a favor, Ritchi," I said.

"I knew that when I heard your voice."

"You know the Smith case I've been working on?"

"The one you lost?"

"Yeah, asshole, the one I lost."

"I know it."

"I want you to go up to see him."

"For what?"

"He's been in solitary confinement for over two years . . . and Ritch, I just got another break in the case that I'm not going to bore you with . . . but I think I'm going to win this case in the long run."

"Yeah."

"Well, Ritch, it's going to take *a lot* longer than I thought, and what I need to know from you, since you're a shrink, is can he hold on?"

"You're going to owe me, buddy," Ritch said.

"Thanks, Ritch. By the way, one other thing."

"I knew it."

"When I told Jay that I wanted you to go see him, he asked that you write him a letter to make an appointment. He said he was kind of busy these days."

"You've gotta be shitting me," Ritch said, incredulous.

I wasn't. When Smith finally called me, and we talked about Graci's letter, I told him that I wanted him to talk to my friend, Dr. Morris. Smith *did* tell me that Morris would have to make an appointment with him because he was kind of busy.

That's what I loved about Smith. He had a lot of style. The son-of-a-bitch was in solitary confinement with nothing to do, and my best friend needed to make an appointment to see him.

★ ★ ★

The discovery of the sand-lifters in mid-July 1988 was good news and bad news. The good news was that the cloud of wrongdoing by the defense was going to be lifted, maybe. The good news was that this physical evidence of sand removed from Susan Reinert's feet during the autopsy was consistent with what we were saying all along—that Susan Reinert was at the shore on the weekend in question, where Jay Smith *wasn't* and Bradfield and others were.

The prosecution had conceded, at least during Smith's trial, that Smith couldn't have done it if Susan Reinert was at the shore on the weekend in question. Guida's memo to Bob Keuch during the trial emphasized the "extreme materiality" of the sand-lifters to the defense for that reason.

And we were finally exposing the prosecution of Smith for what it was: a manipulated trial, a controlled trial, a trial in which the most critical physical evidence was intentionally concealed and intentionally withheld to engineer the guilty verdict. It didn't matter to the prosecution that it was a death penalty case and that Smith might have been innocent. The only thing that did matter was a conviction—certain members of the Pennsylvania State Police and the attorney general's office *needed* that conviction.

I believe that Wambaugh's book and the call of Hollywood added fuel to the fire which initially burned Smith but would ultimately burn *them*.

The media was going crazy. Evidence intentionally withheld by the prosecution in a death penalty case? Evidence planted by the defense to cover their asses? The media could smell a lot of upcoming bloodshed in the courtroom, and the media loves bloodshed, especially from the heroes they helped create. The upcoming hearing in Courtroom 6 of the Dauphin County Courthouse would be mobbed with reporters, and their lethal cameras would be positioned on the courthouse steps and corridors.

The bad news was the additional, inevitable delay with Smith on death row. We would be back in court; the name-calling and finger-pointing would be incredible; the arguments would be caustic and personal; and the mutual, defamatory accusations of wrongdoing and grandstanding would be out of control.

I actually thought Graci had lost his mind during those hearings, or his "marching orders" were to cast all caution and honor to the wind, because his tactic, in part, was to suggest and argue that those lifters might have been *planted* with sand on them in the Pennsylvania State Police evidence locker.

Planted! With sand on them! Now how crazy was that?!

Instead of simply coming forward and saying, "We had these lifters all along, with just a little bit of sand on them. Here they are now. We shouldn't have done that." Or, "We agree, this violated the rules and maybe Smith should be given a new trial. Let's get him off death row immediately and pick a jury." Or, "Let's put some honor back in the criminal justice system instead of making a mockery out of it with our planter theory."

Instead of doing *that*, the prosecution reached back into their old bag of tricks. Graci's position—which I believe he was *told* to take—was that these lifters might have been planted by the defense or by friends of Balshy to protect him from a perjury conviction, and that the prosecution did nothing wrong.

Those assholes.

The bad news was that the threat of Smith's execution for something he might not have done was still there.

· 23 ·

DESERT STORM

John Balshy and Bob Keys went to the attorney general's office in Harrisburg at Graci's request one week before the sand-lifters hearing, which was scheduled for February 16, 1989.

It did not go well.

First, Balshy and Keys had to wait in the reception area for two hours.

Then, as soon as they walked in, Graci read Balshy his Miranda rights again. The prosecutors liked reading Balshy his Miranda rights, whether it was required or not. After Bob Keys laid out the truth from day one, Keys and Balshy were asked to leave and were never contacted again.

"Costopoulos called me again," Keys said to Balshy, on their way back to Lebanon.

"I know. He's been trying to get hold of me too," Balshy said, looking straight ahead.

"What do you want me to do?" Keys asked.

"Avoid him *for now*," Balshy said, torn.

"Why?"

"Because I'm still a cop, and I always will be," Balshy answered like the 27-year veteran that he was.

★ ★ ★

February 16, 1989, in the Dauphin County Courthouse, Harrisburg, Pennsylvania.

We were back in court. Dave Foster was with me this time. The tension had been building for months. Smith would be there, but he had nothing to do with this fight. This one was personal. "Bob," I said in the corridor, "you know I have a lot of respect for you."

"Save your breath, Bill," Graci snapped, in a fighting mode.

"You're making a mistake," I fired back.

"I have a job to do," he said, bristling.

"For who, Bob?"

"Knock it off," Graci said angrily, and meant it.

Robert Tarman had asked to see Graci and me in Judge Lipsitt's chambers at 10 a.m. on Thursday morning, February 16, 1989, before the sand-lifters hearings got underway. Tarman was a former public defender in Harrisburg with a lot of experience in criminal courtrooms. He was one of the best criminal defense lawyers in the area, and he also had a job to do, which was to protect his client from a prosecutorial threat. His client was Corporal Ron Colyer, and the Pennsylvania State Police were setting him up as the sacrificial lamb.

We hadn't even gotten out of the locker room, and it was getting ugly. It appeared the prosecution wanted to take Corporal Colyer to the showers, a man who had been a loyal Pennsylvania State Police officer for almost 20 years, to give him a little old-fashioned therapy, like they did to Balshy.

Tarman knew the stakes on the table in the Smith case. He knew the prosecution was capable of destroying one of their own to protect favorite sons. He also knew what the Smith verdict meant to the Pennsylvania State Police and the attorney general's office that they helped to showcase on the CBS mini-series *Echoes in the Darkness*.

"Your Honor," Tarman began in chambers. "My name is Robert Tarman. I requested this in-camera on behalf of my client, Corporal Ron Colyer, who is a member of the state police.

"I have been notified by Mr. Graci and by Mr. Costopoulos that they both intend to call him as a witness in today's proceeding. I have also put both parties on notice that I've advised him to invoke his Fifth Amendment privileges. Mr. Costopoulos has indicated to me that he has no problem with that at all or a grant of immunity. Of course, that would have to come from the attorney general."

Graci made an issue out of *that*. He advised Tarman that he had a prepared list of questions that he wanted Corporal Colyer to answer.

Tarman went on to explain to Judge Lipsitt what Colyer had been through. He told the judge that there had been two investigations, one in 1986 and one that was ongoing. Judge Lipsitt started shaking his head back and forth as Tarman laid out what had been going on.

"Colyer has submitted himself to numerous questioning sessions and interrogations since that time, and they have taken place up until just recently. He has received threats of prosecution by the state police investigators. They have told him that they feel they have enough on him to charge him with various crimes. At one point, they read him his Fifth Amendment rights at the state police barracks. He's still a member of the state police. He still goes to work every day, but they have gone so far as to read him his rights."

Graci rudely interrupted Tarman, insisting that Colyer's rights be read to him on the witness stand. Instead of just agreeing that Colyer be given immunity, Graci wanted Judge Lipsitt to make that determination. He then handed the judge a list of prepared questions for Colyer.

"Your Honor, we also haven't heard what Mr. Costopoulos wants to ask him," Tarman said angrily, interrupting Graci.

"I can tell you, Your Honor," I said, getting in the fray, "I'm going to ask Colyer if he planted those lifters and all questions related to that ultimate question."

"Your Honor," Tarman asked, "what more do you need to grant Colyer immunity? Mr. Lewis, the district attorney of this county, will come up here right now and say Colyer's a suspect in this case. That alone would be enough. His handwriting is on the lifters. He's been threatened. He's had his rights read to him by these people. They've told me that they don't believe him. And they're going to ask him these questions, and they're going to say, well, no, they don't incriminate him when they don't believe him."

"You know he's been threatened," Tarman added, shifting his gaze to Graci.

"I didn't say that he wasn't. It came from the state police investigators, not me," Graci snapped back defensively.

Finally, Judge Lipsitt threw up his hands and agreed that Colyer could invoke his Fifth Amendment privileges.

Then, in chambers, Graci wanted a ruling from Judge Lipsitt that nothing would be said in open court about any activities after the trial. Graci didn't want one word said about what had happened to those lifters after the verdict. According to Graci, "any activities after the trial are completely irrelevant to this proceeding."

The guy was dreaming.

Dave Foster, who was waiting for the right opportunity, jumped in. Foster argued that the prosecution's misconduct not only took place *during* the trial, but that their actions—which consisted of manipulating and concealing evidence and twisting the truth—were continuing to that day, and in fact, had intensified.

Dave Foster had been with the firm since 1976. He seldom got excited, except over baseball, and never had a harsh word for anybody. But this planting of the evidence theory really got to him.

One thing was made clear to Judge Lipsitt in chambers—the gloves were off.

★ ★ ★

11 a.m.

Our bloodbath in chambers spilled onto the courtroom floor.

We were all back in Courtroom 6 to create a record. The Supreme Court of Pennsylvania, pursuant to our emergency petition alleging that the prosecution *fixed* the outcome of Jay Smith's trial by intentionally concealing the most critical physical evidence in the case—the sand, had ordered this evidentiary hearing.

The reason?

The supreme court had some questions they wanted answered forthwith: Did something happen, and if so, what? How did it happen? Why did it happen?

The courtroom was packed. The audience wanted to see lions eating Christians in the arena, but they didn't know one from the other.

Graci had brought two sharpshooters along to back him up: John Cherry and Anthony Sarcione. On January 1, a newly elected attorney general, the Honorable Ernest Preate, had taken the oath to uphold the laws of the Commonwealth, and these boys were his top lieutenants.

I had Dave Foster and Charles Rector along with Skip and Nick.

Jay Smith sat impassively in his crumpled gray suit and burgundy tie, the same ones he had worn during his trial. He looked like an old man sitting there.

"Your Honor," I began, "We are prepared to go forward, but before doing so, I would like to make a brief opening statement."

"By all means," Judge Lipsitt said, nodding.

I then laid out the history of the case for the judge, reminding him of Balshy's testimony, including the effort Guida had gone to during the trial to call him, and us, liars and perjurers. I told Judge Lipsitt that those lifters were found during the trial, that nobody told us, or even Graci, until *after* we had argued before the Supreme Court of Pennsylvania in May 1988, two years after the verdict of death. I told the judge about Graci's letter telling us about the lifters in July 1988. That's why we had petitioned the Pennsylvania Supreme Court for these hearings; and thereafter, the Pennsylvania State Police and the attorney general's office came up with a phony planting theory to explain and defend their reprehensible conduct.

I also intended to show with my first witness, Dr. Otis Donald Philen, Jr., one of the nation's foremost soil experts, what was on those lifters. That was critical physical evidence that Susan Reinert had been at the shore when she was murdered.

It took almost half an hour to get Dr. Philen's credentials on the record. His doctorate was in soil science and soil chemistry; he was a research analyst with the Tennessee Valley Authority; then he was in charge of research in the x-ray diffraction lab at North Carolina State University; he was a forensic chemist from 1972 to 1975 with the North Carolina State Bureau of Investigation; and from 1975 on, he was a soil scientist. In his vocation he needed the ability to use x-ray diffraction instrumentation, the scanning electron microscope, differential thermal analysis, and petrographic microscopy—all part of the total chemistry of soil and minerals.

Yes, he could identify sand when he saw it.

Dr. Philen had been given the lifters used by Balshy on the feet of Susan Reinert. He had been given access to these lifters before this hearing to do his examination, but it was under the watchful eye of the Pennsylvania State Police. The state police would not allow the lifters to be removed from their custody.

First, he examined them with a scanning electron microscope, which is used to examine the surface of particles, using the source of the electrons rather than light. The instrument also has the capability of photographing particles in a magnified state, which Philen did and handed Judge Lipsitt the enlarged photos of the granular substance on the lifters.

Dr. Philen then explained what we were looking at, because we had no idea, but nobody would admit it. We weren't even sure what he was saying. He used terms like "subangular surfaces," "abrasional types of forces," and "an exhibition of conchoidal fracture."

With my prepared questioning, I tried to clear things up for the Supreme Court of Pennsylvania, Judge Lipsitt, the prosecution (especially Graci), and for the court of public opinion.

Q. Now, Doctor, in the common vernacular, in layman's terms, what were the two particles that you looked at?

A. Sand.

Q. Is there any question in your mind that the two particles that you looked at under the scanning electron microscope were sand?

A. No.

Q. Doctor, do you have an opinion as to the most likely environment from which these two particles of sand originated?

A. Yes, I do.

Q. And what is your opinion as to the most likely environment that these particles of sand originated from?

A. My opinion is the two sand particles which are quartz are constituents of a sandy soil that's probably found in the coastal plain.

Q. A coastal plain environment?

A. Yes.

At that point, the boys to my right at the prosecution's table could feel their asses puckering. The sand storm was stinging them in the face, getting in their hair, getting on their nice pin-striped suits, and forcing them to shut their eyes and hold onto the table.

Another gust was coming.

Dr. Philen defined "coastal plain environment" as an area consistent with the resort area of Cape May, New Jersey and inconsistent with downtown Philadelphia or Smith's home.

Graci objected. Actually, Graci blew up.

I had no further questions. The prosecution was done for.

★ ★ ★

Trooper Victor Dove *hated* getting up on that witness stand. He was in a no-win situation and had been since he found those lifters during the Smith trial in 1986. He either had to tell the truth and put it on Holtz, admitting that he gave the lifters to Holtz when he found them during the trial, or take full responsibility for the cover-up in a death penalty case. Either way, this team player for the Pennsylvania State Police was sick. I called Trooper Dove, a member of the state police for 19 years and a key witness for the Commonwealth in the prosecution of Smith. He was at the crime scene, he was at the autopsy, he said he found the pin in Jay Smith's car, he identified and authenticated the blue comb for Guida, and he was the one who "found" Balshy's lifters with sand on them during the trial.

Q. Did you give a statement that when you found these lifters you knew you found a hot potato?

Graci: Objection!

Lipsitt: Overruled.

A. I said . . . I said words to that effect. I'm not sure if I said hot potato or not. Perhaps I did. I don't remember whether I did or not. I knew it was a hot item, yes, that's correct.

Dove knew how important the Balshy lifters were to the defense. He knew how much effort Guida and the Pennsylvania State Police went to during the Smith trial to call Balshy a liar. He knew Balshy had testified that he had gone between the toes of the victim, Susan Reinert, with hinge lifters and had found what looked like sand to him.

Graci was objecting to every question I asked Dove.

Lipsitt stopped paying any attention to him, and we just kept going.

Q. Did you find the hinge lifters that are in dispute?

A. Yes, sir.

Q. When?

A. On April 24, 1986.

That's exactly what he told the attorney general's office in 1986, immediately after the verdict.

Dove acknowledged that he found those lifters six days *before the verdict*, while the prosecution's case was still ongoing and before the defense had called its first witness. He said he found the lifters "in a box of evidence which was located in the evidence locker, the ID Evidence Locker. The box was placed in there by myself, and I had created different folders and labeled them with different categories. I had labeled one category miscellaneous, and to the best of my recollection they were found in that folder categorized as miscellaneous."

Yes, Dove admitted the box was located at the barracks, Troop "H" Barracks of the Pennsylvania State Police, and it was in the identification unit.

Yes, Dove admitted there were other items in that box related to the Smith case; such as the autopsy tape that was dictated by Balshy during the autopsy.

I then handed Dove a white envelope that contained the lifters.

Q. And in the upper corner where it says case number on this envelope, what does it say?

A. It just says Host Inn.

Q. And was the writing which indicates foot lifts on this envelope at that time?

A. Yes, sir.

Q. Okay. And then you went into that envelope, right?

A. Yes, sir.

Q. And you pulled out these five hinge lifters which we've now marked six through 10.

A. That's correct.

Q. And you looked at them?

A. Yes, sir.

Q. And just go through each one of those hinge lifters for Judge Lipsitt and tell him what writing appears on them. I don't care what order you do them in, trooper. Would it make it easier if I gave them to you one at a time?

A. I like to keep them in chronological order.

Q. All right.

A. Exhibit number 6 is a white rubber lifter which is marked left foot heel, w/f, 6/25/79.

Q. Now, that's written where, up at the top?

A. Yes, sir, that's correct.

Q. Now, you, of course, know that Susan Reinert was a white female?

A. Yes, sir.

Q. And the body was found on June 25, 1979?

A. That's correct.

Q. And you knew that when you found these lifters on April 24, 1986?

A. Yes, sir.

Q. And indeed you also knew that the body was found at the Host Inn?

A. Yes, sir.

Q. And on the outside envelope we've got Host Inn?

A. That's correct.

Q. All right. Go to Appellant's Exhibit 7.

A. Exhibit number 7 is a white rubber lifter with writing on it, left foot toes, w/f, 6/25/79.

Q. Keep going.

A. Exhibit number 8 is a white rubber lifter with writing on it, left foot, w/f, 6/25/79.

Exhibit number 9 is a white rubber lifter with writing on it, right foot toes, w/f, 6/25/79.

Exhibit number 10 is a white rubber lifter with writing on it, right foot w/f, 6/25/79.

According to Trooper Dove, the morning after he found these he told Trooper Colyer what he found and showed the lifters with Colyer's handwriting on them to Trooper Colyer.

Colyer simply told Dove, "Turn them in."

Q. Referring to the lifters?

A. That's correct.

Q. Had you ever given a statement that you told Holtz about these lifters on the same day that you found them?

A. Yes, sir.

There had never been any question in Dove's mind when he gave them to Holtz until Shimko and Clancy got done with him!

My questions to Dove that followed were simple enough: What did you tell Shimko and Clancy the first time? What did you tell Shimko and Clancy the second time? Did something happen to your memory between the first and second time? The last time Dove was interviewed by Shimko and Clancy was the previous month, January 1989.

Q. Last month?
A. That's correct.
Q. '89?
A. That's correct.
Q. And you made it clear last month as to when you found them?
A. Yes, I made it clear at that time. I also made it clear to them on December 27, 1988. I was interviewed at that time. I told them exactly when I found them. I was reinterviewed in January and told them again.
Q. And exactly when you found them, which you reaffirmed in December and again in January, was April 24, 1986?
A. That's correct.
Q. And there's no question about that?
A. Yes, sir, that's correct.

The internal boys—Shimko and Clancy—filed a report that Dove told Holtz one day after the verdict.

Shimko and Clancy must have gotten confused. Maybe the passage of time caused Dove to forget.

Bullshit.

I screamed "Cover-up!"

Graci objected.

Judge Lipsitt told us to "knock it off."

I immediately called Dr. Robert S. Bear, the pathologist who had performed the autopsy on Susan Reinert and the director of the lab at the Community General Osteopathic Hospital in Harrisburg. He testified: "I absolutely remembered Balshy got under the toenails of Susan Reinert . . . and around the feet."

Dr. Bear was so concerned at one point about John Balshy that he wrote him a letter confirming what he saw at the autopsy and vowing to be a witness for him *anytime* on that issue.

Q. Were you visited, Dr. Bear, by a Captain Shimko and one Corporal Clancy regarding your knowledge about this case during the autopsy?

A. I was visited by two state troopers whose names I think
   are that.

Q. Let me show you a report prepared by them indicating that they interviewed you on August 4, 1988, and this is their summary of their
   interviewing you. Do you understand that?

A. Yes.

Q. And they indicate that you said the following: "I don't
   recall Balshy doing anything with the feet while I was in
   the room." Do you see that in that report?

A. I do.

Q. Did you tell them that?

A. Not to my recollection.

I screamed "Cover-up!"

Graci objected.

Judge Lipsitt told us to "knock it off."

The only thing I felt like knocking off was Shimko's and Clancy's heads.
I was furious at their internal investigation which was an ongoing twisting
of the truth.

Their planting theory helped keep my blood pressure up, too. I called
Trooper Colyer to the witness stand; by that time he was badly shaken at
what he was being put through, and he simply denied that he had planted
those lifters. Trooper Colyer was suspended that evening by the Pennsylvania State Police after 23 years of service. Those lifters hadn't been planted,
and the state police and the attorney general's office knew that from day
one. The FBI lab reports—confirming that the lifters and ink predated '79
and that there was sand on those lifters—should have buried their planting
theory, which was another fraud on the court.

Judge Lipsitt wrote the following to the Supreme Court of Pennsylvania
regarding Corporal Colyer and the planting theory:

"The theory that the lifters must have been planted by Corporal Balshy
and/or others was set forth in a worksheet provided Corporal Clancy and
Captain Shimko by Major Hickes, Bureau of Professional Responsibility, at
the outset of their investigation.

"Corporal Clancy and Captain Shimko did not investigate on what date
Trooper Holtz actually first learned of Trooper Dove's discovery of the
lifters. Rather, as part of their marching orders from their state police superiors, Corporal Clancy and Captain Shimko were instructed at the outset of
the investigation that Trooper Holtz was given the lifters the same day they
were found by Trooper Dove which, according to their state police superiors, was May 1, 1986.

"Corporal Colyer did not plant the lifters and had nothing to do with the
planting of any lifters."

★ ★ ★

Holtz couldn't get off the witness stand quickly enough during the sand-lifters hearings. He basically called Dove a liar. He testified, under oath, that he had first learned about the lifters the day after the verdict.

No, he gave no receipt to Dove to document that critical evidentiary transfer.

Yes, he called Guida the same day he got them.

★ ★ ★

For the next two days of hearings, from morning to night, we argued and we fought. Paul Yatron testified that he closed the file out in 1986 because he didn't think it was relevant to the Smith case. The FBI experts— Agent Ronald Duncan, Agent Robert Webb, and Agent Christopher Fiedler—testified that the lifters were *real*, and they had sand on them.

Clancy then testified about his worksheet and internal investigation.

And finally, Rick Guida took the witness stand to conclude the hearings. I knew what Guida had been going through. I knew his world was falling apart, and the stress on his face said it all.

Guida testified that he learned about the lifters from Holtz the day after the jury sentenced Smith to death. Guida testified that he did not believe the lifters were real.

I felt sorry for Rick, but what is reality? Is the ostrich that sticks its head in the sand seeing reality?

24

MERRY CHRISTMAS

In August 1988 (two years after the '86 drug scandal involving Guida), a small task force in Harrisburg raided the house of a suspected local cocaine dealer and found an ounce of cocaine, an unregistered Uzi assault rifle, and a small address book filled with the names of local businessmen and others, with a series of bookkeeping entries next to them.

They arrested Jack Hull, who started out as a drug intermediary for a small group of long-time buddies, but then found out that dealing in cocaine was much more lucrative than anything he had ever done.

"Jack was so open about drug dealing," one client-friend said of him. "He was like 'Jack the Dealer.'"

Well, the authorities busted "Jack the Dealer's" game largely on information gathered by his next-door neighbor, who wrote down the license plate numbers of Jack's frequent visitors, and "Jack the Dealer," hoping to cut his losses, hired Richard Guida to represent him.

After Guida left the attorney general's office in 1986, he was in private practice and doing okay. *Echoes in the Darkness* had made him a local celebrity of sorts; and Rick Guida, 40 and still single at the time, was hanging out at the local yuppie singles bars which dotted the Harrisburg area. Although he was enjoying his life as a private citizen, he missed the action and power of the attorney general's office.

Through interviews with the businessmen and others, the law enforcement boys learned that Jack Hull had bragged about being protected by his friends in the attorney general's office.

That's all the feds needed to hear, and they jumped into Hull's investigation to get a piece of the action. Public corruption was right down their lane, especially if it involved politicians or prosecutors who commanded front-page attention.

The feds didn't know that Hull actually had a little customer, a small-time user in the attorney general's office. His name was Michael Trant. And he had been an assistant prosecutor until 1987. So they began investigating Guida to determine whether he had compromised his office while in that position of power. Guida was like a four-point buck in buck season, and the feds were gunning for him. In the meantime, Guida was representing Hull, and it got kind of awkward.

Acting United States Attorney Jim West was the 47-year-old chief federal prosecutor for the Middle District of Pennsylvania. He had a full head of silver hair, a medium build, and he rambled when he talked. He and I went to Duquesne Law School in Pittsburgh together, and we had been friends throughout our careers. He was an excellent prosecutor and specialized in prosecuting high-ranking politicians who violated the letter and spirit of the law. However, he recused himself from the investigation of Rick Guida, LeRoy Zimmerman's top dog, because he knew Guida personally and needed him to testify in an unrelated grand jury case. Avoiding the appearance of impropriety was of the utmost importance to Jim.

But Assistant United States Attorney Gordon Zubrod, an ex-marine who walked and talked like an officer and a gentleman, didn't know Guida, and he was assigned to investigate the rumor that Guida may have corrupted his office. Zubrod was 40 and married, with children who were athletes; he had short-cropped, dirty blond hair, and his heels clicked when he walked. He never lost that marine training or look.

Gordon Zubrod, once he took command, escalated the federal investigation of Rick Guida. That investigation would take almost three years.

★ ★ ★

Winter, 1989.

The media blasted the Pennsylvania State Police and the attorney general's office after every session of the sand-lifters hearings. But that wasn't going to get Smith a new trial or get him off of death row. Those hearings were now over.

It was a harsh winter in Pennsylvania in '89. The temperatures were dropping day by day. The trees were all barren, and darkness would set in before most children got home from school. The nights were crystal clear, however, and the stars were forever playing in the sky above.

What was going on outside was of no concern to Jay Smith. Inside his cell each evening he sat wrapped in his only blanket waiting for his meal. Smith felt pretty good under the circumstances. He had taken a lot of notes during the sand-lifters hearings, read the media accounts, and he had hope for a new trial. But the hearings had been over for weeks, and he hadn't heard a thing since then, not from anybody, except for an occasional letter from me that didn't say too much.

My last letter was in my own handwriting. Smith could hardly read it and would have flunked me on penmanship, but what he could read said, "we should be done with evidentiary hearings . . . your record is with the Pennsylvania Supreme Court . . . and now, we can only wait."

In the meantime, Smith had read all 10 of Joe Wambaugh's books, and he fantasized that someday the two of them would talk face-to-face, and he would tear up Wambaugh because of his lies. Smith's brother, William, had brought him those books, and he was allowed only so many at a time in his cell. In addition, approximately 10 women, whom he had never met, were writing him letters telling him that they loved him and were looking forward to his release.

One day Smith heard keys rattling in his cell door.

"Get up, Jay," the guard ordered.

"Where are we going?" Jay asked, bewildered.

"Don't worry about it."

"I don't have anything on."

"It doesn't matter."

"Should I bring any of my stuff?"

"You won't be needing it," the guard answered.

A cadre of guards in blue-gray uniforms took Smith, naked, handcuffed and shackled, to another cell in the prison system. Nobody told him anything. Not where he was going, how long he would be there, or why.

When his new cell door was slammed shut on him and Smith looked around, he knew *exactly* where he was. He was in the Phase II holding cell.

Jay Smith trembled with fear. That could only mean his appeal had been denied by the Pennsylvania Supreme Court and the governor had signed his death warrants. Smith knew that in the morning he would take that short walk across the plank and into the van to be driven to his death in the electric chair at Rockview.

That night Smith could not sleep. He lay down on his steel bunk staring at the ceiling and wondering what happened. Why hadn't Costopoulos called? Maybe he did but couldn't get through. Smith had visions of being shaved, diapered, strapped into the chair of death, and electrocuted with such voltage that his hair and skin would burn and smell of ugly flesh, throwing-up in the process, his bowels emptying, filling the diapers.

Early the next morning, a new cadre of guards came to get him. Smith was so weak he could hardly walk. He did not say a word—he was still too proud—but inside he was screaming, protesting his innocence.

Instead of turning right to go to the death van, they marched him back to his old cell. The one wall had been repainted.

Nobody ever told him anything in there.

★ ★ ★

On May 10, 1989, Guida got his target letter from the United States Attorney's Office in Harrisburg, Pennsylvania, informing him that he was the subject of a grand jury probe into public corruption. A target letter from the federal government lets one know that the cross-hairs are on them, and because the feds are a good shot, that can be very threatening.

Guida contends that at the end of the summer of '89, four months after he received the target letter, Zubrod told him they had no evidence that he had compromised his office. That didn't stop Zubrod, however, from shifting his investigation from public corruption to a drug use and distribution probe.

"Failure to prosecute officials for drug use would breed two standards," Zubrod said publicly, "one if you're a private citizen, if you are black or

Hispanic, but another for law enforcement officials who do the same thing and get away with it."

Under the direction of Assistant United States Attorney Gordon Zubrod, as many as 50 witnesses were called to testify before the grand jury under the federal government's subpoena power. Many of those witnesses were long-time friends and associates of Guida, pressured under the threat of perjury charges to tell what they knew about Guida's cocaine use and suspected distribution, no matter how long ago or how small the amount.

I was hearing all the rumors. Friends and associates of Guida were calling me. The media personnel whom Guida and I had gotten to know through the Smith case were calling me. And my own sources—that old, reliable network on the street that I had been tapped into all my life (especially because I was a criminal defense lawyer who represented street people)—were calling me.

I felt bad for Rick. Being investigated by the feds or a grand jury is like getting cancer. It's a fight for your life. I was plenty upset with Guida for the way he had tried the Smith case, but I intended to deal with that bullshit prosecution my own way: head-to-head in the courtroom, no holds barred, with the gloves off.

One of the things that I kept hearing was that Rick was cooperating with the feds and was telling them everything he knew about everybody: his childhood friends; his college friends; his professional associates; people he had worked with and worked for; even his past girlfriends, including his most recent, a 27-year-old sales rep.

I had a talk with Guida one time about the rumors, long before he got his target letter. I had actually called him to my home. That's how concerned I was about what I was hearing about him. I told him we should have a talk about the calls I was getting.

Not one word was said between us about the Smith case.

I told Guida as we strolled through my archery course and then in the kitchen over coffee, to "quit pissing in bottles . . . no more lie detector tests" and to be careful in his dealings with the feds because I didn't trust them. I told Rick that I had seen bucks that had been shot out of season, while lying down, and left to die bleeding where they lie.

"I really appreciate your concern, Bill," Guida said with the worry of the past weeks etched on his face.

Guida seemed to mean it. I was hoping he did and that he would listen to me. I have never trusted *those* kinds of investigations, which fast become modern-day witch hunts. Guida also seemed to appreciate my concern for him because it gets lonely out there when you're on your way down.

Gordon Zubrod was still calling witnesses in December 1989.

★ ★ ★

The Times Leader, Wilkes Barre, Pennsylvania, June 27, 1989:

PITTSTON MAN PLEADS GUILTY
TO PERJURY AND CONSPIRACY

Wilkes-Barre—A Pittston man serving up to 20 years for armed robbery pleaded guilty Monday to perjury and conspiracy for offering to pay off witnesses at his parole hearing.

Charles Montione, 29, was sent back to prison for violating his parole in 1986 after urine tests determined he had used cocaine, according to court documents.

Montione offered to pay witnesses at his parole hearing to testify that they had slipped cocaine into his drink without his knowledge, the documents said.

He pleaded guilty in Luzerne County Court Monday to conspiracy and perjury in the parole case and was sent back to the State Correctional Institution at Cresson, where he continues to serve his armed robbery sentence. His sentencing on the latest charges has yet to be scheduled, but he could face an additional 10 years.

Montione, of Landon Street, was convicted in 1979 of two local robberies and sent to state prison for 6 to 20 years.

In 1985, shortly before his release on parole, he testified against Jay C. Smith, a Montgomery County school principal convicted in the 1979 killing of English teacher Susan Reinert and her two children.

Montione testified Smith, who was his fellow inmate at the State Correctional Institution at Dallas, talked in general terms of how to commit a murder, but never admitted to the Reinert killings.

Montione's name surfaced in another murder case earlier this year during the murder-for-hire trial of another Pittston resident, Frank Montione. Montione, 23, was found guilty of offering $5,000 to an Exeter man in 1976 if he would kill Ned Tracy, of Pittston.

The Exeter man rejected the offer, but Tracy, 29, was later found beaten to death in a shed in Lackawanna County, according to police. No one has been arrested for the killing.

Montione, who's free on $190,000 bail while awaiting an appeal of the jury's verdict, faces up to 10 years in prison.

At Montione's trial, police testified they had tapped the phone of Paul Cavanaugh, an Exeter man they identified as a suspect in the Tracy murder, and taped phone calls between Cavanaugh and Montione dealing with narcotics trafficking.

Police said they believe Tracy was killed because he owed money to drug dealers.

Cavanaugh is to be sentenced today on unrelated drug charges.

Jay Smith snickered for real this time when he read this story in the Wilkes-Barre newspaper.

So did I. The perjury conviction of Montione knocked him out as a Commonwealth witness in the event of Smith's retrial. Convicted perjurers aren't allowed to testify in Pennsylvania, ever.

★ ★ ★

December 22, 1989 was the Friday before Christmas. Outside, on the mountain, snow squalls swirled and danced before resting peacefully on the ground. Our Christmas tree was brightly decorated by Jill and the girls; the mantel was adorned with pine branches that I had gathered in the woods and woven with white lights; under the tree our presents wrapped in festive paper and bows contained wonderful surprises; and in the fireplace a log cracked, adding to the spirit of Christmas.

Jill was out running around with the girls, getting the last-minute shopping done, and I had decided to stay home for the day. I was looking forward to an entire weekend of peace and joy and goodwill toward men. That night, as a family, we were supposed to go to my parents' house for dinner and hook up with all the relatives.

I called the office frequently in the morning and talked to Tammy, getting my mail and my messages, and to my partners who were still around. Everybody was expecting to go home at noon for the holiday weekend. It was a very quiet day, but nobody seemed to mind. Everybody was enjoying an office party.

Around lunchtime, Leslie and Nick went out delivering gifts to some lawyer friends and courthouse personnel, like the prothonotary and the clerk of courts; and finally they ended up at the supreme court office in the capitol building to deliver a bottle of brandy.

When they arrived in the majestic prothonotary's office of the supreme court on the fourth floor, they were cheerfully greeted by the ladies at the desk, who had their own party going.

"Merry Christmas," Nick said to everybody.

"Merry Christmas," Mrs. Williamson wished back, smiling.

Mildred Williamson, an attractive black woman with her own quiet class, was the Deputy Prothonotary of the Pennsylvania Supreme Court. She has always been polite and friendly with everybody in our office because that's just the way she is.

Our office was closed for Christmas. Nick was back at the office at 2 p.m., alone, about to leave for the weekend, when the phone rang jarringly. He debated whether to answer, then did.

"Kollas, Costopoulos, Foster & Fields," he said.

"Hello, this is Mrs. Williamson from the supreme court. Is Mr. Costopoulos there?"

"No, Mrs. Williamson, he's not," Nick answered, thinking maybe that she was calling to thank him for the gift.

"It's urgent that I speak to him," she said in a business-like manner, and then Nick knew. This was no thank you call.

"I know where to reach him," Nick said, "and I will have him call you right away."

"Thank you," Mrs. Williamson said as she ended the conversation.

Either Dr. Jay Smith was about to get the best Christmas present of his life or more electrical current than all the Christmas tree lights in Pennsylvania.

Nick immediately called me at home. I had just taken a nap and was still a bit groggy when the phone rang. I was about to get my own voltage.

"Bill," Nick said excitedly, "Mrs. Williamson just called from the supreme court. She will only talk to you. It's gotta be Smith."

"Nick?"

"I mean it, Bill."

"Don't go anywhere. Just stay where you're at. I'll get right back to you," I said, putting the phone down at the same time.

Now my heart was racing. It had to be Smith. They had that case long enough. It had to be.

I resented the possibility of a denial by the court, especially on Christmas Eve. What kind of Christmas would that be?

It was the Smith case all right. That's what Mrs. Williamson said. She also said that the court had called her to give me advance notice, that the opinion had just been faxed to her.

"Can you tell me what it is," I asked her nervously.

"I'm sorry, Bill, but we're not allowed to do that."

"I understand. I'll send Nick right over."

Nick drove over to the capitol for the second time that day, bounded up all four flights of marble stairs, and raced breathlessly into the office. Mrs. Williamson handed him the opinion without expression, and Nick, knowing how to read opinions from the Supreme Court of Pennsylvania, went right to the last page.

NEW TRIAL.

★ ★ ★

Word traveled fast, even on Christmas weekend. The capitol newsroom picked it up immediately, as well as the wire service, and all the phones at our office were ringing off the hook. Nick had gotten hold of Leslie, who got hold of Dave and Charlie and Skip and Kollas, and everybody agreed that a news conference was in order. Including the media.

Jill wasn't crazy about that idea. The girls certainly weren't. But they all wanted to come along, which was fine with me. After all, it was Christmas for everybody, except the attorney general's office.

That night, my office was packed with cameras and microphones and reporters. Market Street was lined with news vans and trucks displaying their call letters, and the TV networks had their towering antennas positioned for live coverage. It was a great night. It was a great Christmas weekend.

"Mr. Costopoulos, the opinion is 22 pages, can you tell us in a nutshell what the reason is for the new trial?"

"The inadmissible hearsay . . . it was flagrant . . . it was prejudicial . . . and according to the court, Smith was unfairly tried for that reason alone."

"You must be pretty excited," a reporter exclaimed.

"I am."

"Did they say anything about the Martray deal?"

"No . . . it appears as though they didn't have to. They granted Smith a new trial on the *first* issue we raised and argued. To have gone any further would have been superfluous."

"Did they address the concealment of the sand-lifters?"

"No."

"Have you told Smith yet?"

"I called his counselor, who was very cooperative. This opinion has been faxed to the prison, which should take Smith off of death row tonight. At least, the counselor told me, in light of Smith's new status, they're going to let him call me tonight."

"How long has he been on death row?"

"Since May 1, 1986—three years and eight months, almost four years."

"Merry Christmas, huh?"

"Big time, ladies and gentlemen. It truly is a Christmas present I will never forget, and I can't wait to tell Jay Smith."

★ ★ ★

That night, after everybody left—including my trusted staff and Jill and the girls—I sat alone with one lamp on at my desk, waiting for Smith to call. The counselor kept his promise by 10 p.m.

"Jay Smith here," Jay said, sounding like a recording on a machine.

"Jay, Bill Costopoulos. I have wonderful news for you."

"This must be pretty important."

"We won, Jay."

"We did?"

"Yes."

"What grounds?"

"The hearsay."

"When will they take me off of death row?"

"I'm hoping tonight."

"I can make it now."

"I knew you would."

"I wasn't so sure for a while."

"I know."

"Bill, I . . . ah . . . I don't know what to say."

"How about Merry Christmas?"

"Is it Christmas?"

"Yes."

"Then I'll say Merry Christmas."

· 25 ·

CRAPSHOOT

January 2, 1990.

Ten days later, early in the morning, our legal staff—Kollas, Foster, Fields, Rector, Welch, Nick Ressetar, Skip Gochenour, and I—gathered in the conference room adjoining my office. I had this idea, but sometimes my ideas are off-the-wall and everybody in my life ends up paying for them.

This brainstorm was a real crapshoot. But if it paid off, Jay Smith could walk out of jail a free man without having to run the gauntlet of a second trial.

It was a longshot. The odds were heavily against us, because the law was against us; and the dice would roll for months and months, and bounce off three appellate walls before coming to a final stop for all to read.

It was one day after New Year's, and we were all there to discuss my idea. Nick and Leslie looked puffy under the eyes. It was much too soon after New Year's Eve for them. Skip, Dave Foster, and Charles Rector were sipping their fresh coffee from Dunkin' Donuts down the street. Even Bill Kollas, who rarely involved himself with criminal matters, sat in on this one. They all knew somehow they were going to pay for this high-stakes roll.

"Happy New Year, everybody," I said cheerfully.

"Oh, please," Leslie groaned.

"How about another martini?" Skip asked her jokingly.

"Oh, please," Leslie groaned, louder.

"Okay, you two," Nick said, reminding them that this was serious business.

"Skip," I said, getting right down to the Smith case, "you read the supreme court opinion?"

"Yes, sir."

"Where does that leave them?"

"In a world of shit," he answered, "that knocks out the hearsay, all the testimony from the friends and lovers of Bradfield, and I can't wait to try this case again."

"What else?" I asked.

"Martray's done," Rector answered. "Now that we know what his deal is, nobody in the world is going to believe him, not only because of the deal he was given, but because of the lies he told during Smith's trial that he didn't have one."

"Keep going," I said to everybody at the table for all of us to assess the Commonwealth's case since the '86 verdict.

213

"The sand on Reinert's feet is coming in," Skip said and added, "and if you can get in their cover-up effort, they don't have a chance at a conviction."

"What *do* they have left?" I asked.

"They still have the pin. They still have the comb. They still have that bullshit hair and fiber evidence. Martray has to say that Smith confessed, or they'll throw Martray's ass back in jail for sure . . . and . . . ," Foster said.

"They still have two children unaccounted for and the murder of their mother," I said, interrupting Foster, "and that's my biggest problem. Somebody has to be made accountable. Forget the evidence. Forget the fact that Smith may be innocent. Somebody has to be made accountable."

"That's the problem with our fucking case," I continued. "The presumption of guilt once you're arrested is overwhelming. People don't believe that police arrest innocent people. That's why I don't want to try this case again, *ever*, if I don't have to."

"I honestly believe that we can win this time around because the prosecution has nothing left!" Skip said emphatically.

"There are no sure winners when you pick a jury," Leslie countered.

"Keep going, Bill," Nick said, sensing a legal maneuver.

"Well," I began—everybody was listening and I felt like an old law professor from Duquesne, "I have this idea. Maybe we won't have to try this case again. It's a longshot, and I want to take it, but tell me what you think."

We then discussed the law of double jeopardy in Pennsylvania. Historically, and it's always been the law of this Commonwealth, a defendant could only preclude a retrial if the prosecution *provoked* a mistrial. Once a jury reached a verdict, if you could show wrongdoing by the prosecution, the only relief in the past was the granting of a new trial.

But I wanted to believe that our supreme court would be willing to change that law in *this* case.

"What makes the Smith case different," I said, getting excited, "is we can show the supreme court a pattern of prosecutorial misconduct. The supreme court is going to go crazy when they learn that the prosecution *fixed* the first trial by concealing critical physical evidence, the sand-lifters, in a death penalty case. That critical physical evidence was not only withheld during the trial, but was withheld from *them* when Graci argued before them in May of 1988, asking that they uphold the death penalty."

"You want to expand the law of double jeopardy?" Kollas asked, very interested. "Expand it to preclude a retrial where there has been a conviction?"

"Exactly," Nick answered.

"Smith sits in the meantime?" Kollas asked.

"Yes," I answered.

"Have you talked to him about it?" Leslie asked.

"Not yet," I answered.

"You're going to be asking the supreme court to let *Smith* out?" Foster asked, incredulous. "Dr. Jay Smith, the Prince of Darkness?"

"Exactly," I answered.

"You're dreaming."

★ ★ ★

That same day in the attorney general's office, Harrisburg, Pennsylvania.

Merle "Skip" Ebert sat patiently while "The General" ranted and raved. He had seen plenty of generals do a war dance in his career. Ebert, though only 41 years old, was a retired army captain and had served as an intelligence officer in the early '70s. He was also a paratrooper and could feel another big jump coming on. His only hope was he'd be given a parachute for this one.

Attorney General Ernest Preate was furious. He had the supreme court opinion granting Smith a new trial on his desk. He had been in his elected office for less than one year, and between the sand-lifter hearings and this reversal, the media was hammering *him*, when in fact he had had nothing to do with that damn trial in '86.

Now his office was stuck with a high-profile death penalty case, with very little evidence and a marred record. He wasn't going to throw it out and take *that* hit; nor did he intend to lose it.

"Ebert," The General snapped, "I want *you* to try the Smith case. Graci does not want to try it since all he does is handle appeals."

"Yes, sir," Ebert answered, gulping.

"You came with me to try cases," The General reminded him.

"Yes, sir."

"You prosecuted cases in two counties for seven years before I hand-picked you to come with me."

"Yes, sir."

"You've tried hundreds of cases and put some defendants to death, right?"

"Right, sir."

"Ebert?"

"Yes, sir?"

"Don't lose this one."

"Yes, sir."

"Ebert?"

"Yes, sir?"

"Watch Costopoulos."

"I know him, sir."

You bet your ass he knew me. Skip Ebert was an old "friend" of mine from his days as a prosecutor in Cumberland County.

I went to a preliminary hearing for a drug client in the fall of 1988. The state police had a surprise in store for me at the conclusion of my client's preliminary hearing. As I was leaving the hearing, the cops grabbed me and said they had papers to serve, not on my client, but on *me!*

To my astonishment, they handed me a court order directing that my fee in this drug case be frozen. The order was a test case under Pennsylvania's Drug Forfeiture Law to determine whether criminal defense lawyers' fees could be seized by prosecutors in drug cases. The law provided that any monies or assets derived from drug sales were seizable by prosecutors.

Fifty thousand lawyers in Pennsylvania, and they grabbed my money—a legitimate defense fee—to test this law.

The prosecutor who singled me out and got that court order was my buddy Skip Ebert. That test case was on its way to the Supreme Court of Pennsylvania when I heard that Ebert was going to try the Smith case.

He was five feet 11 inches tall and weighed 200 pounds. He jumped at The General's command but would float in mid-air for a long time to come before he would hit the ground running into the legal jungle below.

★ ★ ★

February 1, 1990.

Nick and I arrived early on the morning of February 1, 1990 for our pretrial conference with Judge Robert Walker. The meeting was set for the lawyers' lounge in the Dauphin County Courthouse, a vast, ornate room with dark wood paneling from floor to ceiling, the site of the judges' annual Christmas reception. In the wall opposite the windows was a solid marble fireplace with the inscription "Do as adversaries do in law—strive mightily, but eat and drink as friends."

This morning, however, there wasn't going to be any eating and drinking as friends.

Judge Robert Walker, 60, was a senior judge from Crawford County in the western part of the state. He was specially appointed by the Pennsylvania Supreme Court to handle the new trial recently awarded to Smith. His reputation preceded him as a bright and fair-minded trial judge who ran his courtroom with an iron fist. He certainly wasn't impressed with the might of the attorney general's office or the Pennsylvania State Police.

Although the conference was called to discuss Jay Smith's new trial— possible pretrial motions, setting a trial date, etc.—we had a surprise arranged for Judge Walker and the attorney general's office: a massive motion to dismiss all the murder charges on the grounds of double jeopardy as a result of a pattern of prosecutorial misconduct. It was a bold legal move calculated to establish constitutional precedent in Pennsylvania. None of us knew at the time, however, that we would be engaging in a meeting with historic legal ramifications.

Nick and I were the first ones there. Bob Graci and Skip Ebert of the attorney general's office soon entered the room. We all shook hands. Greetings were exchanged. Good-natured verbal barbs were volleyed back and forth, and even congratulations were extended on the grant of the new trial.

"Skip Ebert, my good friend," I said, standing up, putting my arm around him. "Are you ready to get your ass kicked?"

"You're an asshole," Ebert answered, laughing.

I actually liked Skip Ebert from the day I met him.

That was the tone of things, but the tone was soon going to change.

Finally, Judge Walker and Jack Minnich, the Dauphin County Court Administrator, made their way into the lawyers' lounge. Walker was a big man, rotund with a full, pink face and the demeanor of the experienced trial judge he was. He looked a little like Santa Claus without a moustache and beard, but sported long, flowing white hair. He even had a glint in his eye when he smiled and laughed, but when it came to the law, that glint disappeared, and you knew "you better watch out."

We all exchanged handshakes with the new judge and with Jack Minnich; we talked pleasantries for a little bit to get a feel for each other; and then we got down to business.

"Bill," Jack began, "I am responsible for having a courtroom available to you guys, assuming there is no change of venue, so I have to know when do you think you'll be ready?"

"The rules require the Commonwealth to retry a defendant within 120 days of the granting of a new trial," Graci noted.

"Well, next month is probably too early. At least for me it is. How about April?" Jack suggested.

"Gentlemen," I interrupted, as Nick handed me copies of the two-volume dismissal motion, "not so fast. We have something else to discuss before we start setting a trial date."

I looked over at Skip Ebert and winked. He looked at me like I was nuts.

I then gave a review of the basis for our motion, the facts supporting it, and the legal theory justifying the discharge of Jay Smith. Bob Graci immediately interjected that these claims had all been raised, briefed, argued, and rejected by the supreme court in a footnote of their opinion granting a new trial. He vociferously insisted that the second trial should be held and held soon. Skip Ebert sat silent, apparently realizing that his chance to prosecute Smith would be postponed for perhaps a few months. He had no idea, nor did any of us, whether his opportunity would ever come.

True to his reputation, Judge Walker at once grasped the significance of our argument and knew that he would have to spend considerable time reviewing the voluminous court record of transcripts, findings of facts, and conclusions of law and exhibits. He suggested that we formally file our motion to dismiss later that afternoon.

"Mr. Costopoulos, I want your position in writing within 30 days," Judge Walker ordered. "It is certainly intriguing."

"Yes, Your Honor," I said.

"Mr. Graci, your response will be due within 15 days after that," Judge Walker added.

"Yes, Your Honor," Graci said.

"Oral argument is hereby set for March 15, 1990; and Gentlemen," the judge warned, leaning forward, with no glint in his eye, "there will be no delays."

"Jack?"

"Yes, Your Honor."

"I want you to have Jay Smith at this oral argument."

"Yes, Your Honor."

Judge Walker was not fooling around. That was *his* style.

After we said our goodbyes and were in the car on the way back to the office, I said, "I like Walker, Nick. I like him a lot. I was very impressed with him. You know, maybe we should try the case before him alone, without a jury. We'd have a good shot."

"Bill," Nick said prophetically, "we may not have to retry Smith again."

"You're dreaming," I retorted.

* * *

Many years ago when I was in law school, I wrestled an Alaskan brown bear in the Civic Arena in downtown Pittsburgh. The bear was seven feet 11 inches tall and weighed 675 pounds. I had read an ad in the local newspaper offering a $2,000 prize to anyone who could wrestle and beat the bear.

Dressed in white silks, calling myself "The Golden Greek," and taking eight years of amateur wrestling experience with me into the ring—for the three longest minutes of my life, I was thrown around like a rag doll. Thousands of fans cheered for the bear, and all I had to show for it was a claw mark on my chest, which I proudly displayed for years as a badge of courage.

After that match in Pittsburgh, I befriended the bear's trainer, "Gorgeous George" Allen, who called me two weeks after I started my first job as an assistant district attorney under Roy Zimmerman.

Gorgeous George, who had the same name as the famous wrestler of the 1940s and '50s, requested a rematch with his bear at the Farm Show Complex in Harrisburg and I agreed, but only if he brought the bear to the Dauphin County Courthouse so I could show him off around the office.

I was joking.

Gorgeous George wasn't, and before I could tell him otherwise, he hung up.

My conference with Roy Zimmerman was a classic.

"A bear?!" Roy said, incredulous.

"Yes, sir."

"Coming to this courthouse?!"

"Yes, sir."

"Are you fucking nuts?!"

"Yes, sir."

I had asked Roy to make arrangements for the bear to be brought through the basement of the Dauphin County Courthouse, which he did by calling his friend Bill Livingston, who was the Dauphin County Sheriff in charge. The bear was so big, however, that they couldn't get him on the elevator, and everybody started to freak-out. Finally, the sheriffs put him in an empty holding cell in the basement for everybody to see, safely, behind bars.

Jay Smith was being held in the bear's holding cell the day we were to argue before Judge Walker. I had gone to the basement to talk to him after wading through an army of security. I hadn't seen Jay Smith since the sand-lifter hearings, which was over a year ago, and when I saw him in the bear's cell, I was astonished. Jay Smith had gotten younger by at least 10 years!

"How in the hell did you do that?" I asked Jay.

"I look pretty good, huh?"

"Good, I . . . I can't believe it."

"Well," he said, "since I am going to trial again, I decided to look good for it."

"Yeah?"

"I doubled my workouts, and I have a positive attitude."

"Jay, I work out all the time. I watch what I eat, and I am an eternal optimist. *I'm* not getting younger-looking," I said, and meant it. And yet there was something else about him that was different.

"Your hair's getting grayer," Jay said, smiling.

"Maybe just a little."

"You should try some Maxwell House coffee on it like I do."

"What?"

"If you take the coffee grounds and mix them with water, then rub the mixture into your hair, it works perfectly, at least until you shower," Jay answered, giving me that youthful look.

Then we got down to the serious business at hand. I explained to him that I wanted him to sit behind bars while I waded through the ocean of appeals that would eventually bring his case before the Pennsylvania Supreme Court a second time, maybe. I explained that the double jeopardy issue I was raising was a longshot. To win would require changing the law of Pennsylvania; to win was also the biggest legal gamble of my life, one that *he* would have to pay for.

"My God, man . . . two or three more years in this place . . . I . . . I don't know . . . I . . . I have to trust you, I guess," Jay said, uncertain.

"Not really, Jay, but I want you to."

"Can I think about it?"

"No, Judge Walker wants to know today."

"Can you get me a case of Maxwell House coffee?" Jay asked, shaking his head.

"Absolutely," I answered, smiling.

That's what I loved about Jay Smith. He had style.

★ ★ ★

On May 15, 1990, Judge Walker issued his opinion.

By then he knew the Smith case cold. He knew all about Bradfield and his friends and lovers. He had read the thousand-page transcript of Bradfield's trial. He knew Smith's history, how the prosecution tried him, why the Pennsylvania Supreme Court gave him a new trial, and all about Martray and the sand-lifters.

Judge Walker also knew the law. He knew that he could not change the law of Pennsylvania as a trial judge. He also knew that if he determined our issue had merit, we would be back in the appellate court system for *years* to come, with no trial in the meantime.

Judge Walker, true to his reputation, called it the way he saw it. He ruled that the Commonwealth's position on Martray's deal was "a matter of semantics."

"Suffice it to say," Judge Walker wrote, "that Martray benefited substantially from his cooperation with the Commonwealth in the instant case, whether or not that benefit is properly called a 'deal.'

"Furthermore, it ultimately was established that the sand on the lifters was in fact consistent, at least, with sand from the New Jersey shore. Given the Bradfield alibi that he was at the shore and Reinert was not, the existence of sand on the soles of the victim's feet or between her toes consistent with New Jersey ocean sand was an extremely important factor in the case.

"Neither the attorney general's office nor the Pennsylvania State Police can take any great pride in the manner in which this case was handled during the first trial and the subsequent appellate process. To say that there was no deal with Martray is to fly in the face of logic. Whether it is denominated a deal or not a deal, certainly the very substantial benefits that Martray received for his cooperation with the Commonwealth in this case would have made wonderful grist for the cross-examination mill in the hands of competent defense counsel. It is equally illogical to say that the existence of the lifters and the sand had no relevance to this case and did not have to be revealed. Anyone with an ounce of common sense could see the importance of those items and to argue, as the Commonwealth now does, that they were deemed evidence only in a proposed perjury prosecution against Corporal Balshy is equally untenable."

Judge Walker ruled that our motion had merit. That ruling would keep our dice rolling, first to the Superior Court of Pennsylvania, and, ultimately, to the Supreme Court of Pennsylvania in our quest to change the law to secure Smith's freedom.

Walker's ruling, however, did not mean we were going to win.

· 26 ·

SNAKE EYES

Proctor Nowell entered the apartment of his girlfriend, Monica Hines, age 23, and without any warning pulled a knife and stabbed her once, and again, and then again. Her blood splattered him with each thrust of the knife. Her body was not found until four days later.

It didn't take the police very long to find Nowell roaming the dark streets of the Philadelphia outskirts. Nor did it take the prosecutor very long in the Delaware County Courthouse to convict Proctor of first-degree murder.

Nowell had admitted killing Monica in her apartment in the 1300 block of Renshaw Street, Chester, but said he committed the crime "while under a witchcraft spell."

Juries in Delaware County don't believe in witches or voodoo.

The defense lawyer brought to the court's attention at sentencing that Nowell was a key prosecution witness against William S. Bradfield, Jr. in the Susan Reinert murder case. The judge was not impressed and promptly sentenced Proctor Nowell to life imprisonment.

I guess Monica's terminal condition—the sickle cell anemia that he told me about in my office during the Smith trial—wasn't acting fast enough for good ole Proctor Nowell.

★ ★ ★

August 1990.

"I knew when he was going south," James Diebold said of Guida. "I called him after they announced me as a target. I just wanted to talk to him. All he said to me was, 'Jad, you need to talk honestly about what you know about Hank and me.' My response was, 'Rick, I'm afraid I have a bit of an ethical problem with that.'" It was the last time Diebold ever spoke to Rick Guida, his childhood pal, his college fraternity big brother, his best friend.

Guida had given a proffer letter to the government, outlining the people he could testify against in exchange for a deal to plead to misdemeanor possession. Among them were Mr. and Mrs. Jim Diebold; John Connelly, Rick's law partner in private practice and long-time friend; Melinda Reese, a former girlfriend; and Henry Barr, a very good lawyer friend of Guida's for years, who was Attorney General Dick Thornburgh's top aide in Washington, D.C.

"I think it was a cowardly act," says one source close to the investigation, "by an individual who was willing to betray his best friends, his best friends' wives, his lovers, and basically everybody who ever extended an act of kindness to him—all in a desperate attempt to keep from taking responsibility for his own conduct."

"Rick did *his own friends*," Diebold says. "When they told me what he said, I cried. I couldn't believe it. It hurts me about him. But it hurts me more that the government can do this to people."

The Associated Press quickly named Henry Barr—Thornburgh's top aide—as the next target of the Guida probe. Having resigned from his law firm, Barr began waiting at home for his phone to stop ringing with reporters' queries and start ringing with support from friends. But he knew full well that was never going to come.

I knew of one exception. I had known Henry Barr for years, and he was a great career prosecutor who devoted his life to the criminal justice system. I also liked Henry a lot and called him to let him know how sorry I was, because I knew what was coming—Henry Barr was going to be destroyed.

On August 10, 1990, Barr was indicted for possession of cocaine, and conspiracy to obtain and use cocaine, by a federal grand jury in the Middle District of Pennsylvania. He was sentenced to federal prison for a term of 16 months.

On August 15, 1990, Rick Guida plead guilty to possession of cocaine, and to a felony distribution count, pursuant to a plea agreement in the Middle District of Pennsylvania.

★ ★ ★

The evening of February 27, 1991.

It was freezing outside. Nick didn't wear a coat, and by the time we had walked the windy, blustery streets of Philadelphia to get to our destination, he was turning blue.

Morton's Steak House in downtown Philadelphia at 19th and the Benjamin Franklin Parkway is one of my favorite restaurants, even though it is not owned by Greeks. The two-level dining room has big-city charm, is dimly lit with pewter oil lamps in the shape of pigs, and has white linen tablecloths and comfortable leather booths divided by etched glass. Blackened Cajun rib-eye steak with mushrooms, a huge baked potato, and buttered spinach is what I like to eat there.

Nick ordered grilled swordfish with stewed tomatoes and salad, plus a loaf of warm bread, two orders of escargot, a crab hors d'oeuvre, fried hash browns, and strawberries with whipped cream for dessert. This was after three vodka martinis with olives, which he had at the big walnut bar while we waited for my friend Ritchi Morris to arrive.

Nick knew I was picking up the tab.

So did my friend Ritchi. He must have intended to make up for his trip to Huntingdon to see Jay Smith. No wonder he's so damn fat.

"Quit bitching," Ritchi said after he had ordered a second entree of lobster and steak.

"Yeah," Nick added, calling the tuxedoed waiter over for an after-dinner drink.

"I drove three hours from White Plains to see you," Ritch reminded me.

"Yeah," Nick said, rubbing it in.

"He's just getting old, Nick, but he's still the same as when I met him, always bitching and tight with his money," Ritch added as he jabbed his second 22-ounce filet mignon.

"Yeah," Nick said, laughing.

Those two guys were lucky I loved them. They were also lucky I owed them. Otherwise, I would have quit raising them years ago.

The next day, Nick and I were going to the Superior Court of Pennsylvania to ask *them* to hear us out on the Smith case. We had been assigned an eminently qualified three-judge panel—Cavanaugh, McEwen, and Montgomery—and they could kill our chances to get to the Supreme Court of Pennsylvania; or they could send a signal to their higher brethren to consider changing the law of double jeopardy in the state because of *this* case.

That's why Nick and I were going to be there.

Bob Graci would be there in the morning, too. I don't know why Ritchi was going, except I did invite him.

"And what is it that you want to know from me?" he finally asked, now sounding like the doctor of the mind that he was.

"I want to know, Ritch, how much more Smith can take. He's been on death row in solitary confinement for almost five years. He's over 60 years old and the prison system is a rough son-of-a-bitch on anybody. I didn't realize when I took this legal gamble that it was going to take *years*. I talked him into sitting it out, and if he dies while he's in there, or comes unglued, we lose.

"And I believe the son-of-a-bitch is innocent. I don't believe in my heart, however, that the Supreme Court of Pennsylvania is going to change the law and walk him. That means a second trial that we could have had over a year ago . . . and won!"

"Bill," Ritch said, seeing a need to calm me down, "Jay Smith is a survivor, a *real* survivor. He's not even getting, and would refuse, any kind of counseling. Bill, they can control his body in there, and they do, but they *can't* get to his mind though they fuck with it every day."

"Keep going," I urged, feeling a little better already.

"He's plenty angry," Ritch continued, "with the system, with the stripping of his dignity, with the humiliation he has suffered. He also feels betrayed by Joe Wambaugh who has portrayed him as a monster and a sexual pervert.

"And he's a proud man, a man of many accomplishments with a driving need to make it. He's clever too, Bill, and some of the greatest thinkers in my field maintain that intelligence is the capacity to adapt to life's situations.

"Smith has done exactly that, and though his frustration and anger will forever continue, with some short-term bursts of satisfaction, and though he will never be able to recoup his sense of pride, dignity, and superiority that prison strips a man of in an inhumane way, he *is* going to make it."

"Thanks, Ritch," I said, and meant it. I needed that, because I was feeling guilty playing in a legal crap game against all odds with Smith's life.

"You're welcome," Ritch answered, feeling pleased with himself, "and now I'm going to have a big bowl of strawberries, like Nick, with whipped cream."

"Yeah," Nick said.

* * *

February 28, 1991, in the Superior Court of Pennsylvania, Philadelphia.

We were last on the argument list, but far from least. When Judge Cavanaugh called the Smith case late that morning, an army of legal clerks entered the courtroom from the side door. The argument between Graci and me was heated.

I accused the prosecution of fixing the Smith case. I alleged "intentional, willful, and deliberate prosecutorial misconduct," for withholding the Martray deal and concealing the sand-lifters in a death penalty case, for playing to the media and to Wambaugh, for wanting to win at any cost, including the will to put a man who was innocent to death. I asked the superior court to preclude the Commonwealth from trying him again, even though that meant changing the law of double jeopardy in Pennsylvania.

Graci gave an emotional and prepared response. He said that if the prosecutor did anything wrong—"And I'm not conceding that he did"—the remedy is a new trial and nothing more. "Justice demands that Smith be brought to trial a second time," and Graci added, "the Commonwealth promises Smith a fair trial this time around."

The superior court didn't seem convinced of that promise.

Within three months, on May 22, 1991, the Superior Court of Pennsylvania issued their published opinion, concluding that it had no authority to free convicted murderer Jay C. Smith, but then issued a sharp rebuke to the prosecutors and state police for intentionally mishandling the evidence.

Superior Court Judge James R. Cavanaugh wrote that the matter could only be resolved by the Pennsylvania Supreme Court and described the defense arguments for voiding Smith's conviction as "compelling."

The superior court had sent the signal to their higher brethren, which kept the dice rolling toward the Supreme Court of Pennsylvania.

Thereafter, in a surprise ruling, the supreme court said they would consider our position to change the law and free Jay Smith, which sent shock waves throughout the Commonwealth.

The Pennsylvania Supreme Court's decision to hear the case marked another in a steady stream of post-trial victories for Smith, who had once faced the death penalty.

Those rulings, however, did not mean we were going to win.

* * *

August 1991.

Nick put it on my desk without saying a word, an August '91 issue of the *TV Guide*.

There it was. CBS was going to air *Echoes in the Darkness* that weekend, nationally, over two nights for the second time.

We had a long string of post-verdict victories, but we had had to assume, all along, that someday we were going to pick a jury and try Jay Smith again. He had already been convicted once and sentenced to death in Dauphin County; then again by Joseph Wambaugh in his book; and a third time when the CBS mini-series had aired nationally in 1987.

The portrayal of Smith was that of a monster, a lurking sexual beast who wore satanic suits, a psychotic killer who made people disappear. I didn't want CBS giving the nation another dosage of *that* months before we were to pick our second jury.

"Nick," I said, "file a petition in federal court *today* seeking an injunction."

"What?!" Nick said, astonished.

"You heard me. Allege that CBS airing *Echoes in the Darkness* poses a conflict between competing constitutional rights. In other words, if they air it again, there is no way in hell we're going to be able to get a fair and impartial jury."

"I've never heard of such a petition."

"I've never heard of a mini-series convicting a guy and sentencing him to death *before* his trial."

"Where am I going to find such a petition?" Nick asked frantically.

"Make one up," I answered, smiling, but not joking.

"Today?! You want it filed today?!" Nick asked, now hysterical.

I shook my head, yes. CBS was going to air *Echoes in the Darkness* that Sunday night, and it was already Tuesday.

The next day, the CBS lawyers were on the phone with a federal judge, then with me, then back to the federal judge, then to their offices in New York, and then back to me.

I threatened to sue them. I reminded them of Jay Smith's pending lawsuit in Huntingdon County against Joseph Wambaugh, his publisher, and CBS. I told them I was going to own them.

CBS pulled the show. The decision came after a telephone conference call involving United States District Judge Sylvia Rambo; Harrisburg attorney Steve Shadowen, representing CBS, and myself, a day before the court had scheduled a hearing on the issue.

Shadowen said the network decided it would "take the high ground" and voluntarily cancel the show. He said the decision was not made because CBS thought it would lose the lawsuit. "We strongly believe there was no legal basis for Mr. Costopoulos to get an injunction. It would have been a prior restraint on free speech," Shadowen avowed.

He was probably right.

Nevertheless, there was no *Echoes in the Darkness* that Sunday and Monday. Reruns of *Gunsmoke, Rescue 911,* and *Beverly Hills Cop II* aired instead.

Treat Williams and Gary Cole were given the weekend off. CBS's decision to pull the show also kept my "Greek islander" friend, Chuck Samatos, in Canada which is where I wanted him, and was the main reason I gave Nick this assignment.

★ ★ ★

May 31, 1991, in the Middle District Court of Pennsylvania, Scranton.

Guida sat nervously in the courtroom waiting to be sentenced. His short dark hair and moustache were beginning to show gray. He had lost weight that he could not afford to lose and was experiencing shooting pains in his right hip and leg. The final blow to his dignity and career was about to be dealt by the federal judge who had sentenced Hank Barr the day before.

Barr, 49, who had refused to cooperate and had gone to a trial by jury, was convicted after Guida and others testified for the government. When the judge asked him if he had anything to say, Barr began to rise but then shook his head no. He was sentenced to 16 months in prison and given a $10,150 fine.

Guida was sitting in the same chair the next day.

Guida's lawyer, Paul Killion, a prominent Harrisburg defense counsel and former United States attorney, delivered an impassioned plea for mercy in front of the packed courtroom.

"Now is the time and the place for the sentencing of a man whose record prior to this was unblemished. He was formerly a chief prosecutor for the Attorney General's Office of Pennsylvania. He has been married for over a year, and he has cooperated fully with the United States Government."

Gordon Zubrod, Guida's prosecutor, sat patiently at the next table with his FBI personnel. They knew they had him. They had been before this sentencing judge months earlier in the Guida case, with Guida and his lawyer present, to revoke the plea agreement they had originally entered into. The original plea agreement was cooperation against *everyone* in exchange for a plea to a misdemeanor possession.

Zubrod had told this judge that Guida had failed three polygraph tests. The federal judge agreed with the government that he had violated his plea agreement. This "snag" forced Guida to continue to dime out his friends *and* accept a plea to felony distribution.

"Your Honor," Guida responded when asked by the judge if he had anything to say, "all I can say is that I am unemployed and unemployable. The media has harmed me. The system has harmed me. It would have been less expensive and more humane if they would have just taken me out back and shot me."

Rick Guida was sentenced to 11 months in prison and given a $5,000 fine.

It was a tragic ending to an illustrious career.

· 27 ·

THE BOX

On March 8, 1992, two months before the long-awaited argument before the Supreme Court of Pennsylvania, an ad in the *Harrisburg Patriot-News* caught his eye—"Cash For Your Trash"—advertising trash and junk removal. He picked up the phone, dialed the number listed, and made arrangements for someone to come to his house to clean out the basement and attic. Soon a white male and a white female arrived to view the areas to be cleaned out, and they made arrangements to return in two days. The white male was named Mark, and he said to call him at the number in the ad if there were any changes.

Mark explained he was a junk man. He sold the metal he collected for scrap, and almost everything else went to the incinerator to be burned.

On March 10, 1992, a few minutes before 8 a.m., Mark arrived at the customer's house with a big van, a rented U-haul truck, and two helpers—a young white male and a young black male. Mark removed items from the basement and the attic according to his customer's instructions and under his watchful eye. The white male carried the items from the residence to the van and truck. The black male loaded the items onto the van and the truck. Mark and his helpers left the residence before noon.

And everybody was happy.

★ ★ ★

March 17, 1992, 9 a.m.

"What's this message on my desk?" I asked Allen, who had been with our law firm for over two years. He had been the chief public defender in Huntingdon County, and the first assistant public defender in Dauphin County—a position he held for many years. I saw him cross-examining a witness one day in Harrisburg, and I recruited him on the spot. He is a tall, good-looking Fred Flintstone, who had been going through a mid-life crisis since he was 20—and was 40 when I met him. Allen is a true courtroom player.

"Well, boss," he said, "all I can tell you is I was in the office on Saturday working on my files. Some guy calls, refuses to give his name, did leave a number, and said he's got some information for you on the Smith case."

"It wasn't the Sly Fox, was it?" I asked jokingly.

"Nah," Allen answered, laughing, "but he did sound mysterious as hell."

"Al?"

"Yes, boss."

"There's a lot of crazy sons-of-bitches out there."

"I know, boss. That's what keeps us in business."

I almost threw that message away, but when I did call Mr. Anonymous at the number on the slip, a male answered and told me that he had a box of evidence in the Smith case. He wanted to know if I wanted it. I said sure and didn't press him for any details. I never expected to hear from him again.

Within a half hour, a tall young guy with curly blond hair came walking up the steps of our law office carrying a cardboard box about the size a 20-inch TV might come in. He wore a clean plaid flannel shirt, new blue jeans, penny loafers, and a friendly smile when I greeted him at the door.

"Here's the box," he said, like a Fedex guy, as he handed it to me.

"Thanks," I answered, laughing to myself at this crazy son-of-a-bitch.

"You're welcome."

"What's your name?" I asked, just being friendly, not really caring.

"I'd rather not say," he answered furtively.

"No problem, thanks again."

And he left. That was it.

I carried the box into my office, put it in the corner, and started returning calls that had accumulated over the weekend and answering correspondence.

Before noon I opened my box.

Immediately, I became excited.

I gulped.

I buzzed for Nick. I called Skip. I wanted to talk to Dave and Leslie.

Inside the box were Holtz's original notebooks in the Reinert case—23 of them, all in his handwriting, and dated—a glassine bag with evidence tape on the outside, a blue "79 USARCOM" comb on the inside with two lifters that were used on the comb, and a bunch of previously unknown documents related to the Bradfield/Smith case.

"Holy shit," I thought, astounded.

I rummaged through my trash can looking for the telephone number of Mr. Anonymous and found it crumpled near the bottom. I didn't know what in the hell was going on or what this box was doing in my office. But I knew things were going my way in the Smith case. I knew that the supreme court was going to hear the Smith case in less than two months, and win, lose, or draw, I would appear before them with a good argument and credibility.

But I was suspicious. Could this be a set-up? Was the blond, curly-haired guy a disgruntled state employee or police officer who had broken into the evidence locker to make somebody look bad?

I intended to find out, and fast.

"Hello," I said, when the same guy answered on the second or third ring. "Excuse me, are you the guy that brought me the box?"

"Yes, Mr. Costopoulos," he answered.

"I . . . uh . . . I really appreciate everything you've done, and I promise to protect your identity, but I have to know where this box came from. It's not stolen, is it, or anything like that?" I asked, holding my breath.

There was a long pause on the other end. For a second, I thought the guy had quietly hung up.

"No, Mr. Costopoulos, you've got it all wrong . . . I . . . I really didn't want to get involved . . . but here's the whole story on it."

He said his name was Mark Anthony Hughes and that he was a junk man and an antiques dealer. He said he ran an ad in the local papers—"Cash For Your Trash"—and a guy called him in response. Mark said the caller was moving and wanted his attic and basement cleaned out and that the caller *personally* showed him what he wanted disposed.

Mark said he did the job for the guy, and hauled junk and trash bags out of the house while the caller watched. Mark assured me there was nothing unusual about their arrangement.

"Who was the caller, Mark?" I asked, holding my breath.

"Jack Holtz," Mark answered, like it was no big deal.

I did not let Mark hear the explosion in my head or the pounding of my heart. This was a *very big* deal.

"Then," Mark said, "before I took the junk and trash bags to the incinerator to burn, I went through the trash bags looking for treasures—like baseball cards, relics, antiques, stuff like that—and that's how I came across the box."

"Did you take anything you weren't supposed to, maybe by accident?" I asked, incredulous, almost bursting out laughing at the insanity of it all.

"Mr. Costopoulos, I removed nothing from that house that I wasn't asked to. The guy watched the whole time and directed us to the piles of trash bags and boxes he wanted out of there," Mark answered calmly.

"How did you know to bring me the box . . . Why me? . . . Why didn't you burn it?" I asked, wondering where in the hell this guy was coming from.

"I almost did," he answered. "Maybe I should have, but when I found it, there was 'Murder' written all over the notebooks, and there was evidence in that box, and I didn't know what to do . . . so I called a lawyer friend, and I talked to my brother's lawyer too. One told me to burn it and not get involved. One told me to take it to you because you would know what to do with it. I . . . I decided not to burn it, and I don't feel I did anything wrong."

"You didn't do anything wrong, Mark," I said reassuringly.

"Thanks," he answered.

I told Mark that I appreciated what he did and that I thought it took some courage. I also asked him to call me if anything came up that he wanted to talk about.

I was blown away by this development. Everybody in my office was going crazy. We agreed to keep a tight lid on that box until we figured out what to do with it.

Was Mark telling the truth?

I believed him, but he had to be checked out.

What was our ethical duty?

Tactically, what I wanted to do was keep the box and not tell anybody I had it. This was in contemplation of a second trial. I would lay back and let the prosecution introduce a phony blue comb, which they did during the first trial, and then dramatically produce the real one which came from Holtz's attic. Then I would confront Holtz with his notebooks which conflicted with a lot of his testimony, and then prove to the jury this evidence had been on its way to the incinerator before it was intercepted by the junkman.

But I called the disciplinary board—I could see myself before the Pennsylvania Disciplinary Board, sitting on a box of state police evidence in a triple murder case, telling them it was junk. They referred me to the Advisory Ethics Committee and Professor John M. Burkhoff, a Pittsburgh law professor who wrote the book on ethics.

They had never heard of anything like this. They thought it was pretty wild. They felt that I should take the higher road and not sit on it.

In the meantime, Nick was frantically going through the box item by item, page by page; Leslie was labeling everything, getting herself and Nick confused; Tammy was typing up an inventory list; and Skip was on his way to the incinerator to go through 60 more trash bags before they were burned, hoping to find more "treasures."

"Jesus," Nick said, excited, "look at this letter from Joe Wambaugh to Sergeant VanNort."

Leslie grabbed the letter from Nick and almost tore it. Nick grabbed it back and ran to me with it. They both were breathing down my neck as I read it.

JOSEPH WAMBAUGH
40 Chandler Place
San Marino, California 91108

January 29, 1981
Sgt. Joe VanNort
4221-A Catalina Apts.
Catalina Lane
Harrisburg, PA 17109

Dear Joe:

Here is my proposal regarding the factual book I hope to write concerning the Reinert case:

1. You and I would meet for two or three evenings in Philadelphia and discuss the case. Our conversation would be taped for future use in case we

go forward with the project. You keep the tapes until such time that we sign a contract.

2. If I decide after our meetings that this would not be a suitable book for me, we say good-bye. You keep the tapes which might be valuable at a later time if you decide to give the story to some journalist.

3. If I decide after these meetings that we do have a suitable book project, you sign a legal release giving me all exclusive rights to the story. I pay you $5,000 on signing.

4. I would then begin to follow up on information you've supplied, interviewing witnesses, attempting to interview Smith and Bradfield, etc. During this period of time you would reveal to me everything you know about the case and supply me with any documents which might help me. I realize that there may be some documents which cannot be copied. As soon as you have told me all you know and pointed me in the right direction, I would pay you an additional $45,000.

5. The book would not be submitted to a publisher until the final chapter is written. This could not occur until a judge rejects a criminal complaint, or until a trial wherein a guilty or innocent verdict is brought. It would be pointless to publish a book without an ending.

That's about it. I have never envisioned spending the kind of money I'll have to spend on this case. I think all 65 witnesses in *The Onion Field* case cost me a total of $25,000. But that was a cold case long past. This one is current and hot which is why I'm offering you this kind of money. I wouldn't like anyone to learn about our arrangement. I'll be trying to make deals with Smith and Bradfield and probably 100 minor witnesses to this story. I wouldn't want *anyone* to learn how much money I've paid to you or my funds would be depleted before I half finished my work.

Best regards,

Joe Wambaugh

P.S.   Since I would start the leg work immediately we should be very careful about being seen together for the sake of your job. As far as witnesses would know, I received all my information from news stories and anonymous tips.

"Can you believe this shit?" Nick said.

"VanNort died in September 1981, Nick," I answered, reacting. "No one had been arrested then."

"What was that letter doing in Holtz's box?" Nick asked, accusingly.

"I don't know," I answered.

"Do you think Holtz got any money?" Leslie asked.

"I don't know," I answered.

Pandemonium was setting in. I still wanted to keep all of this quiet until we decided how to handle it. We didn't know where "the higher road" was yet. Then everything got *really* crazy!

Mark Hughes was on the line. He said that Richard Lewis, the District Attorney of Dauphin County, left word on his answering machine to call him immediately. Mark said that his brother's lawyer had tipped Lewis off about "a box of evidence in the Smith case." Mark was furious that such a call had been made without consulting with him.

So much for keeping the box a secret until we found "the higher road."

I told Mark that I would call Rich Lewis. That was fine with him. He was going looking for his brother.

Rich Lewis was also a friend of mine. Our wives even gave birth to our daughters on the same day, in the same hospital, and had befriended each other over the years.

Rich had started his career as an assistant district attorney under Roy Zimmerman with Guida and me. That was 20 years ago, and he had never left that office. He kept his good Italian looks, but his hair and thick mustache had turned completely white. Rich had a great sense of humor, and I looked forward to talking to him as I dialed his number.

"Rich, my good friend, how are you this fine spring day?" I said, jesting.

"Hey, Costy, it's always good to hear from you," Rich answered, laughing.

"Thank you."

"What can I do for you?"

"Stay the hell away from my friend Mark Hughes," I said to Rich, mocking him, letting him know that I knew.

"Oh no," Rich answered, knowing that all hell was about to break loose.

"Right," I said, confirming his worst nightmare.

"Greek, you have the fucking box?"

"That's right," I answered, now unable to control my laughter. This whole thing was unbelievable to me. I was having a lot of fun with this because of my excitement, but it was tempered with the seriousness of the situation.

"Only in America could this happen," Rich said.

"I love America."

"You would. How in the hell . . . you aren't going to tell me anyhow. I can't believe this. They're going to shit."

"When you tell them, tell them not to come looking for it with a search warrant, because it's not in my office. It's not at my home. Tell them they'll never find it, but they *will* see it again. They can bet their asses on that!"

"That's what I was afraid of, Greek."

"Good," I said, and hung up laughing.

★ ★ ★

March 18, 1992, 2 p.m.

Everybody started calling everybody. District Attorney Richard Lewis called the state police to tell them about my call, then called Holtz himself and filled him in. I called Skip Ebert and Bob Graci. Then they called Holtz in a frenzy. And finally, although Holtz dreaded to make the call, he had to tell his Troop Commander, Captain Kathryn E. Doutt. Captain

Doutt directed Trooper Holtz to prepare an immediate Uniform Investigation Report, and then fainted.

It was the most difficult report Holtz ever had to file with his superiors, but he did it. The report read as follows:

On 03/18/92, between 1600 and 1620 hours, this officer received a phone call from Dauphin County District Attorney, RICH LEWIS. At this time LEWIS said he received a phone call from WILLIAM C. COSTOPOULOS, the attorney who defended JAY C. SMITH in the REINERT homicides. COSTOPOULOS said he had a man come to him with items he removed from this officer's residence. These items were from the REINERT investigation. LEWIS said some of the items mentioned by COSTOPOULOS were a blue comb, a lifter, and a letter from JOSEPH WAMBAUGH. LEWIS said COSTOPOULOS told him that he contacted two legal professors for their ethical opinion. LEWIS said he told COSTOPOULOS he should be telling this to either ROBERT GRACI or SKIP EBERT of the attorney general's office.

On 03/19/92, SKIP EBERT of the attorney general's office contacted this officer by phone. EBERT said COSTOPOULOS sent a letter to ROBERT GRACI. That COSTOPOULOS has items that were removed from this officer's residence. Among them are this officer's notebooks, a blue comb, and a letter from JOSEPH WAMBAUGH. EBERT said he had been in contact with ERNIE PREATE, the attorney general. That PREATE is not concerned or excited at this point. EBERT requested I contact COSTOPOULOS and inform him that I want my property returned.

This officer contacted COSTOPOULOS by phone. COSTOPOULOS admitted to having items that were removed from my residence. COSTOPOULOS said it was his impression that I discarded the items and wanted them destroyed. This officer informed COSTOPOULOS that the items he had were removed without my knowledge or permission. That I was not surrendering ownership or claim to the items. COSTOPOULOS said he had contacted the bar association and he has not made up his mind on what he would do with the items. Again this officer claimed ownership of the items and this conversation ended. This officer contacted EBERT and informed him of the conversation with COSTOPOULOS.

On the morning of 03/20/92, EBERT contacted this officer by phone, at his residence. EBERT said COSTOPOULOS visited him this morning at 0900 hrs. COSTOPOULOS said he would return the items, but gave no date or time. COSTOPOULOS said he had my notebooks, a blue comb with a lifter, a letter from JOSEPH WAMBAUGH to JOSEPH VAN-NORT, newspaper articles and depositions. That the items were not in his office because he expected the state police to show up at his office yesterday. EBERT also said a hearing might be held and I would have to identify my handwriting in the notebooks. EBERT said COSTOPOULOS indicated that the man he got the items from might have more things connected with the REINERT case and he would soon be getting them. EBERT asked that I contact MARK and determine if he had any other property from the REINERT investigation and get it back.

This officer then contacted his troop commander, Capt. KATHRYN E. DOUTT. At this time Capt. DOUTT was given all the information and details this officer had.

On 03/20/92, this officer was informed by Capt. DOUTT that he is not to have any additional contact with COSTOPOULOS or MARK, unless ordered.

★ ★ ★

Jack Holtz was sick. He couldn't tell Captain Doutt that he arranged to have critical evidence in the Smith case burned. He couldn't tell her that he had mistakenly given the box to a junkman either, especially a junkman who ended up in my office.

I can't imagine what he said to explain what that evidence was doing in his attic or basement.

That's not where the Pennsylvania State Police keep their evidence.

The Pennsylvania State Police have been around for a long time. They are one of the oldest and most honorable law enforcement agencies in this country. Every recruit is put through a rigorous physical examination and training regimen at the Pennsylvania State Police Academy in Hershey, Pennsylvania. They are taught how to dress, carry themselves, and perform their duties; there they are taught pride and honor. Graduation day looks like something out of West Point, and the media is always invited to witness the discipline and pride of their newest battalions.

But the Smith case was making them look bad. First, there was the Martray deal which *somebody* lied about; then they got crucified in the media for intentionally withholding the evidence of sand from between Reinert's toes; then the Supreme Court of Pennsylvania threw out their conviction of Jay Smith, which the Pennsylvania State Police had helped showcase in the nationwide CBS mini-series *Echoes in the Darkness*.

And now this!

The Pennsylvania State Police knew the box was pure grist for the media. They also knew to be *very* careful with this one because the box could have a bomb in it—one that could explode their case against Smith.

It did.

And it would soon be delivered. The explosion would rock the Pennsylvania State Police headquarters at its very foundation; the windows in the attorney general's office on the 16th floor of Strawberry Square would shatter. Even Smith, way up in Huntingdon, would see and feel the big iron bars in his windows and doors vibrate and rattle loose.

★ ★ ★

March 19, 1992, at the Pennsylvania State Police headquarters, Harrisburg, Pennsylvania.

Jack Holtz had told his superiors that the box had been stolen by the junkman and delivered to me. That was Holtz's explanation. *Nobody* believed him, but he made the complaint, and it triggered a theft investigation—an investigation that could result in the junkman's arrest, and ultimately mine for receiving stolen property.

"Trooper Kelly?"

"Yes, sir."

"Trooper Brown?"

"Yes, sir."

"You two guys will be handling this one," Corporal Freehling announced.

"Oh great," Kelly answered, knowing what he was getting stuck with.

"I know . . . I know," Corporal Freehling said sympathetically. "Just be careful."

Everybody was going to be watching this one.

· 28 ·

DEPICTIONS

Trooper Kelly called Mark Hughes to interview him about a theft complaint, and that's all Hughes needed to hear. Mark immediately called me so the police interview could be conducted at our law office.

Mark Hughes told Trooper Kelly that if the interview was not done at our office, there would be no interview.

Mark Hughes, that happy-go-lucky junkman, was no dummy.

Without telling anyone, including me, he contacted Pete Shellem and Laird Leask, two reporters from the Harrisburg *Patriot-News*, and told them the incredible story about the box.

Pete and Laird went crazy. They were two street-smart, young newspaper reporters from the Woodward and Bernstein school of thought. They also knew they were onto something hot when Hughes walked into their offices for help.

And they agreed to protect him. The reporters promised Mark searing front-page coverage of any inappropriate police action toward him, and that seemed to satisfy Mark.

The meeting with Hughes was arranged by our office for the late afternoon of Friday, March 20, 1992. Trooper Kelly and Trooper Brown would be there to do the questioning. I was going to sit in on it; so were Skip, Charlie, Dave, and Leslie. Trooper Kelly didn't like the entourage, but it was either that or no interview.

I had known Trooper Kelly for almost 20 years, and he was one of many state troopers I really trusted. The white hair at his temples made him appear distinguished and he looked like an older Dan Quayle. Kelly also knew how to question suspects with the style of a true gentleman, but if he thought you were lying, he would gently cut your throat and watch you gurgle. All my dealings with him, over the years, had been up-front, eye-to-eye, and honest.

Trooper Brown was another state trooper I liked. He was a big, black body-builder; and his shirts were always tightly pressed against his neck and massive biceps. I saw him at different gymnasiums working out, but he was in a different league than I ever was. Trooper Brown and I spoke the same language, however, and we had the same ball-busting sense of humor.

On the day of the meeting, a heavy rain was drenching the soft, moist ground of spring outside our office. There was lightning and thunder, and streams of water were rushing along the curbs toward the Susquehanna

River. A flash flood watch was announced on all the news stations, but the flooding didn't amount to much.

Inside our law office, three blocks from the rising Susquehanna River, another flood was in the works that would soon open the floodgates to more public scrutiny.

Mark Hughes was running late, but I blamed it on the weather. What I didn't know is that he was in a parking lot up the street, sitting in the back of Pete Shellem's '87 gray Honda Accord. Laird Leask was in the front seat.

The windshield wipers were clicking back and forth as Pete crushed another cigarette into his already too-full ashtray. Laird was hoping the fogged windows would keep occupants of the car invisible.

"Take these two tape recorders in with you," Pete said, handing them to Mark.

"Do you know how to work them?" Laird whispered, excited.

"Yeah," Mark mumbled, "but what do I . . . uh . . . "

"Just tell them that you want to record the interview," Pete answered, reassuring him.

"That's right," Laird added, "Costopoulos will understand that."

"Okay," Mark said, still unsure of himself.

Mark got to my office before Troopers Kelly and Brown and set up his recorders on my conference table. I asked him why he needed two of them, and he said one was for me. That made sense, and I told Kelly that one was mine and one was Mark's, and that I would give Kelly a copy of the tape upon request.

I sat at the head of our conference room table. Mark sat to my right. Kelly to his. Trooper Brown was directly across from me. Foster and Fields and Charlie and Skip were to my left, and they looked like a coroner's jury.

It got dramatic. First, Kelly read Mark Hughes his rights. Mark wanted them read a second time to make sure his tape recorders were working. Then, before Kelly could ask his first question, I demanded to know what *crime* they were investigating, and *who* had filed the complaint.

Trooper Brown looked down to the floor.

Trooper Kelly, with a great deal of caution and diplomacy, made it clear that the complaint was Trooper Holtz's, and they were only doing their job.

After that the interview went fine. Kelly was tense, but polite, and very professional. At times it got funny. Mark Hughes told them that he was just a junkman who cleaned out a guy's attic and basement, and rather than take the box to the incinerator to burn, he looked into it because he thought it contained a gas grill that might have some value. Instead, he found Holtz's notebooks, the blue comb, the lifters used on the comb, and other important murder documents, including the letter from Wambaugh to VanNort offering $50,000.

"So," Mark said, like it made perfect sense, "after talking to some lawyers and friends, I decided to give the box to Costopoulos."

"No," Mark said indignantly, "he didn't pay me for it. I didn't ask for any money. He didn't offer."

"No," Mark said, "I didn't take the box back to Holtz because I thought he wanted it burned."

"No," Mark said, rolling his eyes, "I didn't take it to the state police, because I figured nobody would find out about it if I did. That's why I decided to take it to Costopoulos. I figured if I gave it to Costopoulos, everybody would find out about it and everybody would be happy."

"I'm no thief, I'm a junkman," Mark said angrily, and added, "You guys make it sound like I was a trained Navy seal that snuck into Holtz's home one night and got Costopoulos the box."

Trooper Brown laughed out loud at that one, and Trooper Kelly gave him a hard look.

I told Kelly and Brown that they weren't getting the box. I told them *everybody* wanted that box. Holtz wanted it. The state police wanted it. The attorney general's office wanted it. But it was *my* box, and I wanted to keep it. Trooper Brown laughed again, and Kelly gave him another hard look. We ended the meeting on good terms. They did have a job to do and they had done it, the right way.

Then I got a shocker. When Mark Hughes left, both tape recorders were gone. I couldn't fucking believe it! Somebody stole my tape recorder!

Then Pete Shellem from the *Patriot-News* called me for a comment on the "theft investigation" that nobody knew about. I knew then that the cat had been let out of the bag. My only concern was that I didn't want Kelly and Brown thinking that I had called the media the moment they left my office.

All hell broke loose that Sunday in the *Patriot-News*. The banner headline read, "EVIDENCE SURFACES IN REINERT CASE: Junkman's Find Could Raise Questions About Murders That Riveted Nation."

A box removed from the attic of the lead investigator in the famed Susan Reinert murder case has yielded evidence that seems to raise serious questions about the case and could clear convicted killer Jay C. Smith.

A duplicate of the comb that connected Smith to the crime scene, investigative notes that contradict prosecution testimony and a letter from an author offering an investigator $50,000 before arrests were even made were found in a box that Trooper Jack Holtz was apparently discarding . . .

All evidence from Smith's trial is supposedly sealed by court order and stored by the state attorney general's office . . .

Hughes turned the evidence over to Costopoulos on March 17, believing it showed a police cover-up in the case. Hughes was the subject of a brief theft investigation initiated by Holtz after the trooper learned of the box.

Then *all* the media rallied around the box and wanted to get the story. They were like wild Indians waiting to attack. To cover my ass, I petitioned

Judge Walker, asking him what to do with it, and he set an immediate hearing.

That theft investigation by the police came to an immediate halt. As I said, Mark Hughes, the happy-go-lucky junkman, was no dummy.

★ ★ ★

It was delivered to my office the next week, before Walker's hearing. It was another trash bag of Holtz's that Pete Shellem, Laird Leask, and Mark Hughes had sifted through. Pete Shellem told me that it was coming, and Mark Hughes delivered it.

Mark handed me an IRS 1099 form. The year was 1986. The payor was Joseph Wambaugh. The payee was John H. Holtz. The amount was $50,000! I stared at it, stunned.

Mark just stood in front of my desk and watched me.

"Is there anything else?" I asked, incredulous at what I had.

Mark nodded his head yes and handed me several more documents.

The bill of sale for Holtz's red Porsche 944 was among them. So was documentation confirming the purchase of Holtz's vacation home in Nags Head, North Carolina for that same taxable year.

"Who else knows about this?" I asked Mark, still reeling from the import of it all.

"Pete and Laird," he answered.

"Anybody else?"

"I don't think so."

That meant the world would soon know, which was just fine with me. The court of public opinion was the perfect jury to pass judgment on this atrocity that had made a mockery of the American justice system.

Pete Shellem and Laird Leask released another banner headline the following Sunday in the Harrisburg *Patriot-News*: "AUTHOR PAID TROOPER PROBING REINERT CASE: FBI, State Police Investigating Wambaugh's $45,000 Payment to Holtz."

> The lead investigator in Susan Reinert's slaying was paid at least $45,000 by an author the same year that Jay C. Smith was convicted of her murder.
>
> Documents obtained by the *Sunday Patriot-News* show that State Trooper Jack Holtz received the money in 1986 from Joseph Wambaugh, who wrote "Echoes in the Darkness," a best seller that was the basis for a highly rated CBS mini-series . . .
>
> Records also show that Holtz, a 23-year veteran of the state police, purchased a Porsche 944 and a resort home on North Carolina's Outer Banks in the year after the trial while earning an annual salary of about $35,000 . . .
>
> Agents from the FBI's Harrisburg Office have launched an investigation into Holtz's actions, according to sources familiar with the probe. In addition, the state police are conducting an internal investigation.

Wambaugh's picture looked nice on the front page of the paper that day. He was smiling and looked happy.

I know I was happy. Now it was time to make Jay Smith happy.

★ ★ ★

April 27, 1992.

The supreme court argument was nine days away. I was running out of time.

Courtroom 1 was wall-to-wall with people. The jury box was filled with media representatives. The former media box across from them was filled with local VIPs—such as other judges who wanted to observe this one— and everybody in the courtroom was buzzing and talking about the box which sat ominously on the defense table.

My entire staff was there, and Jill was sitting in the well of the courtroom with them, rooting us on.

The box had taken on a life of its own, with a mysterious and tantalizing personality. It was photographed and filmed by the media as Skip walked up the courthouse steps with it; it was sketched by artists in the courtroom for the evening news segment; but nobody dared touch it for fear of what might happen. The truth is it was just a damn cardboard box that had once contained a gas grill.

At exactly 9 a.m., Judge Robert L. Walker ceremoniously entered the courtroom in his bright blue judicial robe, the likes of which I had never seen, but Judge Walker was no ordinary judge. Everybody stood at attention as the tipstaff hammered the gavel that the proceedings were now in session.

The judge began:

> Good morning. Before we start the hearing, I think maybe it would be wise if I got something on record as to what I perceive that it is we are doing. Since the case is pending before the Supreme Court of Pennsylvania, I have no authority to do very much, except the rules do say that I can still take care of housekeeping tasks, such as the preservation of evidence and things like that.
>
> Therefore, it is the position of this court that we should examine those items that are in the box that wound up with Mr. Costopoulos. I also want to determine how the box ended up with Mr. Costopoulos and, thereafter, *I* will decide what will be done with that box and its contents.

Judge Walker's ground rules were emphatically clear to everybody in the courtroom. Even his tone was commanding, and we all shook our heads yes.

Jay Smith, dressed in his same gray suit and burgundy tie, sat impassively throughout the proceedings. I hadn't seen Jay for over a year. I had gotten older and he had gotten younger with his radiant, coffee-colored hair and vibrant complexion. I don't know how in the hell he made his cheeks rosy; maybe it was with the radish juice that was on the prison menu.

There was also a slight change in the prosecution's line-up to my right. Skip Ebert had switched chairs with Bob Graci. Ebert was going to handle this hearing for the Commonwealth. He had a suit and tie exactly like Jay Smith's (except his was newer), and he was ready to do battle now that his parachute had finally hit the ground.

I was looking forward to the whole thing—I had a pat hand, and aces up my sleeve. Every time I looked over at Ebert and Graci, I patted the top of the box and winked. Ebert just smiled and shook his head in disbelief, and Graci cringed.

The hearing wasn't going to take that long. Judge Walker just wanted to know what was in the box, and how I got it. Then he was going to decide whether I could keep it, or whether Holtz was getting it back, or whether the state police or the attorney general's office could have it.

My first witness was Special Agent Michael P. Malone, whose initials were on the blue comb in my box. He was the senior examiner of the hair and fibers unit of the FBI lab in Washington, D.C. The blue comb had been turned over to him for examination in 1980, shortly after Reinert's body was found, and he used two sticky pieces of tape, which were also in the box, to lift fibers, hair, fingerprints, and things like that from the blue comb.

Malone told Judge Walker that no hair or carpet fibers were lifted from the comb. The lifters used on the comb had rust-colored fibers visible to the naked eye that may have come from a sweater. My questions of Agent Malone continued.

> Q. Agent Malone, what was your purpose for marking that comb
> with your initials?
> A. I marked it for identification so that I could identify
> it if it was used for a trial later on.
> Q. So your specific reason for the marking of it was to
> authenticate it in court?
> A. That's correct.

In the upper left-hand corner in black ink were the letters "D-O-V-E" for the same reason.

Skip Ebert was looking at a different blue comb on his desk, which was the one introduced by Guida at Smith's trial in 1986. It was in an evidence bag, but it didn't have any initials on it. Somebody had decided back then, for reasons that would never be known, to introduce a fraudulent blue comb but represent it to the jury as the real one.

What the real comb was doing in Holtz's attic would also never be known.

Skip Ebert looked astonished at the fraudulent blue comb on his desk, and when he caught me looking at him, I grinned menacingly.

I called Trooper Victor Dove to the witness stand. This guy Dove was starting to get under my skin. He was the one who found the sand-lifters during the trial. He was also the one who *authenticated* the fraudulent blue comb for Guida at Smith's trial in 1986 when he should have known better.

Yes, he testified after examining the comb with a magnifying glass that he had produced from his pocket, that was his name on the real blue comb from Holtz's attic.

Dove admitted that the blue comb they showed the jury in 1986 had no name, or initials, or any other identifying letters. He didn't know who put that fraudulent blue comb in an official evidence bag to make it look real or why it was done. He just wanted the hell out of there, because he had been on the force for 22 years and didn't want his walking papers that day.

Dove wasn't the one I wanted, anyhow. The one I wanted was waiting in the hallway, pacing back and forth, refusing to talk to anybody, and dreading this moment of truth. The one I wanted was Jack Holtz—the one who heard Smith sentenced to death 36 times and told Wambaugh for his book, "I loved it; I wanted to hear it 36 *more* times . . . Death . . . Death . . . Death"—that's the one I wanted.

"*When* did he get the $50,000 from Wambaugh?" Smith whispered to me softly as Jack Holtz was being sworn in.

"We're about to find out," I whispered back, not so softly.

"What was it for?" Smith asked.

"I don't know that either," I answered.

"Boy," Smith added, "Holtz looks bad to me . . . he's getting old-looking."

"It's the gray in his hair," I said to Smith, smiling.

I could tell that Jay Smith was enjoying the moment. He was no longer expressionless, emotionless. Jay was slowly coming back to life.

Jack Holtz *didn't* look good up on that witness stand. He looked tired, puffy in the face, and he kept clearing his throat to testify. He also kept adjusting the microphone and facing the jury box out of habit—except the people in that jury box were out to lynch *him*.

Holtz hated his jury who had once been his friends. Pete Shellem and Laird Leask were in the jury box with the rest of the media, writing furiously in their little notebooks.

It only took about five minutes for Holtz to find out that the judge on the bench was no baby-sitter. Holtz testified that he didn't bring his written memo setting forth the dates and chronology of the events leading up to the hearing.

"Why wouldn't you bring a copy when this hearing is all about what you did?" Judge Walker asked, obviously annoyed.

"Because I had no idea what was going to be asked here today," Holtz answered, feigning innocence.

"Now, Mr. Holtz, I can't accept that," Judge Walker snapped, "but go ahead. I can't believe that you didn't know what you were going to be asked."

Holtz looked like a kid who had gotten his first public scolding. I don't think any judge had put him in his place before, but that was Judge Walker's style, and I loved it.

And Jay Smith, who nudged me during that exchange, loved it.

After that, Holtz was a little more cautious up there. He told Judge Walker that Mark Hughes went into a closet in his basement—or must have because that's where the box was, and his notebooks were on shelves in the closet, not in the box—without his permission or knowledge and secreted the box and his notebooks out of the house.

That's what he had also told Captain Doutt.

Hence the theft investigation by Troopers Kelly and Brown.

"Why was the real blue comb, the one with Malone's initials, and Dove's, together with the lifters, in your basement?" I asked Holtz.

"After the Smith trial," he said, trying to sound convincing, "I picked it up from the evidence room on the 15th floor of the attorney general's office. It was just in there, and I didn't know what it was, and I took it home with me."

Yes, he said, there was blaze-red evidence tape on it.

No, he said again, he didn't know and didn't bother to look at what he had.

"What about the fraudulent blue comb that was introduced at trial?" I asked Holtz with obvious disbelief.

Holtz, the affiant, the one who was assigned this case full time for seven years, acted like he never heard of any blue comb and that it had nothing to do with the Smith case. His testimony put the fraudulent blue comb on Dove, who by now was out of sight running for cover.

Q. Trooper Holtz, let me direct your attention to a photocopy of the original letter that was found in your home, dated January 29, 1981, from author Joseph Wambaugh to Sergeant Joseph VanNort. Did you ever see the original of that?

A. I did see a letter from Joseph Wambaugh to Joe VanNort.

Q. Did you see that letter dated January 29, 1981?

A. Yes.

Q. When?

A. It would have been after Joe VanNort's death. He died in October of 1981. I cleaned out his desk in late 1981 or the beginning of 1982.

Q. Did you read it?

A. Certainly.

Everybody in the courtroom knew what *that* letter was about. I marked a photocopy of the Wambaugh letter to VanNort as an exhibit and read it into the record, because I wanted the Pennsylvania Supreme Court to know what *that* letter was about.

Now it was time to get into Holtz's pocket.

And everybody sat up. Judge Walker folded his hands and leaned toward the witness. Skip Ebert and Bob Graci folded their hands too, in prayer. I looked over at Jill, and she winked "get him."

"Mr. Holtz, was there an *arrangement* between you and Mr. Wambaugh?" I asked, getting straight to the point.

"Yes, there was."

"Was that arrangement ever reduced to writing?"

"By writing, I don't know what you mean," Holtz answered, attempting not to sound guilty.

"Exchange of letters," Judge Walker snapped, "a correspondence, anything in writing?"

"I signed a release for him to depict me in a movie the way he saw fit," Holtz answered quickly.

"When was that release signed?" I asked, picking up the tempo.

"I think it was signed on the 19th of April of 1986, and I gave it back to Joseph Wambaugh on the 27th of April, 1986 or later," Holtz answered, trying to slow things down.

"Was this before or after the jury had come in?" Judge Walker asked with obvious determination to get to the truth.

"The Commonwealth rested its case on the 24th of April," Holtz answered softly.

The scriveners in the media box wrote furiously. Some of the reporters ran for the phones. Others in the media box sat there in stunned silence.

Holtz admitted that Wambaugh discussed VanNort's letter with him. Holtz further admitted that Wambaugh's terms with VanNort depended upon VanNort's revealing everything he knew about the case, providing Wambaugh with any documents which might help him and result in an arrest or verdict.

"Yes," Holtz testified, "I think at one point in time, Wambaugh did tell me he had some type of deal with VanNort over the telephone. I really didn't discuss it with him."

"But," Holtz continued innocently, "my $50,000 was so Wambaugh could characterize me in a book. He came to my house on April 19th . . . No, I never met him before . . . Yes, that was during the Smith trial before the Commonwealth rested, and he gave me a check for $5,000 and told me I was getting another $45,000. I got the check for $5,000 on April 19th. I got the other $45,000 that summer.

"Then I got another $1,000 from New World Productions for the movie."

And that was Holtz's explanation. The junkman stole the box. He stole the notebooks which were on shelves in his closet, stuck them in the box, and delivered everything to me, which made Holtz the victim of a house burglary.

As to the comb and the lifters in his basement, Holtz didn't know what that was about. The fraudulent comb produced at trial was not his problem.

As to the money from the author, Wambaugh walked into his house one day during Smith's prosecution, unannounced and unexpected, handed him a check for $5,000 and committed another $45,000 so Holtz could be in Wambaugh's book.

And to think, I signed the exact same "character depiction waiver" for nothing.

★ ★ ★

Everybody loved Mark Anthony Hughes. He was the junkman, the antique dealer, and the only thing he stole was the show and the hearts of everyone who heard him testify. He had no motive to lie about anything.

Mark took the witness stand in the jam-packed courtroom and politely told everybody the truth. He carried out of Holtz's house *exactly* what he had been told to.

"Yes," Mark testified, "the notebooks were in the same box with the comb, and the VanNort letter was in the same box as the notebooks, and that box would have been burned if I didn't think there was a gas grill in it."

"Yes," Mark testified, "there was also a letter in that box dated September 10, 1985 . . . from a guy by the name of Bernie Bales to Joseph Wambaugh who said he was Ray Martray's cellmate."

Q. After you discovered what was in the box, Mr. Hughes, what did you do with the box?

A. I had it sitting on my counter where everybody walks through the door for about a day because everybody in the store was reading through it and shuffling through it, and then I gave it to a friend of mine, and he kept it at his house until . . . Do you want the rest of the events?

Q. Go ahead.

A. He kept it at his house until I gave it to you on Tuesday.

"Anonymity is not a strong suit of mine," Judge Walker said to Mark. "You gave it to a friend. Who is this friend?"

"Do I have to give it?" Mark asked guilelessly.

"I have told you that you're on the witness stand as a witness. You got yourself involved in this, and you are going to tell me anything I ask, and I am asking who the friend was," Judge Walker said scoldingly.

"His name is Ron Doyle," Mark answered quickly and apologetically.

Mark Hughes was in another world in that courtroom. He was the epitome of innocence. He didn't know it, but what he did took a lot of courage.

At the conclusion of the hearing, Judge Walker issued an order right from the bench directing the court reporter to transcribe the testimony and promptly make it available to the Pennsylvania Supreme Court.

He then sentenced the box to confinement in a locked room at Dauphin Manor, a county home for the elderly in Harrisburg.

That meant I wasn't getting the box to take home with me, which was okay, because I had photocopied everything in it anyhow. That meant Jack Holtz wasn't getting the box he said had been stolen from his home.

That meant the Pennsylvania State Police and the attorney general's office weren't getting the box either.

Judge Robert L. Walker might have looked like Santa Claus without a beard, but he wasn't giving anything to anybody that day. I felt sorry for my box when the sheriffs took it into custody to lock it up in a closet at a home for the elderly.

But with all due respect for this newly assigned judge, he acted swiftly and fairly, without fear or favor, without sympathy or bias, and he left the ultimate fate of Jay Smith to the Supreme Court of Pennsylvania.

"I'm glad you got him, that lying son-of-a-bitch," Jay said, shaking his head angrily and bitterly.

"He got himself, Jay," I answered, giving Holtz some credit for his self-destruction and fall from grace.

"Thanks for the photocopies of his notebooks," Jay added. "You know, I went through every one of them."

"I knew you would," I said, smiling.

"He wrote in there that Martray said, 'Smith did *not* say that he killed the fucking bitch.'"

"I know."

"His notes also have in them that several children early in the investigation told him that Karen Reinert owned a *blue* pin with a white 'P'."

"I know."

"There's a lot more in those notebooks that was lied about at my trial."

"I know that too."

"Well . . . why are you holding back?" Jay asked, wanting to know.

"Jack's notes are locked up. We have them and he doesn't. If I have to try this case again, I'm going to nail him with his own notes in front of the jury."

"I see," Jay said, now understanding, "but . . . "

"What is it, Jay?"

"No more delays, Bill."

"No more delays, Jay."

THE SUPREMES

$\mathbf{M}$ay 6, 1992.

The chandeliered lights glistened and the early morning sun was streaming through the stained-glass dome. It was 7:45 a.m. and no one was present in the quiet Supreme Court Room on the fourth floor of the capitol.

I stood at the podium looking up at the seven black leather chairs above me. I was dressed in a dark blue, double-breasted suit with a blue paisley silk tie. I was alone, and I wanted to be alone.

Today was the day. I was first on the list. It had been a sleepless night for me, and I had been up since 4 a.m.

I had some final thoughts to put together and some talking to do at that podium—before anybody got there—to myself, to *them*, to the vast empty gallery behind me, to the 16 mural panels on the walls by Violet Oakley portraying the evolution of law through the ages.

Four years had gone by since I had stood in that courtroom arguing the Smith case. Four years ago, I had asked the Supreme Court of Pennsylvania to give Jay Smith a new trial.

And they did. It was right before Christmas, 1989. I will always remember getting that order. I will always remember telling Jay Smith and getting him off death row.

"But Your Honors," I said, now fantasizing, now talking out loud at the podium, to myself, to *them*, "that wasn't enough for me.

"You see, I needed complete victory. It wasn't enough that I retry the case, believing I could win it. I wanted to change the law. I wanted to do something with my life that made a difference in the criminal justice system.

"I have children that mean something to me, three daughters. The criminal justice system means something to me. I fear deranged killers, rapists, drug dealers, drunk drivers, but I'll take my chances with them. What I fear more is abusive government, corrupt prosecutions, and the power to arrest and destroy without competent evidence.

"Fifteen years ago, when I was a young lawyer with hopes and dreams, I defended a boy charged with killing his mother. I represented him to the best of my abilities, zealously within the bounds of the law, and secured his acquittal, but thereafter, a more zealous police officer in a highly publicized move arrested me for tampering with witnesses and obstruction of justice, in that death penalty murder case. I will never forget the pain and hurt that malicious arrest brought my parents and loved ones. Nor will I forget the fear of total destruction for something I did not do. It took years of my life to extricate myself, but the scars run deep and will always remain.

"I vowed then to get even, to fight corrupt prosecutions without fear of reprisal, which forever looms.

"That's why, Your Honors, I took the biggest legal gamble of my life and asked a 62-year-old man that I believe is innocent to wait in prison for me to do what I thought was right. Now I am asking *you* to change the law of this Commonwealth and send a message to all of law enforcement—the Pennsylvania State Police, the attorney general's office, the 67 district attorneys throughout the Commonwealth—and tell them that if they intentionally conceal evidence during a trial, and *fix* the outcome of a case, that in those instances where they get caught, the ultimate sanction will be imposed, discharge of the defendant.

"Wambaugh made his money. CBS made theirs. Holtz made his. That money may be stained with the blood of an innocent man.

"Yes, Your Honors, I am asking you to free Jay Smith who has been convicted of murdering a woman and two children.

"Yes, I believe Jay Smith is innocent and was framed.

"No, I can't prove his innocence.

"Yes, Your Honors, I *can* prove he was framed!"

I looked around the courtroom. I turned around and faced the vast empty gallery.

"I'm doing this for you too," I said, raising my voice, hoping they would understand, "because most of you have children that will inherit what we pass on to them. Our forefathers founded this country in fear of government. We owe to our sons and daughters a criminal justice system that we do not fear, one with integrity and honor, one in which the search for truth is paramount.

"What you don't understand is that in a criminal courtroom anything can happen, and innocence is no defense. We can't allow prosecutors in a death penalty case to conceal physical evidence intentionally to assure a conviction so books can be written or movies made about them. We can't allow arresting officers to get $50,000 from authors during the trial and write it off as a character depiction.

"Whether *you* believe Jay Smith is innocent doesn't matter to me.

"Jay Smith will not live forever. Jay Smith will not outlive our children. The criminal justice system will.

"And that's what I'm saying. That's what I care about.

"This legal gamble to change the law will make a difference."

An old, black tipstaff had come in through a side door and was watching me. His hair was white and he had a beautiful, brown, pin-striped, three-piece suit and a gold chain in his vest pocket. I had known him for many years, and he knew me, and though we had said very little to each other for the past 20 years, we knew each other well. He had tears in his eyes. So did I.

"Are you okay, Mr. Costopoulos?" he asked.

"I'm okay," I answered, smiling, letting him know I appreciated his concern.

"Give 'em hell!" he said with a great deal of emotion in his voice.

"I will, John," I said with confidence.

"You got 10 minutes."

"Thanks."

★ ★ ★

By 9 a.m. the Supreme Court Room was filled to capacity. Lawyers, law clerks, and other legal personnel were sitting and standing throughout the gallery waiting for the court crier to announce that court was in session. Everyone there was respectfully quiet.

Jill was there in a conservative two-piece, black suit. I was glad she had made it. She was sitting in the front. She too was nervous and anxious. She knew that the attorneys, when appearing before the Supreme Court of Pennsylvania, would come under intense fire with interruptions and questions from any one of the seven jurists at any time.

Nick, Leslie, Dave, Charlie, Allen, Bill Kollas, and his wife Diane, all managed to get seated but not together.

Skip Gochenour was standing in the back and nodded when I saw him.

Bob Graci stood nervously in the front, whispering to Ebert and other pin-striped prosecutors from the Pennsylvania Association of District Attorneys who had joined his position on the record.

And media representatives—from *The Philadelphia Inquirer*, *The Philadelphia Daily News*, the Harrisburg papers, the Associated Press, the United Press International, television and radio correspondents with artists doing sketches, and their camera crews in the hallway—were scattered throughout the courtroom. I recognized most of them and liked them all. Their coverage had been fair and highlighted this momentous legal issue.

"All rise, please!" the court crier announced loudly, pounding his gavel. "The Honorable Supreme Court of Pennsylvania is now in session!"

Justice Cappy, the newest supreme court member from Pittsburgh, entered first and took the far-right chair as viewed from the podium. He was followed by Justice Zappala, then Justice Flaherty, then Chief Justice Nix, then Justice McDermott—Justice Larsen was absent due to illness—and finally, Justice Papadakos.

My heart was racing. The palms of my hands were cold. No longer was the courtroom an empty forum where I could fantasize. This was it.

"*Commonwealth versus Jay Smith*," Justice Nix pronounced, and I immediately walked to the podium. Bob Graci sat to my right with a suitcase full of briefs and documents.

And that room of quiet dignity immediately became tense. Those supreme court jurists were like a firing squad of six. Somebody was going to die.

Once again the proceedings exploded into a heated, legal argument where the accusations of "intentional concealment of physical evidence ... prosecutorial misconduct ... planting evidence ... falsehoods, fabrications, and lies" were exchanged with venom.

"Mr. Costopoulos, the sand-lifters were found *during* the trial. Is that what you're saying?" Judge Cappy asked.

"Yes, Your Honor, specifically on April 24, 1986, by Trooper Victor Dove, and the prosecution had not rested its case yet."

"The intentional concealment of physical evidence. That's pretty bad," Justice Papadakos commented from the opposite end of the bench as he threw his pen down on his pad.

"Yes, Your Honor, that's pretty bad."

"When did Dove tell Holtz?" Justice Zappala asked.

"The first time Dove was asked, he said, 'The following morning, during the trial.' After that, when the internal boys got done with him, Dove couldn't remember," I answered, driving my point home.

"I bet," Zappala said, shaking his head.

"Is Martray back in jail yet?" Justice Flaherty asked.

"No, Your Honor."

"Why not?"

"Ask Mr. Graci, Your Honor. I have no idea *why* he's still out or *how* he's still out *legally*."

"The prosecutor told you he wasn't given any favorable consideration?"

"No deals whatsoever is what Guida said, and he told the jury in his closing the same thing, and further told them that Martray had done *all his time* when in fact he didn't."

"I would call *that* a falsehood," Justice Flaherty said, shaking his head, looking at Zappala on his left.

"I would call that a lie," I said, emphasizing what that trial was all about.

"Mr. Costopoulos," Justice Cappy interjected.

"Yes, Your Honor."

"Are you saying Holtz got $50,000 from Wambaugh?"

"Yes, Your Honor."

"Holtz admitted that last month in front of Judge Walker," Justice Papadakos said angrily.

"What was that money for?" Justice Cappy asked.

"To depict his character," I answered, mocking Holtz's testimony.

Bob Graci wiped his forehead with a white, silk handkerchief that adorned his black, two-piece suit. He knew he was in for it. I could not see the gallery behind me, but their silence was deafening.

"We've seen the letter from Wambaugh to VanNort, and *that* $50,000 had conditions attached to it, like the filing of a criminal complaint to effectuate an arrest," Papadakos interjected, helping me out.

"Did Holtz get any of it *during* Smith's trial?" Justice Zappala asked me.

"Holtz admitted that he got $5,000 from Wambaugh *during* the trial and a $45,000 commitment in writing *during* the trial," I answered.

The questions from the bench were exciting to me. Once again the supreme court knew the entire record and was blowing away the Commonwealth's smoke and continuing deception, like their planting theory and their argument that payments to Holtz by Wambaugh during the trial to depict him in a movie were irrelevant.

Everything that day was happening so fast. Seven years of legal skirmishes and bloody battles—the trial, the Martray hearings, the first argument before the Supreme Court of Pennsylvania, the sand-lifter hearings, the argument before Judge Walker, the argument before the Superior Court of Pennsylvania, the box hearings—were being condensed in replay action by the supreme court, in fast-forward mode, with full sound and color.

The normal 15-minute allotment per counsel was forgotten. My argument was almost an hour long, and then Chief Justice Nix put the cross-hairs on me and pulled the hammer back with his next question.

"Mr. Costopoulos," he asked, "doesn't society have a paramount right to have one accused of heinous murders answer to the law?"

Justice McDermott, who hadn't said a word during the argument and who was sitting at the right hand of Justice Nix, sat up and folded his hands awaiting my reply.

The other four justices fell silent.

I could have heard a pin drop in the back of the courtroom.

"Yes, Your Honor," I answered, "but in this country one accused of any crime, including heinous murders, must only answer to the law of the land, not to the law of prosecutors who control the outcome of a case. Jay Smith answered the accusations six years ago but was denied a fair verdict, and I am asking this court to change the law of this Commonwealth and preclude a retrial in *any* case where it is proven the prosecution controlled the outcome of the first proceeding by intentionally concealing critical evidence.

"Yes, I am asking you to set Jay Smith free in the name of the law.

"Society's paramount right in this country is to a criminal justice system that we can trust and believe in."

I could feel from their silence that it was time for me to sit down, that I had done all that I could for Jay Smith, for the principles I believed in. I respectfully nodded and thanked the justices for the honor of appearing before them.

I was hoping that Chief Justice Nix would put his hammer down gently.

I believed that it went extremely well, but it wasn't over yet. The outcome that I wanted was the release of Jay Smith, and to do that, the Supreme Court of Pennsylvania was going to have to change 200 years of precedent.

* * *

It was Bob Graci's turn to face the Supreme Court of Pennsylvania.

Over the years I got to know Bob Graci. He was a bright appellate advocate with a sensitivity that would make him an excellent judge someday (in fact, I would vote for him). He was married with children of his own, and he had a real sense of honor, integrity, and credibility. He rubbed me the wrong way plenty of times, but I really learned to like him as a person because of his sincerity and dedication.

But sometimes honorable men are put in positions that aren't so honorable. That's the position Bob Graci was in before the Supreme Court of Pennsylvania on that May 6th.

He hadn't tried the Smith case. He didn't find the lifters. He didn't even know about the lifters when he argued before the supreme court the first time asking that Smith be put to death. In fact, he was the one who wanted to come forward with the lifters.

I still felt that his pursuing the planting theory—no matter who gave him those marching orders—was the wrong thing to do. It compromised his honor and credibility.

I felt that he was wrong in denying that Martray had been given a deal.

I also felt he should have quit covering up and protecting Holtz, knowing what the truth was.

A prosecutor has no duty to win at all costs. A prosecutor's obligation to the system is on a higher level, where truth is paramount, above all else.

Bob Graci took the short walk to the podium from the counsel table. He adjusted his tie, and his papers, but had barely begun his oral presentation when he was abruptly interrupted by an irate Justice Papadakos.

"Mr. Graci," the justice asked sternly, "what do we do with the intentional concealment of critical physical evidence by the prosecution *during* the trial?"

"Under the existing law of this Commonwealth, the defendant's remedy is a new trial, and nothing more. Mr. Costopoulos can't cite one case to the contrary. A trial will serve the purpose of getting to the truth," Graci answered, hoping that would satisfy the court.

"Nobody from the prosecution seemed to care about the truth when Smith was tried in 1986," Justice Flaherty remarked, shaking his head, obviously not satisfied.

"Mr. Graci," Justice Papadakos said, now angrily, "I know what the existing law of this Commonwealth is, but what do we do with the intentional concealment of critical physical evidence by the prosecution *during* a trial?"

"Assuming that, Your Honor," Graci said carefully.

"Oh, we're assuming *that*," Justice Papadakos interrupted, wanting his question answered.

"I didn't try that case, Your Honor," Graci said defensively.

"We're not blaming you, Mr. Graci," Chief Justice Nix noted, sympathetically, "but now *we* have a real problem on our hands."

"Yes, Your Honors," Graci said in deferential agreement.

Chief Justice Nix looked at his brothers on the bench. They all shook their heads indicating "we understand the issue . . . we have no further questions . . . we have heard enough."

Graci retired to the back of the courtroom, exhausted and dejected.

Jill breathed a sigh of relief as I approached her, and shot me a wink. I felt good, but I knew I would be restless until the supreme court ruled, which would take months.

And that was it.

★ ★ ★

Before I left the supreme court late that afternoon, I argued the seventeenth case on the list, which was *Commonwealth v. Hess*. This case went back to when Skip Ebert, who was working for the District Attorney of Cumberland County at the time, got a court order under Pennsylvania's Drug Forfeiture Law seizing my fees in a drug case—fees which the prosecution agreed were legitimate. This was the test case to determine whether prosecutors, in the name of the drug war and under this new legislation, could seize defense attorneys' fees.

This was an important case to the entire bar.

Prosecutors were waiting throughout the Commonwealth with their forfeiture petitions.

Defense lawyers were threatened and riled up.

The Pennsylvania Association of Defense Attorneys joined my position, and David McLaughlin came in from Philadelphia on behalf of that association to see me through it. I will always be grateful for their support. David McLaughlin looked like a sharp Philadelphia lawyer, dressed in a three-piece, pin-striped, Pierre Cardin suit with a red silk tie—and he was.

The prosecutor against me in this case was Mike Eakin, the District Attorney of Cumberland County, where the case originated. Mike was a good friend of mine from my home county. Mike had recently been elected President of the Pennsylvania Association of District Attorneys. That association of 67 district attorneys was there to get my money. The Attorney General's Office of Pennsylvania sent lawyers in from their forfeiture department, and they also argued on behalf of the Commonwealth to make sure of it.

Skip Ebert watched this one too, with apprehension.

★ ★ ★

The next day, I telephoned Jay Smith at the Huntingdon State Correctional Institution to let him know how our argument went before the supreme court.

"How did it go?" Jay asked me.

"Pretty good," I answered.

"How long will it take them?"

"Maybe six months, Jay."

"Maybe more?"

"Yeah."

"Now what?"

"Now we wait."

· 30 ·

VINDICATION

September 18, 1992.

Even the end was strange.

Before daylight, I had worked out in my gym. I was back into my lifting routine on a regular schedule.

That early fall morning, I put on my blue jeans, a black T-shirt, and a black leather jacket and rode my 1340 cc, midnight blue Harley-Davidson—a full dresser, with extra lights and chrome, and an eagle's head on the front fender—to my unassuming office in Lemoyne. The 30-minute ride from my mountain-top home was brisk, and I loved it.

I was hoping to be home by early afternoon to ride horses with Jill and the girls across the power-line on top of Sterrett's Gap. But then my plans were changed.

Around 11:40 a.m., Nick told me that Mildred Williamson, the Deputy Pro-thonotary of the Supreme Court of Pennsylvania, was on the phone. She asked me if I was going to be in my office for the next 20 minutes.

I said yes.

She said, "I'll be right over."

It was a long 20 minutes. I didn't know why she was coming. Not *for sure*, I didn't.

Everybody in my office was anxious, and everybody was telling me their thoughts at the same time.

"It has to be Smith," Dave said, excited.

"No, I don't think so. It's only been four months," Nick countered.

"Maybe it's a personal thing," Leslie suggested.

"No, she never would have said 'this is the Prothonotary's Office of the Supreme Court' if it was a personal thing," I added, not thinking for one second it was a *personal* thing.

"That's true," Leslie agreed.

"Maybe it's the Hess case," Charlie remarked, reminding us all that the Hess case had been argued on the same day as Jay Smith's.

"Yeah," Dave said, nodding his head in agreement with Charlie.

"It's one or the other, since it's not personal," Leslie conceded.

"Well, if it is Smith, maybe it's *bad* news, and because she likes you, maybe she wants to tell you herself," Nick said cynically as my blood pressure skyrocketed.

"Maybe it's Smith, and she wants to be the first to tell you the *good* news,"

255

Tammy, my dear secretary, volunteered, just to make me feel better.

"Everybody, please, get out of here. I can't take it!" I pleaded, desperately needing time to myself.

I watched out my front window, refusing to take any calls. I watched Mildred walk up the front steps of my office and I greeted her at the front door. I was nervous and tried not to show it, but she knew.

She had in her right hand a large manila envelope. I politely showed her into my office and she began to admire a piece of stained glass in the window, which depicted the head of a Texas longhorn with an Indian feather dangling off one horn. Please, take it, I thought, just give me the envelope.

We walked into my conference room, and I sat at the head of the table. She sat to my immediate right. I still didn't know *for sure* why she was there, or what was in the envelope. I was too nervous to think about *that!*

Mildred Williamson handed me the envelope that would change my life. I took out the stapled document. The caption at the top of the page read, *Commonwealth v. Jay C. Smith.* My heart was pounding a mile a minute, my stomach tightened, and I wanted to flip to the last page to get to the order because I couldn't take the pressure anymore—but I was afraid to.

I didn't have to.

My eyes had automatically drifted to the first sentence of the opinion, written by Mr. Justice Flaherty, dated September 18, 1992: "In this infamous murder case, we are compelled to order the discharge of appellant Jay C. Smith."

Discharge flashed on the page and the voltage jolted my body.

"Despite our prior holding granting a retrial, we now hold that the prosecutorial misconduct during appellant's first trial was not only impermissible, but had constitutional implications under the double jeopardy clause which prohibit retrial," Justice Flaherty continued on page one.

I could feel Mildred Williamson watching me closely.

Now I *did* flip to the last page, just to make sure my eyes weren't playing tricks on me, or that the supreme court didn't say something different in the middle of their 12-page opinion, and then reverse themselves.

ORDER REVERSED AND APPELLANT DISCHARGED.

No dissents.

The supreme court did it.

The supreme court changed the law of Pennsylvania and sent law enforcement a stunning message.

"I . . . uh . . . Mrs. Williamson . . . I . . . I must tell you that this is the highest point of my legal career and I . . . I don't know what . . . I don't know what to say," I stammered, and meant it.

"It was an honor for me to be the one to bring this to you. Mr. Costopoulos . . . I was asked to deliver it in person by the Supreme Court of Pennsylvania because it's a discharge order," she said, smiling, with sincerity.

"Does the attorney general's office know yet?" I asked.

"*Nobody* else knows yet," she answered, "and this will not be filed of record until 1 o'clock . . . and the supreme court doesn't want anything released until then."

"I understand," I said, shaking my head, still stunned.

I kissed her on the cheek, and kept myself as composed as possible—it was damn tough not to let out a scream—until she left. I knew everybody in the office was within walls of me, not knowing, waiting.

Never before had a court order been hand-delivered to me in 22 years of practicing law.

Nick, who had put his life and soul into it; Dave, Leslie, Charlie, Allen, Jeff, and Tammy—all of them rushed me at the front door the moment Mildred Williamson left.

I didn't have to say a word.

They knew.

We did it.

We just stared at each other in stunned silence.

Jay C. Smith was going home. He just didn't know it yet.

★ ★ ★

We were to tell no one until 1 o'clock. They were my strictest orders, and then I immediately called home to tell Jill. The phone rang and rang and no one answered.

I asked Tammy to get me a suit and a white shirt and tie from my house, and maybe find Jill. I couldn't be talking to the media in a black Harley T-shirt with an eagle flying on my chest.

But time was flying like that eagle, fast and furious.

Skip Gochenour was on his way over, and within hours he would be driving his cobalt blue BMW 525, at a high rate of speed, to the prison in Huntingdon where Smith was waiting to be brought to my office and then home. Jay Smith would arrive at 9:28 p.m. a free man.

In the meantime, his brother William was on his way in from Wilmington, Delaware with a new suit of clothes for Jay.

Jill was on the phone and when I told her, she screamed, "Oh my God!"

Attorney General Preate also called and offered sincere congratulations. We talked like two generals might talk at the end of a seven-year war. We both agreed that he had nothing to do with the "egregious prosecutorial misconduct" referred to by the Supreme Court of Pennsylvania in its landmark opinion.

But now it was time to bring the troops home and celebrate.

At 1:01 all eight lines at the law office lit up at the same time. The Smith opinion had just been filed at the Prothonotary's Office and copies had been delivered to the media room in the capitol.

★ ★ ★

The attorney general's office hunkered down when the manila envelope was delivered to the 16th floor of Strawberry Square. All was quiet down the hallway of prosecutorial offices. The casualty list would never be made public.

The supreme court concluded that "an examination of the record establishes the bad faith of the prosecution beyond any possibility of doubt; indeed, it would be hard to imagine more egregious prosecutorial tactics."

That's why the supreme court changed the law of the land and set Jay Smith free.

It was not a question of his guilt or innocence.

The Supreme Court of Pennsylvania just wasn't going to tolerate the intentional concealment of critical physical evidence in a criminal case, especially a death penalty case.

Bob Graci felt a sharp pain in his stomach as he read the opinion on his desk.

Skip Ebert just shook his head in disbelief.

Ken Reinert, the ex-husband of slain Upper Merion teacher Susan Reinert, got the call telling him the man he believed murdered Susan and his two children was going free, and he felt a murderous anger.

His stepdaughter, Lisa Kelso, was so shaken at the news of Smith's release she said, "I'm deathly afraid . . . I'll take precautions now wherever I go and keep an eye out for who is behind me."

Then she asked the media whether she and her family could get a court order to keep Smith away from them.

Ken Reinert's new wife, Lynn, said it wouldn't surprise her if Smith hurt her family or someone else. "He's a sick man," she told Philadelphia's Channel 6 TV news, "He's going to go after someone else."

Early that same afternoon, Jack Holtz, not knowing, took the elevator to the 16th floor of Strawberry Square to return a file in another murder case that had been taken from him. That's where *he* got the news, and the blood drained from his face. Without saying a word, he left quickly.

Skip Ebert was so concerned that Holtz might commit suicide, he called his superiors to keep an eye on him.

★ ★ ★

I immediately called Jay Smith from my office. It was 1:10 p.m. I had no trouble getting through to him *this* time.

"Jay," I said.

"What's going on?" he asked.

"Let me read you something."

"Go ahead."

"In this infamous murder case, we are compelled to order the discharge of appellant Jay C. Smith."

"What's that?"

"We won," I said. "The supreme court has ordered your discharge. You are a free man, Jay," I said, but there was no answer. For a second, I thought he might have had a heart attack. That would have been terrible.

"Jay . . . Jay . . . are you still there?"

"When . . . when can I go home?" Jay asked, barely audible.

"Tonight," I answered. "Skip's on his way up."

"Bill, please call my brother right away."

"I already did, Jay."

"Good," he said thankfully. "Now what?"

"Pack your stuff," I said.

"They can keep it," he answered.

It was dark when Skip Gochenour pulled into the visitors' parking lot at the State Correctional Institution at Huntingdon. Several media vehicles were in position with telescopic lenses aimed and focused at the front gate. Their wait was over.

Within minutes Smith emerged out of the darkness at the front gate wearing his baggy prison denims with blue tennis shoes. That picture made every paper in the country by morning with headlines reading "JAY WALKS."

The word was out on all the wire services.

The media was tracking him from Huntingdon to our offices with two-way radios and car phones. Their flash news bulletins made it sound like an unguided missile was on its way to Harrisburg and everybody should lock their doors and pull their blinds, and maybe get out of town.

They had also sent a convoy of vehicles to Market Street in Lemoyne to await his arrival. Their vans, trucks, and jeeps—all with call letters, some with towers to film his arrival "live"—took over several blocks. It was a warm, still evening. Dozens of reporters from every network, and curiosity seekers, were milling around and sitting on the lawns, eating pizza and submarines and drinking soda while they waited.

Inside, the conference room table had dozens of microphones clustered together for Jay Smith's comments.

The two-hour ride from Huntingdon was delayed. En route to the office, Smith asked Gochenour to stop at a Roy Rogers for black coffee with sugar and a quarter-pound hamburger. It was the first time in 13 years that Smith had ridden in the front seat of a car or in any vehicle without being handcuffed and shackled. Before they entered the Roy Rogers, Smith went over and touched a tree.

Outside my office, the crowd swelled. My 17-year-old daughter Kara was standing on the sidewalk, looking up and down Market Street, waiting for their arrival. Her leather skirt was a little too short for me, but she said I was old-fashioned. Me? Old-fashioned?!

Somebody kept the parking space at the bottom of the office steps open, and finally, at 9:28 p.m., Skip Gochenour pulled in.

Smith got out of the car, still wearing his baggy prison denims with blue tennis shoes. He was embraced by his brother, William, a retired Philadelphia Electric Company supervisor, as they stood in the glare of lights from Philadelphia and Harrisburg television stations.

Jay Smith waved to everybody, overwhelmed by it all, and immediately walked up the steps, between the lions, and into the office where I was waiting. We shook hands, but said nothing. His brother accompanied him upstairs to change into his new clothes.

A few minutes later, Smith came downstairs to face the press. He wore a solid gray suit that his brother brought him, a maroon tie, and cordovan wingtips. His coffee-colored hair was neatly combed to the side. The cameras flashed and clicked in his face as he took the chair before the array of microphones in the conference room. I sat to his left, but this was *his* press conference. I was excited for him, for me, for everything I believed in.

"What's the first thing you're going to do, Jay?" a reporter shouted.

"Be with my brother and my family," Smith said without hesitation.

"And what will you do with your life now?"

"I haven't given it any thought. I don't know where I'll go from here," Smith answered, shaking his head pensively.

"Are you angry?"

"Yeah, I'm angry."

"How angry?"

"I would like to drop a nuclear bomb on Pennsylvania."

"Why's that?"

"The state of Pennsylvania and the state police tried to kill me."

Oh no, I thought. Great, I thought. This is the last thing in the world the people of Pennsylvania wanted to hear from Dr. Jay Smith, the "Prince of Darkness."

Throughout the press conference, Smith laced his answers with how *certain members* of the state police framed him and tried to kill him.

When someone asked what he meant, he replied, "I thought the electric chair was pretty close."

Smith's comments on other aspects of his case were equally pointed.

On the Reinert family's negative reaction to his release, Smith said, "Susan Reinert was a good teacher, one of my best. I had nothing to do with her death. The Reinert family was also duped and deceived by the state police."

I thought Jay Smith's answers were excellent. I was actually proud of him. He was on a roll.

"Mr. Smith?"

"Yes."

"Now that the Supreme Court of Pennsylvania has discharged you, you could go public with anything you know about Susan Reinert's two children and never be prosecuted."

"I have no information, none whatsoever, regarding those children. I did not kill those children. I did not harm those children in any way," Jay answered calmly, without any hostility toward the reporter who asked it.

On codefendant William Bradfield, Smith said, "He is right where he belongs . . . in prison doing three life sentences."

Smith said that Bradfield and Jack Holtz "were the two guys who tried to kill me."

At another point, he added Joseph Wambaugh, author of *Echoes in the Darkness* to his list of would-be Jay Smith killers.

On whether he was bitter, Smith said, "Yes, pretty bitter. Bradfield tried to kill me, the Pennsylvania State Police tried to kill me."

He ended the conference by thanking me, several times, and said he was thankful the supreme court had the courage to make the right decision. "Everyone is out for blood when someone is killed."

Smith described prison as "a world worse than a nightmare or hell. They are breeding criminality in prison. When they come out, they're in a rage."

★ ★ ★

Midnight.

Everybody had gone home, except Jay's brother, who was waiting downstairs.

Jay and I sat alone in an upstairs office. We had some talking to do.

"Bill, I . . . I don't know how to . . . ," Jay said, breaking the silence.

"It's okay, Jay," I answered.

"It was rough."

"I don't know how you did it."

"I feel like I have returned from hell."

"You did."

"Will you stay in touch?"

"Of course."

"I have a lot of thinking to do. I have a little life left. This is all so sudden."

"It's okay now, Jay . . . your brother is waiting downstairs to take you home."

"Thanks, Bill."

"We've got plenty of time to talk now that you're out."

"It's hard to believe."

It was time to get my grade. Over seven years ago, after the jury pronounced Death 36 times, Jay Smith tapped me on the shoulder before the sheriffs took him away and told me that I had flunked. I never got over that.

"Before you go, Jay?"

"Yes."

"Do you remember back seven years ago when you flunked me?"

"Of course. I will never forget being sentenced to death 36 times. I also never forget students that flunk."

"Well, what's my grade now?" I asked, grinning and proud, knowing an A+ was coming.

"I knew you were going to ask me that."

"Good."

"So, I gave it a lot of thought on the way down here, and I have decided to give you a B+."

I couldn't believe it. I spent seven years of my life on this son-of-a-bitch. I changed the law of Pennsylvania for him. I walked him out of prison, and he gives me a B+.

"B+?!" I exclaimed, astonished.

"Correct," he said sternly. And I knew the Principal was back.

"Why?" I asked.

"Tardiness of work."

Then I understood. It took me too long to get him out. That's what I loved about Jay Smith. He had style.

★ ★ ★

My suit was hanging in the coffee room, along with my white shirt and tie. My Harley T-shirt and black leather jacket felt tighter than they ever had. I was really pumped.

Outside the streets were desolate. All the residential lights were out. Most sane people were sleeping soundly.

That midnight blue steel monster roared when I hit the ignition switch. I jammed a Garth Brooks tape into the sound system on the dash and turned it up loud. It was time for the Eagle to fly once again.

For Jay Smith, it was the first time in 13 years.

Freedom, and a system to protect it, is what the Smith case was *really* about.

· 31 ·

REFLECTIONS

The Chester County apartment house where William Bradfield had been living with fellow teacher Susan Myers when Reinert and her children were murdered was a potential gold mine of evidence. It has been converted into a convent. That apartment house was *never* searched.

William Bradfield continues to be housed in the State Correctional Institution at Graterford, Pennsylvania, tucked away under three life sentences. He was found guilty of scheming to inherit Reinert's million-dollar estate and having plotted her death, while secretly planning to make it appear as though Smith alone had been responsible.

Susan Myers, prior to the Smith trial, said that Bradfield loves prison, that he is now a poet in exile and has taken correspondence courses in Arabic and astronomy.

As to Myers, the former Upper Merion English teacher who was living with Bradfield on the weekend in question: she reportedly got $10,000 from Joseph Wambaugh to help him with his book. Her whereabouts since Smith's release are unknown.

Joanne Aitken remains resolute. The Harvard-educated architect communicates with William Bradfield to this day, according to the prison records. She continues to enjoy immunity. Her whereabouts are unknown.

Wendy Zeigler, the former Bradfield student and the youngest of his former lovers, testified at the Bradfield and Smith trials. Her whereabouts are unknown, although some people say she has become a nun.

Christopher Pappas, the former Upper Merion substitute teacher, testified at his mentor's murder trial. He had been working a construction job in Montgomery County and has avoided the teaching profession. He may never go back, and his current whereabouts are unknown.

Vincent Valaitis continues to teach at Upper Merion High School. He publicly admitted to a Philadelphia reporter after the box was found that he too got money from Wambaugh during Smith's trial. He said he got Guida's permission. Valaitis significantly embellished his testimony at Smith's trial as Wambaugh watched.

It is to the point now—after two trials, two books, a television mini-series, an ocean of appeals, and over a decade of continuous denials by Smith—that some people finally believe what Smith has been saying all along: that he was framed by Bradfield and others, and that he had nothing to do with the death of Susan Reinert or her children. And that the influence of the media and a famous author and Hollywood and overzealous police and prosecutors corrupted the system for personal gain.

There is no question that some critical physical evidence, the sand on Reinert's feet, was intentionally concealed by the police and prosecution. There is no question that the police and prosecutors were consulted in the production of the mini-series, while Smith was on death row.

The jailhouse confessions have also been exposed for what they were.

Raymond Martray, the former small-town cop from Connellsville, Pennsylvania, continues to enjoy his freedom. He walked out of prison in the middle of a four- to eight-year sentence for masterminding a burglary ring. Martray, also once convicted of perjury, still calls *them* whenever he needs a favor. Holtz's notebooks reflect an entry made during the polygraph test of Martray: "S did *not* kill the fucking bitch."

To this day, Martray owes the Commonwealth more time he will never do.

Charles Montione is still in prison, but not for life. After serving time for perjury and various drug offenses, he was convicted in January 1995 of first-degree murder in Wilkes-Barre, Pennsylvania for a contract hit on a drug dealer. The murder by Montione took place in February 1986, just two months before he testified on behalf of the attorney general's office at the trial of Jay Smith. Interesting.

If Smith had gone to a second trial, the prosecution would have had nothing left. The key physical evidence had surfaced from the shore; the deals had been exposed; the critical hearsay statements had been thrown out; the lead state police investigator had gotten caught with $50,000 from Wambaugh in his pocket—other evidence in his house, destined for the incinerator, had been intercepted; and the lead prosecutor had been jailed.

Some say the prosecution of Smith, and everyone involved in it, was *cursed*. Skip Ebert, the third prosecutor to take over, was plenty concerned about his assignment and the bizarre calamities that continued to plague the prosecution. Ebert remarked: "People came to me and said, 'Don't get involved in this case. It's cursed.' Maybe I should have listened."

Maybe he should have.

Maybe Bob Graci, who still experiences sleepless nights, should have listened too.

Maybe the people who saw to it that the world was safe from Jay C. Smith should have played by the rules.

Jack Holtz now admits—after he was caught red-handed—to taking $50,000 from Los Angeles cop-turned-famous-author Joseph Wambaugh. Whether it was for providing inside information or for his character depiction, Holtz's career has been dashed and his credibility forever damaged.

Rick Guida was last seen by a friend of his crossing the Market Street Bridge in Harrisburg. Rick was on a work-release, out-mate status while serving the last two months of his prison sentence for cocaine possession and distribution. Guida's career has also been ruined and his credibility forever damaged.

In the wake of their self-destruction, Joseph Wambaugh published a *New York Times* best-seller, *Echoes in the Darkness*, and generated a seven-figure sum. Then he bagged an extra $800,000 for helping with the nationally televised mini-series based on his book about the Reinert case. He lives a rich man's life in southern California, where he has declined comment on the twists and turns in Smith's case.

Wambaugh has no idea of the influence his money and power and tickets to stardom had on the lives of so many people involved in the case. I do not believe it was intended.

Someday I am going to say something to Loretta Schwartz-Nobel who also published a book about this case. Wambaugh's book was a tough act to follow, but she managed to get *Engaged To Murder* out there, and it was billed as "the inside story of the Mainline murders." She had interviewed Jay Smith several times while he was in prison before I became involved. All of her handwritten notes on those interviews were in Holtz's box.

Loretta, Loretta, Loretta?!

John Balshy has gone back into retirement, angry and bitter. He attends church every Sunday and encourages his family to do the same. He and Bob Keys came to see me one day and told me everything.

Senior Judge Lipsitt, 71, continues to render competent and honorable service to the citizenry of Pennsylvania as he has for over 25 years. He was unfairly blamed by many for the transgressions of overzealous cops and prosecutors who went on to Hollywood and lost sight of their higher obligations to the system.

Judge Walker died in October 1993. He was an honorable man and an excellent jurist.

★ ★ ★

Smith still has a shady past.

That will never change.

The police say that his daughter, Stephanie, and his son-in-law, Eddie Hunsberger, disappeared from the face of the earth on February 28, 1978, and are presumed dead. Cops have concluded they were murdered and point to Jay Smith.

Eddie Hunsberger's parents have insisted for years that Jay Smith murdered the couple. Some say if you find their bodies, you'll find the children.

Eddie Hunsberger's parents followed Smith's case for 13 years and have gone public with their accusations. Now they are living in fear that they might be next.

Yet there has never been a shred of evidence linking Smith to the murder of his daughter and son-in-law.

Jay Smith has always maintained that his daughter and son-in-law were heroin addicts. Methadone clinics in the Philadelphia area confirm they were patients.

Holtz's notebooks, which were found in the box, contain a five-page interview with one Ruth Rhoades, who told him that she saw Stephanie and Eddie, alive and well, in the spring of 1979.

But the Smith legend continues.

★ ★ ★

Whatever happened to the Reinert children?

Some people say that they were disposed of in a sewer line that was under construction on the weekend in question between Morgantown and Downingtown, which would have been on their mother's way to her final resting place at the Host Inn.

Balshy believes they still may be alive.

Ken Reinert, the children's father, prays for that.

Skip Gochenour believes that they were burned to oblivion at the coke smelting furnaces in Phoenixville, Pennsylvania. Towering blast furnaces loom on the horizon at the Phoenix Steel Company near Bradfield's home. On the right-side quarter panel of Susan Reinert's car, the FBI removed crushed samples of slag, a ferrous material found in coke and iron.

Nick Ressetar agrees with Skip.

Others believe that they were dumped into the mammoth footers of the Marriott Hotel that was under construction directly across from the Host Inn at the time of their disappearance.

Jay Smith thinks that they are somewhere between here and New Mexico and that Bradfield knows exactly where they are.

What I believe doesn't matter.

★ ★ ★

Smith is branded: KILLER.

The public still believes that he murdered Susan Reinert and her two children.

Yet, at its best, the evidence was purely circumstantial. Its chief ingredients: a strand of hair, some tiny rug fibers, a comb, and a pin—and a convicted perjurer, an ex-cop who testified that Smith had confessed to him when they shared a prison cell.

Smith had a dozen combs in his King of Prussia house just like the one found under Reinert's corpse: cheap, plastic combs that bore the inscription of the Army Reserve unit in which Smith had once served as a colonel.

There was no need to present a fraudulent one.

Microscopic rug fibers found in Reinert's hair and car were forced to match those found in a red carpet in Smith's house—a place Smith insisted Reinert had never been. The single brown hair found in sweepings from Smith's basement was forced to match Reinert's hair. A green Philadelphia Art Museum pin found in Smith's car was similar to the pin the 11-year-old Karen Reinert was wearing when she was last seen alive.

And that was the Commonwealth's case, at its best.

Presumed innocent.

Means nothing.

Weeks passed after Smith was set free, and the furor raged on. She called and said that her name was Martha Shultz, shortly after the Smith verdict in May '86. She said that she had been a Smith juror and wanted to see me right away. We met at the Howard Johnson's by the Camp Hill Mall—she brought her husband Stan and I took Jill—and we had the fish dinner, all you can eat. I recognized her right away, early 50s, the sewing machine operator from Halifax, juror number four.

Martha Schultz was distraught. She said that she felt like she had blood on her hands. She felt that she had been deceived by the American criminal justice system, and manipulated and used by the prosecution. She couldn't sleep at night and felt guilty, and she wondered whether she could seek recourse from the authorities for what they had put her through.

I told her no.

Her husband started ranting at the unfairness of it all.

"What did you convict on?" I asked.

"Why, everything Bradfield's friends said about Smith."

"What did you think of their hair and fiber evidence?"

"That was a joke."

"What about the pin in Smith's car?"

"We weren't impressed."

"What convinced you?"

"Well, I personally could not believe that the Pennsylvania State Police would arrest somebody if he didn't do it."

* * *

Jay Smith had 13 of his twilight years taken from him by the justice system. Over seven of those years were on death row for the Reinert murders. He is a bitter man, with good reason. But now that he has had time on the outside to think about his swirling reversal of fortune—a remarkable shift from death row to supreme court-ordered freedom—ex-Upper Merion High School Principal Smith says he'd like to get beyond vengeance to the place where he can disappear. Somewhere in Pennsylvania, New Jersey, or Delaware. Maybe near a community college, where he doesn't need a teaching degree, where he can get a driver's license and an apartment and maybe teach a few classes in education or criminal justice.

"That's a blessing about the name Smith," he said.

"They don't even know who you are after a while."

Jay Smith, convicted seven years ago as the executioner of Susan Reinert and her children, is free. He can think and say and do—within the law—the same things as anybody else. He has a lot on his mind. He says he spent his time in prison consumed with his own defense—reading books, writing letters, working on a criminal justice dictionary. But he is not a man who shares his thoughts or emotions easily.

Is he angry?

Yes.

Is he bitter?

Yes.

He meant what he said about dropping a nuclear bomb on Pennsylvania, but now he would like it dropped surgically, without property destruction, on Bradfield.

What other feelings does he have?

He hopes that maybe someday the truth will come out, and everybody—including Ken Reinert—will realize "I didn't do it."

In the meantime?

"I don't plan to spend my life trying to rehabilitate myself. I'm 64 years old. I'm too old for that.

"The only salvation I have is the name Smith."

Jay Smith seeks refuge in his name. He wants to be forgotten, to go on with what precious life he has left. He believes that in time that's possible.

One day shortly after his release, he decided to go for a walk down the residential street on which his brother lives. It was a beautiful, sunny day, and there were no fences or bars to stop him. He could smell the fresh air and see the green grass, and he never remembered the sky so blue. It was a feeling, a strange feeling from many years ago, when he was a small boy.

The Uni-Mart was only two blocks away. William had asked him to buy a loaf of bread and had given him the money. Jay was nervous, but he agreed and was looking forward to this small task. He entered the busy store, and within seconds, everybody was gone. Not even the cashier stayed. He went home empty-handed.

As Jay walked home, children played on the streets but kept their distance.

An elderly couple saw him coming and pointed, then quickly crossed to the other side of the street.

A police car cruised slowly beside him, not stopping.

Presumed innocent.

Means nothing.

Principal suspect.

Jay C. Smith.

EPILOGUE

The dun mare was breathing heavily as the rocks under her hooves cracked and rolled down the steep cliff behind her. The fall foliage once again on top of Sterrett's Gap blessed the mountain with yellows and reds and golds, and the late evening sun on the horizon ahead of us gave the heavens a fiery glow. Soon that sun would set and the stars above would point the way home.

A brisk cool front was waiting on top of that hill, and the wind softly whistled through the pines. Two young fawns were playing ahead of us, but their mother quickly moved them along to safety, and they vanished into a thicket. The doe had sensed danger where there was none, but she was taking no chances with her children.

I loved it out there, alone, closer to God and in touch with his reminders of all that matters. I believe in my heart that I set an innocent man free.

But sometimes I wonder.

I know in my heart that the system I devoted my life to is better off. I paid the price of endless battles in the courtroom where reputations are won and lost, and dignity and honor, and sometimes lives, are sacrificed. That change in the law and the message to prosecutors will make a difference. But it all seemed up there, on that mountain, to have happened so long ago in a world of another lifetime.

Darkness was setting in, and I had miles to go. The wind was picking up and a storm was threatening. In the distance, heat lightning flashed in the sky and a lone hawk circled and squawked. Even my mare had a young colt at home and was anxious to get back. I gently pressed my right spur into her and she leapt onto the timber road ahead of us, and then I yelled and the mare raised her head and lunged forward faster, and faster, and faster.

Everything became a blur.

We were going home.

CAST OF CHARACTERS

Joanne Aitken—Harvard graduate student in architecture; loved William Bradfield; after Reinert's murder she drove Bradfield's VW across country alone.

John Balshy—Testified at Jay C. Smith trial that he found grains of sand on feet of Reinert at the autopsy using rubber lifters.

Frances Bradfield—William Bradfield's first wife.

Mariel Bradfield—William Bradfield's second wife.

Nona Bradfield—William Bradfield's mother.

William Bradfield—Former chairman of English Department at Upper Merion High School; found guilty of first-degree murder for the killings of Reinert and her two children (October 1983); serving three consecutive life sentences; all appeals denied.

Elizabeth Brook—Susan Reinert's next-door neighbor and granddaughter of Mary Gove; with Gove, last known witness to see Susan Reinert and her children alive on the evening of June 22, 1979.

Ron Colver—Pennsylvania State Police trooper; was present at autopsy of Susan Reinert on June 25, 1979 where he received rubber lifters from Trooper John Balshy; initialed and dated lifters at autopsy.

Louis DiSantis—Pennsylvania State Police trooper assigned full time to assist Joe Van-Nort and Jack Holtz in Reinert murder investigation.

Victor Dove—Found rubber lifters containing sand removed from the feet of Susan Reinert at Pennsylvania State Police lab during the murder trial of Jay C. Smith, specifically on April 24, 1986; testified that he told Trooper Holtz about the lifters the day he found them.

Pat Gallagher—Brother of Susan Reinert.

Isaac J. Garb—Presiding judge during William Bradfield's trial for murder of Susan Reinert and her children.

Stanley "Skip" Gochenour—Private investigator, ex-cop; performed all investigations for Smith's defense at request of William C. Costopoulos.

Mary Gove—Susan Reinert's next-door neighbor; last known witness to see Susan Reinert and her children alive on June 22, 1979 along with her granddaughter, Elizabeth Brook.

Richard Guida—Chief deputy attorney general for Pennsylvania; main prosecutor in Reinert murder case; successfully prosecuted William Bradfield and Jay C. Smith in separate trials; resigned from office amid rumors of cocaine use; convicted by federal authorities in 1991 for cocaine distribution and sentenced to 11 months in prison.

Jack Holtz—Worked the case full time for seven years; chief investigator after VanNort's death; testified that Wambaugh paid him $5,000 during Smith's trial for a "character release" and $45,000 after the trial; retired from state police during internal probe into his conduct.

Mark Hughes—Junkman hired by Trooper Jack Holtz to clean out his house; discovered box of evidence from Holtz's attic related to the Reinert murder investigation and turned it over to Jay C. Smith's attorney.

Stephanie Smith-Hunsberger—Daughter of Jay C. Smith and wife of Edward Hunsberger; vanished with her husband in 1978 or 1979; presumed dead.

Edward "Eddie" Hunsberger—Married to Stephanie Smith, daughter of Jay C. Smith; vanished with Stephanie in 1978 or 1979; presumed dead.

William W. Lipsitt—Dauphin County Senior Judge who presided over trial of Jay C. Smith and evidentiary hearings concerning Raymond Martray and the rubber lifters.

Joshua Lock—Attorney appointed to represent William Bradfield during his murder trial.

Raymond Martray—Former policeman convicted of operating a burglary ring in western Pennsylvania and of perjury; testified that Smith confessed to him.

Charles Montione—Inmate who testified that Jay C. Smith confessed to him. Convicted of perjury and various drug offenses in later, unrelated proceedings. In January 1995, convicted of first-degree murder and sentenced to life for the contract slaying of a drug dealer in February 1986, two months before he testified on behalf of the prosecution and state police against Smith at trial.

Susan Myers—Teacher at Upper Merion High School; lived with William Bradfield for 20 years as friend and lover; went with Bradfield to Cape May on weekend of murders.

Proctor Nowell—Inmate who claimed that William Bradfield confessed to him; has since been convicted of murder in the first degree for killing his girlfriend.

Christopher Pappas—Substitute English teacher at Upper Merion High School; part of the Bradfield circle of confidants; spent alibi weekend with Bradfield at Cape May.

Karen Reinert—Eleven-year-old daughter of Susan and Ken Reinert; last seen outside of her home with her mother and brother on June 22, 1979; presumed dead.

Kenneth Reinert—Ex-husband of Susan Reinert; father of Karen and Michael.

Michael Reinert—Ten-year-old son of Susan and Ken Reinert; last seen outside of his home with his mother and sister on June 22, 1979; presumed dead.

Susan Reinert—Mother of Karen and Michael; loved William Bradfield and named him beneficiary of her $750,000 life insurance policy; found dead at age 36 in the trunk of her car on June 25, 1979 in Harrisburg, Pennsylvania.

Nicholas Ressetar—Chief paralegal to William C. Costopoulos, defense attorney for Jay C. Smith; did all legal research and writing, and is credited by Costopoulos for developing case that changed the law in the Commonwealth of Pennsylvania, which resulted in the release of Jay C. Smith.

Jay C. Smith—Former principal of Upper Merion High School; colonel in U.S. Army Reserves and aide to General John Eisenhower; resigned from school after convictions for theft; incarcerated on June 25, 1979 to serve sentence the same day that Reinert's body was found; arrested and charged with murdering Reinert and her children; has always maintained his innocence; convicted of three counts of first-degree murder and sentenced to death; later granted a new trial by the Pennsylvania Supreme Court; released from prison after the supreme court dismissed charges.

Stephanie Smith—Jay C. Smith's wife of 28 years; died of cancer.

Vincent Valaitis—English teacher at Upper Merion High School; friend, associate and neighbor of William Bradfield; spent alibi weekend of June 22-25, 1979 at Jersey shore with Bradfield, Myers and Pappas.

Joe VanNort—Chief investigator for the Pennsylvania State Police after discovery of Reinert's body; promised $50,000 by noted writer Joseph Wambaugh in 1981 for inside information on the case; died of a heart attack on October 1, 1981 while at police firing range.

Robert Walker—Judge specially appointed by the Pennsylvania Supreme Court to handle the retrial of Jay C. Smith, which was never held; presided over the junkman's "box" hearing; died October 1993.

Joseph Wambaugh—Famous cop-turned-author; attended trial of Jay C. Smith in April 1986; wrote *Echoes in the Darkness,* a national best-seller about the Reinert murder; did screenplay for a CBS-TV mini-series of the same name; hearing in April 1992 disclosed that he paid Trooper Holtz $5,000 during Jay C. Smith's trial and $45,000 more after the trial.

Wendy Zeigler—former student who had platonic relationship with Bradfield but wanted to marry him; hid $25,000 of Reinert's money for Bradfield; eventually testified against both Bradfield and Jay C. Smith.